# Lecture Notes in Artificial Intelligence

Subseries of Lecture Notes in Computer Science
Edited by J. Siekmann

T0241810

## Lecture Notes in Computer Science

Edited by G. Goos and J. Hartmanis

## Editorial

Artificial Intelligence has become a major discipline under the roof of Computer Science. This is also reflected by a growing number of titles devoted to this fast developing field to be published in our Lecture Notes in Computer Science. To make these volumes immediately visible we have decided to distinguish them by a special cover as Lecture Notes in Artificial Intelligence, constituting a subseries of the Lecture Notes in Computer Science. This subseries is edited by an Editorial Board of experts from all areas of AI, chaired by Jörg Siekmann, who are looking forward to consider further AI monographs and proceedings of high scientific quality for publication.

We hope that the constitution of this subseries will be well accepted by the audience of the Lecture Notes in Computer Science, and we feel confident that the subseries will be recognized as an outstanding opportunity for publication by authors and editors of the AI community.

Editors and publisher

# Lecture Notes in Artificial Intelligence

Edited by J. Siekmann

Subseries of Lecture Notes in Computer Science

## 383

K. Furukawa  H. Tanaka
T. Fujisaki  (Eds.)

# Logic Programming '88

Proceedings of the 7th Conference
Tokyo, Japan, April 11–14, 1988

## Springer-Verlag

Berlin Heidelberg New York London Paris Tokyo Hong Kong

**Editors**

Koichi Furukawa
ICOT Research Center
Mita Kokusai Building 21F, 4-28 Mita 1-chome
Minato-ku, Tokyo 108, Japan

Hozumi Tanaka
Department of Computer Science, Faculty of Engineering
Tokyo Institute of Technology, 12-1 Oh-okayama 2-chome
Meguro-ku, Tokyo 152, Japan

Tetsunosuke Fujisaki
IBM, Thomas J. Watson Research Center
P.O.Box 704, Yorktown Heights, New York 10598, USA

CR Subject Classification (1987): D.1, D.3.1−4, F.4.1−2, I.2.3−4, I.2.7

ISBN 3-540-51564-X Springer-Verlag Berlin Heidelberg New York
ISBN 0-387-51564-X Springer-Verlag New York Berlin Heidelberg

© Springer-Verlag Berlin Heidelberg 1989
Printed in Germany

Printing and binding: Druckhaus Beltz, Hemsbach/Bergstr.
2145/3140-543210 – Printed on acid-free paper

# Foreword

This volume of the Springer Lecture Notes in Computer Science contains most of the papers presented at the Seventh Logic Programming Conference (April 11-14, 1988 Tokyo). It is the successor to volumes 221, 264 and 315.

The contents cover various aspects of logic programming such as foundations, nonmonotonic reasoning, programming language/systems, concurrent programming, knowledge base and applications of computer-aided reasoning and natural language understanding.

The first paper in the "Foundation of Logic Programming" section gives theoretical results on "narrowing", a natural extension of unification for handling equalities as well as usual Horn clauses. The second paper gives a proof method of definite clauses. There is some similarity to inductionless induction based on the Knuth-Bendix algorithm, but its principle is different.

The first and second papers in the "Nonmonotonic Reasoning" section deal with the problem of belief revision caused by adding new facts. The third paper gives a new formalism to the problem of nonmonotonic reasoning associated with inheritance and proposes a parallel algorithm to solve it.

"Logic programming Language/System" contains three papers on debugging, explicit control of logic programs and a new programming paradigm called lattice programming. This last one is particularly interesting both from theoretical and practical viewpoints. It associates for each computing path of Prolog programs a value other than true/false, thus increasing its expressive power.

The "Guarded Horn Clauses" section includes two papers. The first tries to realize reflection on GHC, and the second paper gives an implementation of full GHC by communication processes.

The next "Knowledge Base System" section contains two papers. The first one gives inference methods and semeantics for a knowledge base containing disjunctive non-Horn clauses. The latter describes a formalism of conventional network type database access in terms of a refutation procedure.

The "Computer-aided Reasoning" section consists of just one paper. The paper describes a system to assist human reasoning, namely a very interesting and seemingly useful application program written in ESP, a dialect of Prolog that can be used to write programs in object-oriented style.

The last section is "Natural Language Processing", which contains three papers. The first paper concerns lexical analysis of Japanese sentences. An efficient algorithm and its implementation in ESP is given. The second paper presents a system which generates a summary of a given sentence. The system achieves this difficult goal by restricting the reference domain, thus making it possible to understand the described situation. The last paper proposes a new knowledge representation formalism suited for representing dynamic behaviors by extending the frame system. It also points out the necessity of reasoning in different situation which depends on multiple world representation.

We thank program committee members, reviewers and authors for their cooperation and patience. We extend our special thanks to reviewers from IBM Watson Research Center for their thorough efforts to improve the quality of the English as well as the contents.

Tokyo, Spring 1989

Koichi Furukawa
Hozumi Tanaka
Tetsunosuke Fujisaki

# Table of Contents

## Foundation of Logic Programming

## Nonmonotonic Reasoning

## Logic Programming Language/System

# Executive Committee / Program Committee / Editorial Board

# Completeness of Extended Unification Based on Basic Narrowing

## Akihiro YAMAMOTO

Department of Information Systems
Interdisciplinary Graduate School of Engineering Sciences
Kyushu University 39
6-1, Kasuga-koen, Kasuga, Fukuoka, 816 JAPAN

Mailing Address: Research Institute of Fundamental Information Science
Kyushu University 33, Fukuoka, 812 JAPAN

## Abstract

In this paper we prove the completeness of unification based on basic narrowing. First we prove the completeness of unification based on original narrowing under a weaker condition than the previous proof. Then we discuss the relation between basic narrowing and innermost reduction as the lifting lemma, and prove the completeness of unification based on basic narrowing. Moreover, we give the switching lemma to combine the previous algorithm and our new proof.

## 1. Introduction

The main contribution of this paper is a proof that the extended unification procedure based on basic narrowing is complete under some conditions. The procedure was first given by Hullot [2], and then improved by Bosco et al. [1]. The improved procedure [1] was obtained by translating every basic narrowing sequence into an SLD-refutation sequence. It is now very important as a foundation of logic-functional programming languages, but the proof of its completeness is not straightforward.

Hullot [2] proved the lifting lemma for basic narrowing as that of SLD-resolution. However, his proof is incomplete since we found a counter example for Lemma 3 [2]. To prove the lifting lemma for basic narrowing, we need to construct a basic reduction sequence from every term, but its existence is not guaranteed in general. By clarifying the function of innermost reduction, we overcome this difficulty and show the existence.

We first show, under a weaker condition than [2], the completeness of unification based on original narrowing. That is, the term rewriting system is simply assumed weakly canonical. Then we establish the relation between innermost reduction and basic narrowing as the lifting lemma, and prove the completeness of unification based on basic narrowing. Thus we suppose the condition that the term rewriting system is both weakly canonical and normalizing with innermost reductions. Moreover, we show the relation between the completeness theorem and the algorithm in [1] by clarifying the procedure which searches an innermost redex. Thus the relation is stated as the switching lemma.

The paper is organized as follows. In the next section, we explain narrowing and basic narrowing. In Section 3, we prove the completeness of unification based on narrowing under a weaker condition than that in [2], and discuss the problem in the case of basic narrowing. In Section 4, we prove the completeness of unification based on basic narrowing under a weaker condition than that in [2]. In Section 5, we discuss the relation of our proof and the algorithm given in [1] as a form of the switching lemma.

## 2. Narrowing and Basic Narrowing.

In the present paper we treat extended unification in a first order equality theory $E$ using a term rewriting system $R$. An $E$-unifier of two terms $t$ and $s$ is a substitution $\theta$ such that $E \models t\theta = s\theta$, where $\models$ represents logical consequence and the predicate symbol $=$ is interpreted as equality. We consider the case that $E$ is given as a reflexive symmetric transitive closure of the reduction relation on $R$, which is defined below.

The symbol $\equiv$ denotes syntactical identity. The set of all variables occurring in a term $t$ is denoted by $V(t)$. We use the special function symbol $eq$ only for the description of procedures.

We assume that the term rewriting system $R = \{\alpha_i \to \beta_i ; i \in I\}$ satisfies the following conditions:

(i) $V(\alpha_i) \supset V(\beta_i)$,

(ii) $\alpha_i$ is not a variable,

(iii) $I$ is finite.

We define the occurrence of every subterm of a term $t$ as a sequence of positive integers as follows:

(i) The occurrence of $t$ is the empty sequence (denoted by $\Lambda$),

(ii) If the occurrence of the subterm $f(t_1, \ldots, t_n)$ is $u$, then the occurrence of the term $t_i$ is $u \cdot i$.

Let $t$ be a term. Then the symbol $Oc(t)$ denotes the set of occurrences of all subterms of $t$, and $Og(t)$ denotes the set of occurrences of all non-variable subterms of $t$. When $u \in Oc(t)$, $t/u$ denotes the subterm of $t$ whose occurrence is $u$, and $t[u \Leftarrow s]$ denotes the term which is obtained by replacing subterm $t/u$ by a term $s$. A subterm of $t$ whose occurrence is not $\Lambda$ is called a *proper subterm* of $t$.

Let $u$ and $v$ be two occurrences. Then we write $u \preceq v$ if there is a sequence $w$ such that $u \cdot w = v$.

**Definition 1.** Let $t$ and $s$ be terms. Then $t$ is *reduced to* $s$ if there exist $u \in Oc(t)$, $\alpha \to \beta \in R$, and a substitution $\theta$ such that $t/u \equiv \alpha\theta$ and $s \equiv t[u \Leftarrow \beta\theta]$. When $t$ is reduced to $s$, we write $t \to s$, or $t \to_{[u, \alpha \to \beta, \theta]} s$ to give full details. We call $t/u$ a *redex* of $t$.

When we regard $\to$ as a binary relation on the set of terms, we call it the *reduction relation* on $R$.

A term $t$ is in *normal form* if there exists no term $s$ such that $t \to s$. If there exists a finite reduction sequence

$$t \equiv t_0 \to t_1 \to \cdots \to t_n \equiv s$$

such that $s$ is in normal form, then $s$ is called a *normal form of* $t$ and is denoted by $N(t)$. Moreover, let $\theta$ be a substitution $\{X_1 \leftarrow t_1, \ldots, X_n \leftarrow t_n\}$. If each of $t_1, \ldots, t_n$ is in normal form, then $\theta$ is said to be in *normal form*. For every substitution $\theta$, the substitution $\{X_1 \leftarrow N(t_1), \ldots, X_n \leftarrow N(t_n)\}$, if it exists, is called a *normal form of* $\theta$.

**Definition 2.** Let $t$ and $s$ be terms. Then $t$ is *narrowed* to $s$, if there exist $u \in Og(t)$, a variant $\alpha \to \beta$ of a rule in $R$, and a substitution $\sigma$ such that $\sigma$ is an mgu of $t/u$ and $\alpha$ and $s \equiv (t[u \Leftarrow \beta])\sigma$. When $t$ is narrowed to $s$, we write $t \Rightarrow s$, or $t \Rightarrow_{[u,\alpha \to \beta,\sigma]} s$ to give full details.

We assume that for every narrowing sequence

$$t_0 \Rightarrow_{[u_0,\alpha_0 \to \beta_0,\sigma_0]} t_1 \Rightarrow_{[u_1,\alpha_1 \to \beta_1,\sigma_1]} t_2 \Rightarrow \cdots \Rightarrow_{[u_{n-1},\alpha_{n-1} \to \beta_{n-1},\sigma_{n-1}]} t_n,$$

the variables in every $\alpha_i \to \beta_i$ are *standardized apart* ([3]). We also assume that mgu's are computed by the algorithm in [3, 4]. Then the *E-unification of two terms* $t$ *and* $s$ *based on narrowing* is to generate the set

$$\Sigma(t,s) = \left\{ \sigma \;\middle|\; \begin{array}{l} \text{there exists a narrowing sequence} \\ eq(t,s) \equiv t_0 \Rightarrow_{[u_0,\alpha_0 \to \beta_0,\sigma_0]} t_1 \Rightarrow_{[u_1,\alpha_1 \to \beta_1,\sigma_1]} t_2 \Rightarrow \\ \qquad \cdots \Rightarrow_{[u_{n-1},\alpha_{n-1} \to \beta_{n-1},\sigma_{n-1}]} t_n \equiv eq(t',s') \\ \text{such that } \sigma = \sigma_0 \cdots \sigma_{n-1}\mu|_{V(t) \cup V(s)}, \text{ where } \mu \text{ is an mgu of } t' \text{ and } s' \end{array} \right\}$$

where $\theta|_V$ denotes the restriction of a substitution $\theta$ to a set of variables $V$.

For two substitutions $\theta$ and $\tau$, we write $\theta =_E \tau$ if $E \models X\theta = X\tau$ for every variable $X$.

**Definition 3.** A set of substitutions $\Sigma$ is a *complete set of E-unifiers* of $t$ and $s$ if, for every E-unifier $\theta$ of $t$ and $s$, there exist $\sigma \in \Sigma$ and a substitution $\gamma$ such that $\theta|_{V(t) \cup V(s)} =_E \sigma\gamma|_{V(t) \cup V(s)}$.

**Definition 4.** *E-unification based on narrowing* is *complete* if, for every two terms $t$ and $s$, $\Sigma(t,s)$ is a complete set of E-unifiers of $t$ and $s$.

Basic narrowing is introduced in order to improve E-unification based on narrowing.

**Definition 5.** A narrowing sequence

$$t_0 \Rightarrow_{[u_0,\alpha_0 \to \beta_0,\sigma_0]} t_1 \Rightarrow_{[u_1,\alpha_1 \to \beta_1,\sigma_1]} t_2 \Rightarrow \cdots \Rightarrow_{[u_{n-1},\alpha_{n-1} \to \beta_{n-1},\sigma_{n-1}]} t_n$$

is *basic* if there exists a sequence of sets of occurrences $U_0,\ldots,U_n$ which satisfies the following conditions:

(B-1) $U_0 = Og(t_0)$,

(B-2) $u_i \in U_i \subset Oc(t_i)$ $(0 \le i \le n-1)$ and $U_n \subset Oc(t_n)$,

(B-3) $U_{i+1} = (U_i - \{v \in U_i \,;\, u_i \preceq v\}) \cup \{u_i \cdot v \,;\, v \in Og(\beta_i)\}$ $(0 \le i \le n-1)$.

**Example 1.** Let $R = \{f(X,b) \to g(X), \; a \to b\}$. Then a narrowing sequence

$$f(a,X) \Rightarrow f(b,X) \Rightarrow g(b),$$

is basic because the sequence

$$U_0 = \{\Lambda,1\}, \; U_1 = \{\Lambda,1\}, \; U_2 = \{\Lambda\}$$

satisfies the conditions (B-1), (B-2), and (B-3). However,

$$f(a,X) \Rightarrow g(a) \Rightarrow g(b)$$

is not basic because $U_0$ and $U_1$ must be $\{\Lambda, 1\}$ and $\{\Lambda\}$ respectively so that $U_0$ satisfies (B-1), (B-2) and (B-3), but $U_1$ violates (B-2).

The $E$-unification of two terms $t$ and $s$ based on basic narrowing is to generate the set

$$
\Sigma_B(t,s) = \left\{ \sigma \left|
\begin{array}{l}
\text{there exists a basic narrowing sequence} \\
eq(t,s) \equiv t_0 \Rightarrow_{[u_0, \alpha_0 \to \beta_0, \sigma_0]} t_1 \Rightarrow_{[u_1, \alpha_1 \to \beta_1, \sigma_1]} t_2 \Rightarrow \\
\qquad \cdots \Rightarrow_{[u_{n-1}, \alpha_{n-1} \to \beta_{n-1}, \sigma_{n-1}]} t_n \equiv eq(t', s') \\
\text{such that } \sigma = \sigma_0 \cdots \sigma_{n-1} \mu|_{V(t) \cup V(s)}, \text{ where } \mu \text{ is an mgu of } t' \text{ and } s'
\end{array}
\right. \right\}
$$

as in the case of narrowing.

**Definition 6.** $E$-unification based on basic narrowing is *complete* if, for every two terms $t$ and $s$, $\Sigma_B(t,s)$ is a complete set of $E$-unifiers of $t$ and $s$.

[1] has improved $E$-unification based on basic narrowing by using innermost occurrences and has given an efficient algorithm as explained below.

**Definition 7.** Let $U$ be a set of occurrences of subterms of $t$. An occurrence $u$ is *innermost* in $U$ if there is no occurrence $v$ in $U$ such that $u \preceq v$ and $v \neq u$.

**Algorithm 1 (Bosco, Giovannetti and Moiso [1]).**

$unify(t, s, S)$  /* $t$ and $s$ are terms and $S$ is a rule to select an innermost occurrence from $B$ */
$\quad E := eq(t, s)$, $B := Og(eq(t, s)) - \{\Lambda\}$, and $\Theta := \epsilon$
$\qquad$ /* $E$ is a term, $B$ is a set of occurrences, and $\Theta$ is a substitution */
LOOP:
$\quad$ **if** $B = \phi$ **then**
$\qquad \Theta := \Theta\mu$ and return $\Theta|_{V(t) \cup V(s)}$ **where** $\mu$ is an mgu of $t'$ and $s'$ **where** $E \equiv eq(t', s')$
$\quad$ **else**
$\qquad$ select an innermost occurrence $u$ from $B$ according to $S$,
$\qquad$ nondeterministically execute either (1-1) or (1-2), and goto LOOP:
$\qquad$ (1-1) $B := B - \{u\}$
$\qquad$ (1-2) select nondeterministically a variant $\alpha \to \beta$ of a rule in $R$ such that
$\qquad\qquad$ all the variables in $V(\alpha)$ are new and $E/u$ and $\alpha$ are unifiable,
$\qquad\qquad E := (E[u \Leftarrow \beta])\sigma$, $\Theta := \Theta\sigma$, and $B := (B - \{u\}) \cup \{u \cdot v ; v \in Og(\beta)\}$
$\qquad\qquad\qquad$ **where** $\sigma$ is an mgu of $E/u$ and $\alpha$
$\quad$ **end if**

The search space of basic narrowing is decreased in Algorithm 1 by introducing the *computation rule* $S$ (or the *selection rule* in [1]), which selects one of the innermost occurrences from the set $B$. In a basic narrowing sequence, the terms introduced by an mgu may not be selected afterwards. Algorithm 1 satisfies the conditions of a basic narrowing sequence by selecting an innermost occurrence from $B$.

In the following sections, we reconsider the conditions for the completeness of the above three algorithms.

## 3. The Problem on Basic Narrowing

In this section we point out the problem on the completeness of $E$-unification based on basic narrowing. For the purpose of the discussion, we extend the completeness of $E$-unification based on narrowing. It was proved that $E$-unification based on narrowing is complete if $R$ is canonical, that is, confluent and finitely terminating ([2] Theorem 2). The following theorem is the lifting lemma for narrowing proved in [2].

**Theorem 1 (Hullot [2]).** *Let $t$ and $s$ be terms such that $t \equiv s\eta$ for some normal substitution $\eta$. Then for a reduction sequence*

$$t \equiv t_0 \rightarrow_{[u_0, \alpha_0 \rightarrow \beta_0, \theta_0]} t_1 \rightarrow_{[u_1, \alpha_1 \rightarrow \beta_1, \theta_1]} t_2 \rightarrow \cdots \rightarrow_{[u_{n-1}, \alpha_{n-1} \rightarrow \beta_{n-1}, \theta_{n-1}]} t_n,$$

*there exists a narrowing sequence*

$$s \equiv s_0 \Rightarrow_{[u_0, \alpha_0 \rightarrow \beta_0, \sigma_0]} s_1 \Rightarrow_{[u_1, \alpha_1 \rightarrow \beta_1, \sigma_1]} s_2 \Rightarrow \cdots \Rightarrow_{[u_{n-1}, \alpha_{n-1} \rightarrow \beta_{n-1}, \sigma_{n-1}]} s_n,$$

*and a sequence of normal substitutions $\eta_0, \ldots, \eta_n$ such that*

$$\eta_0 = \eta, \quad \eta|_{V(s)} = \sigma_0 \cdots \sigma_{i-1}\eta_i|_{V(s)} \quad (1 \le i \le n),$$
$$t_i = s_i\eta_i \quad (0 \le i \le n).$$

The assumption of Theorem 1 is only that $\eta$ is in normal form. Therefore we can easily weaken the condition for Hullot's Theorem.

**Definition 8.** $R$ is *weakly canonical* if for every term $t$ there exists only one normal form $N(t)$ and for every pair of $t$ and $s$

$$E \models t = s \Leftrightarrow N(t) \equiv N(s).$$

The following theorem can be proved in the same way as in [2].

**Theorem 2 (Extension of Hullot's Theorem).** *If $R$ is weakly canonical, then $\Sigma(t, s)$ is a complete set of $E$-unifiers of $t$ and $s$.*

**Proof.** Let $\theta$ be an $E$-unifier of $t$ and $s$. Because $R$ is weakly canonical, we can let $\eta$ be a normal form of $\theta$. Also we can construct a reduction sequence

$$eq(t, s)\eta \equiv t_0 \rightarrow t_1 \rightarrow \cdots \rightarrow t_n \equiv eq(N(t\eta), N(s\eta)),$$

such that $N(t\eta) \equiv N(s\eta)$. Thus by Theorem 1 there is a narrowing sequence

$$eq(t, s) \equiv s_0 \Rightarrow s_1 \Rightarrow \cdots \Rightarrow s_n \equiv eq(t', s').$$

Then $t'$ and $s'$ are unifiable because there is a substitution $\eta_n$ such that $t'\eta_n \equiv s'\eta_n$. $\blacksquare$

To show that the above theorem is a proper extension of Hullot's Theorem, we give an example which shows the difference between canonicity and weak canonicity.

**Example 2.** Let $R = \{repeat \rightarrow repeat, repeat \rightarrow halt\}$. Then $R$ is weakly canonical. For every term $t$, its unique normal form is a term given by replacing every *repeat* in $t$ by *halt*. Moreover, we can decide $E \models t = s$ by comparing $N(t)$ and $N(s)$. However, $R$ is not finitely terminating, so $R$ is not canonical.

Now our problem is to prove the completeness of $E$-unification based on basic narrowing. A result similar to Theorem 1 is needed for basic narrowing. Thus we introduce basic reduction.

**Definition 9.** Let $t$ and $s$ be terms such that $t \equiv s\theta$ for some substitution $\theta$. Then a reduction sequence

$$t \equiv t_0 \rightarrow_{[u_0, \alpha_0 \rightarrow \beta_0, \theta_0]} t_1 \rightarrow_{[u_1, \alpha_1 \rightarrow \beta_1, \theta_1]} t_2 \rightarrow \cdots \rightarrow_{[u_{n-1}, \alpha_{n-1} \rightarrow \beta_{n-1}, \theta_{n-1}]} t_n$$

is *based on* $Og(s)$ if there exists a sequence of sets of occurrences $U_0, \ldots, U_n$ which satisfies the conditions (B-2) and (B-3) in Definition 5 and the following condition (B-1') instead of (B-1):

(B-1') $U_0 = Og(s)$.

**Example 3.** Let $R = \{f(X, b) \rightarrow g(X), a \rightarrow b\}$ . In the same way as in Example 1, we can show that a reduction sequence

$$f(a, b) \rightarrow f(b, b) \rightarrow g(b)$$

is based on $Og(t)$, but

$$f(a, b) \rightarrow g(a) \rightarrow g(b)$$

is not.

To get a theorem corresponding to Theorem 1, it is asserted in [2] (Lemma 3) that

if $t$ and $s$ have the relation $t \equiv s\eta$ for some normalized substitution $\eta$, then
*every* reduction sequence from $s$ is based on $Og(s)$.

However the second sequence in Example 3 does not satisfy the above assertion. Therefore the proof of the completeness of $E$-unification based on basic narrowing does not work. Algorithm 1 is also incomplete because the proof of the completeness of Algorithm 1 in [1] is again due to the above assertion.

Algorithm 1 is found by using the one-to-one correspondence between SLD-refutation and basic narrowing sequence in [1]. The efficiency of SLD-resolution is due to the *computation rule* ([3]). Algorithm 1 uses not only the computation rule but also innermost occurrences. In the first sequence of Example 3, the innermost redexes only are selected. On the other hand, in the second one, $f(a, b)$ is selected and it is not an innermost redex. This selection makes a counter example for Lemma 3 [2]. In general, when we construct a basic reduction sequence from a term $t$ to $N(t)$, the terms introduced by the substitution at each reduction need to be in normal form because they may not be selected as redexes. From these consideration, we suggest that the innermost occurrence should essentially owe to the completeness of $E$-unification based on basic narrowing.

In the next section, we prove the completeness of $E$-unification based on basic narrowing along the consideration above.

## 4. Completeness of Unification Based on Basic Narrowing

In the context of term rewriting systems, the word 'innermost' is not used as the meaning defined in Definition 7.

**Definition 10.** Suppose that $t \rightarrow_{[u, \alpha \rightarrow \beta, \theta]} s$ for some term $s$. Then $t/u$ is an *innermost redex* and the reduction is called an *innermost reduction* if any proper subterm of $t/u$ is normal.

**Example 4.** Let $R = \{f(X, b) \rightarrow g(X), \ a \rightarrow b\}$. Then the innermost redexes of $f(f(a, b), f(b, b))$ are $a$ and $f(b, b)$. Thus

$$f(f(a, b), f(b, b)) \rightarrow f(f(a, b), g(b))$$

is an innermost reduction, but

$$f(f(a, b), f(b, b)) \rightarrow f(g(a), f(b, b))$$

is not.

We will clarify the relation of the two definitions of 'innermost', which are in Definition 7 and in Definition 10, as an algorithm in Section 5.

As suggested by Example 3, innermost reduction furnishes a way to construct the basic reduction sequence. The following lemma is a key result for our proof of the completeness of $E$-unification based on basic narrowing.

**Lemma 1.** *Let $t$ be a term and $\eta$ be a normal substitution. If a reduction sequence*

$$t\eta \equiv t_0 \rightarrow t_1 \rightarrow \cdots \rightarrow t_n$$

*consists only of innermost reductions, then the reduction sequence is based on $Og(t)$.*

**Proof.** The proof is by induction on the length of the reduction. Suppose first that $n = 1$, and consider the reduction sequence

$$t\eta \equiv t_0 \rightarrow_{[u_0, \alpha_0 \rightarrow \beta, \theta_0]} t_1.$$

Then the occurrence of every redex of $t_0$ is in $Og(t)$ because $\eta$ is normal. Thus the result holds by letting

$$U_0 = Og(t),$$
$$U_1 = (U_0 - \{v \in U_0 \, ; \, u_0 \preceq v\}) \cup \{u_0 \cdot v \, ; \, v \in Og(\beta_0)\}.$$

Now suppose that the result holds for $n$. Consider the sequence

$$t\eta \equiv t_0 \rightarrow \cdots \rightarrow t_{n-1} \rightarrow_{[u_{n-1}, \alpha_{n-1} \rightarrow \beta_{n-1}, \theta_{n-1}]} t_n \rightarrow_{[u_n, \alpha_n \rightarrow \beta_n, \theta_n]} t_{n+1}.$$

From the induction hypothesis there is a sequence of sets of occurrences $U_0, \ldots, U_n$ which satisfies the conditions (B-1'), (B-2), and (B-3) for the sequence

$$t_0 \rightarrow \cdots \rightarrow t_{n-1} \rightarrow t_n.$$

Because $t_{n-1}/u_{n-1}$ is an innermost redex, all of its proper subterms are normal, and $\theta_{n-1}$ is also normal. Thus the occurrence of every redex of $\beta_{n-1}\theta_{n-1}$ is in $Og(\beta_{n-1})$. So because $u_n \in U_n$, the sequence $U_0, \ldots, U_{n+1}$ satisfies the conditions (B-1'), (B-2), and (B-3) by letting

$$U_{n+1} = (U_n - \{v \in U_n \, ; \, u_n \preceq v\}) \cup \{u_n \cdot v \, ; \, v \in Og(\beta_n)\}. \blacksquare$$

If $R$ is canonical, then $R$ has the property that there is an innermost reduction sequence from every term $t$ to $N(t)$ because any reduction sequence from $t$ reaches $N(t)$. However the property is not confirmed in general. Therefore we need to identify the class of term rewriting systems with this property.

**Definition 11.** $R$ is *normalizing with innermost reductions* if for every term there exists an innermost reduction sequence to its normal form.

Then the completeness of $E$-unification based on basic narrowing is proved using the innermost reduction sequence.

**Theorem 3.** *If $R$ is weakly canonical and normalizing with innermost reductions, then $\Sigma_B(t, s)$ is a complete set of $E$-unifiers of $t$ and $s$.*

**Proof.** Let $\theta$ be an $E$-unifier of $t$ and $s$, and $\eta$ be its normal form. Because $R$ is normalizing with innermost reductions, there exists an innermost reduction sequence

$$eq(t,s)\eta \equiv t_0 \rightarrow_{[u_0, \alpha_0 \rightarrow \beta_0, \theta_0]} t_1 \rightarrow_{[u_1, \alpha_1 \rightarrow \beta_1, \theta_1]} t_2 \rightarrow \cdots \rightarrow_{[u_{n-1}, \alpha_{n-1} \rightarrow \beta_{n-1}, \theta_{n-1}]} t_n \equiv eq(N(t\eta), N(s\eta)).$$

By Lemma 1 there is a sequence of sets of occurrences $U_0, \ldots, U_n$ which makes the reduction sequence basic. By Theorem 1, we can construct a narrowing sequence

$$eq(t,s) \equiv s_0 \Rightarrow_{[u_0, \alpha_0 \rightarrow \beta_0, \sigma_0]} s_1 \Rightarrow_{[u_1, \alpha_1 \rightarrow \beta_1, \sigma_1]} s_2 \Rightarrow \cdots \Rightarrow_{[u_{n-1}, \alpha_{n-1} \rightarrow \beta_{n-1}, \sigma_{n-1}]} s_n \equiv eq(t', s').$$

Then the narrowing sequence is also basic by using $U_0, \ldots, U_n$ because the two sequences use the same occurrence at each step. Moreover, $t'$ and $s'$ are unifiable, and there is a substitution $\gamma$ such that

$$\sigma_0 \cdots \sigma_{n-1} \mu \gamma|_{V(t) \cup V(s)} = \eta|_{V(t) \cup V(s)}$$

where $\mu$ is an mgu of $t'$ and $s'$. $\blacksquare$

If $R$ is canonical, then $R$ is weakly canonical and normalizing with innermost reductions because every reduction sequence from a term $t$ reaches $N(t)$. Thus Theorem 3 holds for canonical term rewriting systems.

### 5. Switching Lemma for Basic Narrowing

In this section we discuss the relation between Theorem 3 and Algorithm 1. The most important point of Algorithm 1 is the computation rule $S$. Thus we give the switching lemma that confirms the introduction of $S$ into basic narrowing as in the theory of SLD-resolution.

At first we consider a procedure for innermost reduction. The following Algorithm 2 is the representation.

**Algorithm 2.**

$innermost\_reduce(t)$    /* $t$ is a term */
    $T := t,\ B := Oc(t),$      /* $T$ is a term, and $B$ is a set of occurrences */
  LOOP:
    **if** $B = \phi$ **then**
      return $T$
    **else**
      nondeterministically select an innermost occurrence $u$ from $B$,
      **if** there is no rule $\alpha \to \beta$ in $R$ such that $T/u \equiv \alpha\theta$ for some $\theta$ **then**
        (2-1) $B := B - \{u\}$ and goto LOOP      /* $T/u$ is in normal form*/
      **else**
        nondeterministically select $\alpha \to \beta$ from R such that $T/u \equiv \alpha\theta$ for some $\theta$
        $T := T[u \Leftarrow \beta\theta],\ B := (B - \{u\}) \cup \{u \cdot v \,;\, v \in Og(\beta)\}$, and goto LOOP
      **end if**
    **end if**

In Algorithm 2 the procedure which searches an innermost redex from a term is clarified by using the set $B$ and step (2-1). This step shows the difference between Definition 7 and Definition 10.

Now we apply Algorithm 2 to the construction of the basic reduction sequence in the proof of Theorem 3. The reduction sequence and the basic narrowing sequence in the proof use the same sequence $U_0, \ldots, U_n$. Thus it is clear that we may add a step corresponding to (2-1) to the procedure for basic narrowing. In Algorithm 1 the step is (1-1).

Then in order to prove the completeness of Algorithm 1 using Theorem 3, we need to show that we may restrict the selection of innermost occurrences with a computation rule $S$. This restriction is allowable because of the following switching lemma for Algorithm 1. To explain the lemma, in Algorithm 1, we use symbols $E(S, n)$, $B(S, n)$, $\Theta(S, n)$ to represent the values of $E$, $B$, and $\Theta$ at the beginning of the $n$-th execution of the LOOP when the computation rule is $S$.

**Lemma 2.** *Suppose that there are two innermost occurrences $u$ and $v$ in $B(S, n)$ and that $S$ selects $u$ in the $n$-th execution of the LOOP and $v$ in the $(n+1)$-st. Then we may use the computation rule $S'$ which selects $v$ instead of $u$ at the $n$-th execution of LOOP and $u$ at the $(n+1)$-st. Moreover we can let $E(S, n+2)$ and $E(S', n+2)$ be variants, $\Theta(S, n)$ and $\Theta(S', n)$ be variants, and $B(S, n+2) = B(S', n+2)$.*

It should be noticed that Lemma 2 is proved by translating every basic narrowing sequence to an SLD-refutation and applying the switching lemma for SLD-refutation in [1]. Of course, the false assertion was used in [1]. Thus we omit its proof.

## 6. Conclusion

We have proved the completeness of $E$-unification based on narrowing under a weaker restriction and have proved the completeness of $E$-unification based on basic narrowing, and have given the switching lemma. The discussion in [1] is important but was only half way to the completeness because it showed only the switching lemma.

In the discussions above, we have used the conditions that $R$ is weakly canonical and is normalizing with innermost reductions. Both [1] and [2] treat the case that $R$ is a canonical term rewriting system, which is useful for theorem provers using reduction. In the discussions on narrowing, the restriction for term rewriting systems should be weakened because $E$-unification based on narrowing is a refutation procedure. We have shown that it can really be weakened.

We need to find sufficient conditions under which a term rewriting system is weakly canonical and normalizing with innermost reductions. Especially, we have not clarified any properties of term rewriting systems which are normalizing with innermost reductions. We conjecture that weakly canonical term rewriting systems are normalizing with innermost reductions.

We need also to import the property of SLD-resolution other than the switching lemma into the theory of narrowing. For example, we are considering the complete definitions of functions in the same way as those of predicates in SLD-resolution.

## Acknowledgements

The author would like to thank Prof. Setsuo Arikawa for his constructive comments and encouragements. The author also wishes to thank Dr. Makoto Haraguchi for many discussions on narrowing and SLD-resolution.

## References

[1] Bosco, P.G., Giovannetti, E., and Moiso, C. (1987): Refined Strategies for Semantic Unification, Proc. TAPSOFT '87 (LNCS 250), 276-290.

[2] Hullot, J.M. (1980): Canonical Forms and Unification, Proc. 5th Conference on Automated Deduction (LNCS 87), 318-334.

[3] Lloyd, J.W. (1984): Foundations of Logic Programming, Springer-Verlag.

[4] Martelli, A. and Montanari, U. (1982): An Efficient Unification Algorithm, ACM TOPLAS, 4(2), 258-282.

[5] Yamamoto, A. (1987): A Theoretical Combination of SLD-Resolution and Narrowing, Proc. 4th ICLP, 470-487.

# Proving Definite Clauses without Explicit Use of Inductions*

*Akito SAKURAI   Hiroshi MOTODA*
Advanced Research Laboratory, Hitachi Ltd.
1-280 Higashi-Koigakubo, Kokubunji, Tokyo 185, JAPAN

**Abstract.** We propose an algorithm to prove a definite clause is modeled by an intended minimal model of a set of definite clauses. In the algorithm, no induction scheme will be used explicitly, although in effect a mathematical induction is implied. This algorithm corresponds to an inductionless induction method using the Knuth-Bendix algorithm in an equation problem. It resembles the completion algorithm, but in fact it is a completely different algorithm.

## 1. Introduction

The problem we are concerned with is how to determine if a definite clause is valid under an intended minimal model of a set of definite clauses. Let us call this an implication problem, just as the problem to determine the validity of equalities under some theory is called an equality problem.

The implication problem is the one to be solved by a theorem prover for a first-order logic. It is, however, well known that if the theory includes inductive definitions it is hard to determine the validity of clauses. The reason lies in the difficulties of an inductive proof whose construction is necessary when objects of the theory are defined inductively.

To implement an induction mechanism in a system, you have to implement heuristics of induction pattern or generalization ([2] etc.). Similar difficulties lie in the equality problem. Many researchers have tried adoption of the Knuth-Bendix completion algorithm to the equality problem with an idea that if the system augmented with the new equality to be proved can be completed by the algorithm (and satisfies certain conditions), then the equality is consistent with the original system([6],[8]).

Can the same approach be used in the implication problem? Unfortunately "No" is the answer. For example, Hsiang's system [4] seems not to have enough capability to prove inductive theorems. Although Paul [11] claims his system can conduct inductive proofs, it usually "proves" a theorem by failing to halt.

Hsiang [5] proposed an extension of Prolog to incorporate the ability to conduct inductive proofs. But the ability is quite limited. Firstly, the implication problem targeted by his system is restricted so that an implication to be proved contains only equalities in its consequence part. Secondly, the transformations adopted in the system are so weak that efficient lemmas are not deducible. For example, the system cannot express an implication problem with a non-deterministic predicate in its consequence part, as in the perm-perm problem in Appendix A.3. The rev-rev problem in Appendix A.2 can be expressed but not proved.

We propose in this paper an algorithm to solve the implication problem, by which inductive proof is made without using induction explicitly, which is different from Knuth-Bendix's but to which it bears some resemblance. In Appendix B, we show an example

---

* This paper is a revised and extended version of [12]

which is easy to understand but which conveys key ideas of the proposed algorithm. Readers are advised to read it first. In section 2, we introduce very briefly some terminologies, and in section 3, we describe the algorithm. The conditions necessary to guarantee the validity of a proof or a disproof will be found in section 4. The justification of the conditions is briefly described in section 5.

## 2. Preliminaries

In this section we give necessary definitions of terminology to be used.

### Syntax

We distinguish between sets of variables, function symbols and predicate symbols. A constant is a 0-ary function symbol. A *term* is a variable, a constant, or of the form $f(t_1, \ldots, t_n)$ where $f$ is an n-ary function symbol and $t_1, \ldots, t_n$ are terms. An *atomic formula* (or *atom* for short) is of the form $P(t_1, \ldots, t_n)$, where $P$ is an n-ary predicate symbol and $t_1, \ldots, t_n$ are terms. An atom is *a ground atom* if it contains no occurrence of any variables. A *definite clause* is a clause of the form $A \leftarrow B_1, \ldots, B_n \quad n \geq 0$ where $A, B_1, \ldots, B_n$ are atoms, and variables occurring in them are universally quantified. A definite clause is a *definite ground clause* if it contains no occurrence of any variables. A *substitution* $\sigma = \{X_i/t_i\}$ is an operation defined on an atom, which replaces simultaneously all occurrences of given variables $X_i$ with given terms $t_i$. The result is called an *instance*, and is denoted by $A\sigma$ for an atom $A$. A substitution is a *ground substitution* if the result is ground. This naturally extends to a set of atoms, clauses and programs. We use the following terminology in our own meaning.

- We denote an array of variables with a boldface letter.
- $\forall(F)$ and $\exists(F)$ are the universal and existential closure of any formula $F$, respectively.
- A program is a set of definite clauses.
- A conjunct is a conjunction of atoms, and a disjunct is a disjunction of conjuncts.
- An extended definite clause is a formula of the form $\Gamma \leftarrow \Delta$, where $\leftarrow$ is the usual logical implication, $\Gamma$ and $\Delta$ are respectively a disjunct and a conjunct with some variables existentially quantified in each conjunct, and with all other variables universally quantified in the formula. For the sake of clarity and convenience, existentially quantified variables in different conjuncts are named distinctly. In other words an extended definite clause is $\forall(\exists X_1 \Gamma_1 \vee \cdots \vee \exists X_n \Gamma_n \leftarrow \exists Y \Delta)$, where $\Gamma_i$ and $\Delta$ are conjuncts.
- If it is not ambiguous, $\Gamma_1 \vee \cdots \vee \Gamma_n \leftarrow \Delta$ or $\Gamma \leftarrow \Delta$ is used instead of $\forall(\exists X_1 \Gamma_1 \vee \cdots \exists X_n \Gamma_n \leftarrow \exists Y \Delta)$.
- An internal variable is an existentially quantified variable.
- For a substitution $\sigma = \{X_i/t_i\}_{i=1}^n$, we consider only the substitutions where no $X_i$ appears in any $t_j$. In our context a substitution so restricted is always available if we choose appropriate variants of formulae for $\sigma$ to operate on.
- Equality (=) as a predicate satisfies equality theory [10], and can be considered as defined by the following clauses: $=(\alpha, \alpha)$. $=(\varphi(X_1, \ldots, X_k), \varphi(Y_1, \ldots, Y_k)) \leftarrow =(X_1, Y_1), \ldots, =(X_k, Y_k)$ where $\alpha$ represents an arbitrary constant symbol, $\varphi$ an arbitrary function symbol, and $k$ its arity.
- $M \models G$ denotes that a formula $G$ is correct under the model $M$.
- $M_P$ is a minimal model of a program $P$. For details, see the following "Semantics".

Note that we do not presuppose any interpreter (i.e., computation rule and search rule). So, two conjuncts $A, B$ and $B, A$ (or two disjuncts $A \vee B$ and $B \vee A$) are equivalent in all means.

## Semantics

The concept of "correctness" should be made clear before entering into discussing proofs of "a goal $G$ is correct under a program $P$". It is natural to consider that a closed formula $\forall Z (\exists X \Gamma \leftarrow \exists Y \Delta)$ is correct under a program $P$, if and only if, for any ground substitution $\sigma$ of the variables $Z$, "$P \vdash \exists Y \Delta \sigma$ entails $P \vdash \exists X \Gamma \sigma$" where $\vdash$ will be discussed later. Then what should be the meaning of $P \vdash \exists Y \Delta \sigma$ (or $P \vdash \exists X \Gamma \sigma$) ?

It is also natural to consider a completion of $P$, that is comp($P$), as the meaning of a program $P$ rather than $P$ itself (i.e.,the logical meaning of the program). Especially when a program $P$ is viewed as defining predicates inductively, employing comp($P$) corresponds to adding to a definition of each predicate the statement "Only those defined by the above are $\cdots$".

Defining a transformation, $T_P$ from interpretations to interpretations, associated with a program $P$ under the fixed point semantics, the least fixed point of $T_P$ is considered to be the meaning of the program $P$. Note that, since the optimal fixed point also becomes the minimal fixed point under logic programming, the minimal fixed point semantics is more appropriate [9]. Adding to this advantage, the fixed point of $T_P$ is also a model of comp($P$) if augmented with appropriate equational theories [10]. We adopt this minimal fixed point formalism as the semantics.

An Herbrand universe is commonly used as a domain of interpretations. There are two reasons for this. The first is that the minimal fixed point of $T_P$ on an Herbrand universe coincides with the minimal Herbrand model $HM_P$. The second is that $G$ is a logical consequence of $P$ if and only if $G$ is valid under $HM_P$ [10] when negation of the goal $G$ is of clausal form (general goal clauses of Prolog have this form)

But in our implication problem, naive use of the Herbrand universe is not appropriate. The cause is rooted in the existence of $\sigma$ stated above. Terms substituted for by $\sigma$ can not be restricted to the elements of $HU_P$. In fact if we so restrict, something unpleasant results:

Set $P = \{q(a), \forall X p(X)\}$ and let a goal to be proved $G$ be $\forall X (q(X) \leftarrow p(X))$. Obviously $HM_P = \{q(a), p(a)\}$ implies $HM_P \models G$. But intuitively we believe that $G$ cannot hold since $q(X)$ may not so for some $X$ other than $a$. Moreover, $G$ is not a logical consequence of $P$.

The cure is easy. Since the trouble is ascribed to substitutions which may replace variables with terms consisting of constants other than predicted, we adapt the Herbrand universe to include an enumerable (by Löwenheim's theorem) set of constants including all that we need in future, and call it the extended Herbrand universe $U_P$. We construct the extended Herbrand base $B_P$ in the same way as we construct the Herbrand base. Since the difference between $HU_P$ and $U_P$ is only the existence of additional constants, constructions of models, a least model $M_P$, fixed point and other semantics, etc. are no different from conventional ones. The implication problem is, therefore, to find if $M_P \models \Gamma \leftarrow \Delta$.

## 3. Equiformalization Algorithm

In this section we describe the proposed algorithm. The algorithm proceeds, trying to reduce difference of form on both sides of implication while conserving correctness of implications (the details are not discussed in this paper), to make both formulae be of the same form. Hence we call it the equiformalization algorithm.

Following the equiformalization algorithm, we non-deterministically develop a tree called a transformation tree. If one non-deterministically constructed transformation tree is proved to satisfy a proof-condition stated in section 4, then the algorithm terminates with a positive answer. If one tree satisfies a disproof-condition, then the answer is negative. If all the trees constructed non-deterministically satisfy a failure-condition, then the total algorithm (including all non-deterministic branchings) terminates with failure. There also exist some cases when the algorithm never terminates. In this sense the name 'algorithm' may be inappropriate. Since the name 'Knuth-Bendix algorithm' is used fairly commonly, we use the word too. At each step of the algorithm, a transformation tree is further transformed by expanding a leaf to a subtree.

Throughout this paper, $H$, with possible further qualifications, denotes an atom; $\Gamma$, $\Delta$, $\Lambda$ and $\Pi$, with possible further qualifications, usually denote conjuncts, but denote disjuncts in an implied part of $\leftarrow$; $\sigma$, $\theta$ and $\eta$, with possible further qualifications, denote substitutions.

**Definition 3.1** *A transformation tree is a tree, in which*

*(1) on each node is an extended definite clause (possibly empty on a leaf node),*
*(2) nodes with an empty clause and nodes marked false have no descendants,*
*(3) the descendants of a node are constructed by one of the procedures in Transformations,*
*(4) each branch is marked either "equivalence-preserved" or "equivalence-not-preserved",*
*(5) each node is marked "false" or not marked.*

The equiformalization algorithm proceeds as follows. The algorithm consists of a big loop and twelve transformations. Here, $C_0$ denotes an extended definite clause to prove under a program $P$, where all the predicates referred to in $C_0$ are defined. And in the following, the description is for a non-deterministically obtained tree.

**Algorithm 3.2**
1. *Let $T_0$ be a tree with only a root node $C_0$. $i \leftarrow 0$.*
2. *If $T_i$ satisfies a proof-condition, then the algorithm terminates: the answer is positive. If $T_i$ satisfies a disproof-condition, then the algorithm terminates: the answer is negative. If $T_i$ satisfies a failure-condition, then the algorithm fails (only one non-deterministically selected branch fails).*
3. *Select non-deterministically a non-empty leaf not marked false $C$ in $T_i$ and also non-deterministically one of the procedures in Transformations and apply it to $T_i$. Let the resultant tree be $T_{i+1}$.*
4. *Set $i \leftarrow i + 1$ and go back to step 2.*

Transformation procedures are applied to some non-empty leaf of the tree. The basic idea is to transform a conjunct or a clause on the leaf by "equivalence-preserved" transformations to obtain its descendants, and to repeat the process until all the leaves become trivially valid formulae. Of course, the validity of a root node is equivalent to that of the leaves, and that is preserved by transformations. But in fact we use some "equivalence-not-preserved" transformations, hoping that they will eventually assist us to find good lemmas. Our claim is that even in the latter case, if all the leaves become valid, then under some condition the root node is valid.

**Transformations.**

The transformation procedures, when a tree $T$ and a leaf $C : \Gamma \leftarrow \Delta$ are given, output a resultant tree $T'$. They are one of the following (ones marked with $*$ are equivalence-preserved; the others are equivalence-not-preserved, and a variant is so chosen that its variables do not appear so far in $T$):

*(1) If the leaf is $false \leftarrow true$ then it is marked false. If the leaf is $\Gamma \leftarrow false$ or $true \leftarrow \Delta$ then $T'$ is $T$ with an empty leaf added as a child of $C$.

*(2) Simplification: If $\Gamma$ is a conjunct and there exists a substitution $\sigma = \{X_k/t_k\}$ where
  · $X_k$ is an internal variable of $\Gamma$ and $t_k$ is a term whose variables are of $\Delta$, and
  · for any predicate $P$ in $\Gamma$ there is a predicate $P\sigma$ in $\Delta$,
  then, $T'$ is $T$ with an empty leaf added as a child of $\Gamma \leftarrow \Delta$.

(3) ∨-deletion: Select non-deterministically conjuncts in $\Gamma$ and delete them from $\Gamma$ forming $\Gamma_1$. If all the conjuncts in $\Gamma$ are to be deleted, $\Gamma_1 = false$. $T'$ is $T$ with $\Gamma_1 \leftarrow \Delta$ added as a child of $C$.

*(4) Unfold-right: Select non-deterministically a predicate $H$ in $\Delta$. Assume without loss of generality that $\Delta \equiv \Delta', H$. For every clause in **P** do, $n$ being initialized to 0:
  if $H$ is unifiable with $H'$ of a variant $H' \leftarrow \Pi$ of the clause with m.g.u. $\theta$ (that is, $H\theta = H'\theta$) then
    set $n \leftarrow n+1$, set $\Gamma_n$ to $\Gamma\theta$ and set $\Delta_n$ to $\Delta'\theta, \Pi\theta$
  end-of-do.
  If $n = 0$ then set $T'$ to $T$ with $\Gamma \leftarrow false$ added as a child of $C$. Otherwise set $T'$ to $T$ with $\Gamma_1 \leftarrow \Delta_1, \cdots, \Gamma_n \leftarrow \Delta_n$ added as the children of $C$.

*(5) Unfold-left: Select non-deterministically a conjunct $\Gamma_1$ in $\Gamma$ and a predicate $H$ in $\Gamma_1$. Assume without loss of generality that $\Gamma_1 \equiv \Gamma'_1, H$, and $\Gamma \equiv \Gamma' \vee \Gamma_1$.
  For every clause in **P** do, $n$ being initialized to 0:
  if $H$ is unifiable with $H'$ of a variant $H' \leftarrow \Pi$ of the clause with m.g.u. $\theta$ (that is, $H\theta = H'\theta$) then
    (a) set new $\Gamma_1$ to $X_1 = X'_1, \cdots, X_l = X'_l, \Gamma_1\sigma$ (consequently new $\Gamma_1 \equiv$ new $\Gamma'_1, H\sigma$) where $\sigma = \{X_1/X'_1, \cdots, X_l/X'_l\}$, $X_j$'s are the universally quantified variables in old $\Gamma_1$ to be replaced by $\theta$, and $X'_j$'s are newly introduced variables which have never appeared in $T$,
    (b) If there is no $X_j$ such that it does not appear in $\Delta$ and is to be replaced with a non-variable term by $\theta$, then:
        set $n \leftarrow n+1$ and set $\Gamma_{1,n}$ to $\Gamma'_1\theta', \Pi\theta'$, where $\theta'$ is $\theta$ except $X_j$'s are replaced with $X'_j$'s
  end-of-do.
  If $\Gamma \equiv \Gamma_1$ and $n = 0$ then set $T'$ to $T$ with $false \leftarrow \Delta$ added as a child of $C$. Otherwise, set $T'$ to $T$ with $\Gamma' \vee \Gamma_{1,1} \vee \cdots \vee \Gamma_{1,n} \leftarrow \Delta$ added as a child of $C$.

(6) Cut-right: If there exists an extended definite clause $\Lambda_1 \vee \cdots \vee \Lambda_n \leftarrow \Pi$ which is a variant of a clause on a node $N$ other than $C$ in $T$, and a substitution $\theta$ which satisfies

- $\Delta \equiv \Delta_1, \Delta_2$ and $\Pi\theta \equiv \Delta_1$
- for any internal variable $X$ in $\Pi$, $X\theta$ is a variable and does not occur other than in $\Pi\theta$
- $\theta$ replaces different internal variables in $\Pi$ with different internal variables in $\Delta$

then let $T'$ a tree obtained from $T$ by adding the children $\Gamma \leftarrow \Lambda_i\theta, \Delta_2$ for all $i$ to the leaf $C$. The node $N$ is called a *reference node*, and the node $C$ a *cut node*.

(7) Cut-left: If there exists an extended definite clause $\Lambda \leftarrow \Pi$ which is a variant of a clause on a node $N$ other than $C$ in $T$, and a substitution $\theta$ which satisfies
- $\Gamma \equiv \Gamma_1, \Gamma_2 \vee \Gamma_3$ where $\Gamma_1$ and $\Gamma_2$ are conjuncts, and $\Lambda\theta \equiv \Gamma_1$
- for any internal variable $X$ in $\Lambda$, $X\theta$ is a variable and does not occur other than in $\Lambda\theta$
- $\theta$ replaces different internal variables in $\Lambda$ with different internal variables in $\Gamma_1$ and $\Gamma_2$

then let $T'$ be a tree obtained from $T$ by adding a child $\Pi\theta, \Gamma_2 \vee \Gamma_3 \leftarrow \Delta$ to the leaf $C$. $\Lambda$ is called a cut formula, and $\theta$ is called a cut substitution. Also the node $N$ is called a reference node, and the node $C$ a cut node.

*(8) Replace-right: If it is already proved that $\Lambda_1 \vee \cdots \vee \Lambda_n \leftarrow \Pi$, $\Pi \leftarrow \Lambda_1$, $\cdots$, and $\Pi \leftarrow \Lambda_n$ hold where $\Lambda_1, \cdots, \Lambda_n$, and $\Pi$ are conjuncts and the variables in them do not appear in $T$, and there exists a substitution $\theta$ which satisfies
- $\Delta \equiv \Delta_1, \Delta_2$ and $\Pi\theta \equiv \Delta_1$
- for any internal variable $X$ in $\Pi, X\theta$ is a variable and does not occur other than in $\Pi\theta$
- $\theta$ replaces different internal variables in $\Pi$ with different internal variables in $\Delta$

then let $T'$ be a tree obtained from $T$ by adding children $\Gamma \leftarrow \Lambda_i\theta, \Delta_2$ for all $i$ to the leaf $C$.

*(9) Replace-left: If it is already proved that $\Lambda \leftarrow \Pi$ and $\Pi \leftarrow \Lambda$ hold where $\Lambda$ and $\Pi$ are conjuncts and the variables in $\Lambda$ and $\Pi$ do not appear in $T$ and there exists a substitution $\theta$ which satisfy
- $\Gamma \equiv \Gamma_1, \Gamma_2 \vee \Gamma_3$ where $\Gamma_1$ and $\Gamma_2$ are conjuncts, and $\Lambda\theta \equiv \Gamma_1$
- for any internal variable $X$ in $\Lambda$, $X\theta$ is a variable and does not occur other than in $\Lambda\theta$
- $\theta$ replaces different internal variables in $\Lambda$ with different internal variables in $\Gamma_1$ and $\Gamma_2$

then let $T'$ be a tree obtained from $T$ by adding a child $\Pi\theta, \Gamma_2 \vee \Gamma_3 \leftarrow \Delta$ to the leaf $C$.

(10) Partial instantiation: If there exists a substitution $\sigma = \{X_k/t_k\}$ where
- $X_k$ is an internal variable of $\Gamma$, and $t_k$ is a term whose variables are of $\Delta$,

then, $T'$ is $T$ with a leaf $\Gamma\sigma \leftarrow \Delta$ added as a child of $C$.

(11) Delete:

*(11-1) If $\Delta \equiv \Delta_1, \Delta_2$ and
   (a) the variables appearing in $\Delta_1$ never appear other than in $\Delta_1$, and
   (b) $\Delta_1 \leftarrow true$ is provable, where all variables are existentially quantified,
   then, $T'$ is $T$ with a leaf $\Gamma \leftarrow \Delta_2$ added as a child of $C$.

*(11-2) If $\Delta \equiv \Delta_1, \Delta_2$ satisfies the above (a) and

(b) $false \leftarrow \Delta_1$ is provable, where all variables are existentially quantified, then, $T'$ is $T$ with a leaf $\Gamma \leftarrow false$ added as a child of $C$.

*(11-3) If $\Gamma \equiv \Gamma_1, \Gamma_2 \vee \Gamma_3$ where $\Gamma_1$ and $\Gamma_2$ are conjuncts and

    (a) the variables appearing in $\Gamma_1$ never appear other than in $\Gamma_1$, and

    (b) $\Gamma_1 \leftarrow true$ is provable, where all variables are existentially quantified, then, $T'$ is $T$ with a leaf $\Gamma_2 \vee \Gamma_3 \leftarrow \Delta$ added as a child of $C$.

*(11-4) If $\Gamma \equiv \Gamma_1, \Gamma_2 \vee \Gamma_3$ where $\Gamma_1$ and $\Gamma_2$ are conjuncts and satisfies the above (a), and

    (b') $false \leftarrow \Gamma_1$ is provable, where all variables are existentially quantified, then, $T'$ is $T$ with a leaf $\Gamma_3 \leftarrow \Delta$ added as a child of $C$.

*(11-5) If $\Gamma \equiv \Gamma_1, \Gamma_2 \vee \Gamma_3$ where $\Gamma_1$ and $\Gamma_2$ are conjuncts, and

    (c) $\Delta \equiv \Delta_1, \Delta_2$ and $\Gamma_1 \equiv \Delta_1$ then, $T'$ is $T$ with a leaf $\Gamma_2 \vee \Gamma_3 \leftarrow \Delta$ added as a child of $C$.

(11-6) If $\Gamma \equiv \Gamma_{1,1}, \Gamma_{1,2} \vee \cdots \vee \Gamma_{n,1}, \Gamma_{n,2}$ where $\Gamma_{i,1}$ and $\Gamma_{i,2}$ are conjuncts for all $i$, $\Delta \equiv \Delta_1, \Delta_2$, and $\Gamma_{i,1} \equiv \Delta_1$ for all $i$, then $T'$ is $T$ with a leaf $\Gamma_{1,2} \vee \cdots \vee \Gamma_{n,2} \leftarrow \Delta_2$ added as a child of $C$.

*(12) Equality-elimination: Suppose an equality $X = t$ is included in some conjuncts in $\Gamma$ or $\Delta$ (where $X$ is a variable and $t$ a term). $T'$ is $T$ with a $C$ on which substitution $\{X/t\}$ is executed is added as a child of original $C$, where the conjunct is deleted from the modified $C$ if $X$ is an internal variable and does not appear in the conjunct after the substitution.

Note that a cut procedure is quite similar to a fold transformation [13]. The difference is that the cut replaces an extended definite clause with a prospectively non-equivalent predicate (or another extended definite clause), whereas the fold replaces it with its equivalent predicate.

Also note that although from the above description it seems that there is so much non-determinism that the algorithm generates many lemmas, some restriction of the application of 'unfold' reduces the lemmas generated to no more than those generated by the Knuth-Bendix algorithm (if the problem is an equality problem). The details are not discussed here due to the limitation of space.

## 4. Conditions to support a proof, a disproof or failure

In this section, we present conditions for the transformation tree generated by the equiformalization algorithm to support a proof or a disproof, or to suggest that some transformation applied is inappropriate. Justification for them is described in the next section. Some terminology referred in the conditions is defined afterwards.

### Condition 4.1 (condition to support a proof)
(1) The leaves are all empty and are not marked false.
(2) Any elementary directed closed path in a dependence graph of a transformation tree is a contraction path.

### Condition 4.2 (condition to support a disproof)
(1) There is a node marked false.
(2) All the transformations done between the root node and the node marked false are marked equivalence-preserved.

## Condition 4.3 (condition to suggest a failure)

(1) Condition 4.1 (1) holds, but not Condition 4.1 (2).
(2) Condition 4.2 (1) holds, but not Condition 4.2 (2).

In Tamaki and Sato's Unfold/fold transformation [13], which, in a sense, is included in our approach, replacement of equivalent conjuncts is limited, so that the replacer must be "smaller" than the replacee. In contrast, in our approach, we do not place such a condition on replacements, but on cuts (more precisely, when the cut forms a "loop" with other branches). Clearly our restriction is weaker than theirs. A similar approach may be applied to fold/unfold transformations.

We prove the correctness of these conditions in the next section. The following are definitions and theorems to be used in the proofs.

**Definition 4.4** If for a substitution $\theta = \{X_i/t_i\}_{i=1}^{n}$, $X_i$'s do not appear in any $t_i$'s, a constraint expression $\varpi(\theta)$ of $\theta$ is: $\varpi(\theta) \equiv X_1 = t_1, \cdots, X_n = t_n$.

**Definition 4.5** A substitution $\theta$ is compatible with a first order formula $\Pi$ iff $M_P \models \exists(\Pi\theta)$.

**Definition 4.6** A dependence graph of a transformation tree $T$ is a directed graph whose nodes and branches are those of $T$ with a few more branches added, where,
(1) a direction of a branch originated in $T$ is from a parent to a son.
(2) a new branch is added from a cut node to its reference node for any cut.

**Definition 4.7** An example of an extended definite clause $\Gamma \leftarrow \Delta$ is a substitution $\theta$ such that
· All the universally quantified variables in the clause are instantiated to ground terms by $\theta$, and $\Delta\theta$ is ground, and
· $M_P \models \Delta\theta$
A counterexample is an example $\theta$ but $M_P \not\models \exists(\Gamma\theta)$.

**Theorem 4.8 (propagation of a counterexample)** If there is a counterexample on a node $N$ in a dependence graph, there is at least one successor node of $N$ on which there is a counterexample.

(proof) We have cases according to what transformation is applied to $N$. The numbers used to identify cases in the following correspond to the ones in Transformations in section 3. Let $\sigma$ be a counterexample on $N$ and $\sigma'$ be the one on a successor node, which shall be the required.
(1) In the former case, a son is not generated. In the latter case, we do not have $\sigma$.
(2) We do not have $\sigma$.
(3),(5),(9),(10),(11),(12) Obviously $\sigma' = \sigma$ except that the elements whose replaced variable does not appear in the resultant node are deleted.
(4) Let us assume that $\sigma$ is compatible with $\varpi(\theta)$ for some $\theta$ among $n$ $\theta$'s (for if such a $\theta$ does not exist, $M_P \not\models \Delta\sigma$). Let $\sigma'$ be a ground substitution whose constraint expression is equivalent to $\varpi(\theta)\sigma$ (the existence of such a $\sigma'$ is easily proved).
(6) Let $\eta$ be a substitution which changes a clause on the reference node to the variant used in the transformation. We have two cases:

(a) $M_P \models \Lambda_i\theta\sigma \leftarrow \Pi\theta\sigma$ for some $i$, i.e., $M_P \models \exists(\Lambda_i\theta\sigma)$. Let $\sigma''$ be such that $\Lambda_i\theta\sigma\sigma''$ is ground and $M_P \models \Lambda_i\theta\sigma\sigma''$. Then let $\sigma'$ be a union of $\sigma$ and $\sigma''$ but deleting elements whose replaced variables are not in $\Lambda_i\theta, \Delta_2$. Since $\sigma''$ does not replace internal variables in $\Gamma$, $\sigma'$ is a counterexample.

(b) $M_P \not\models \Lambda_i\theta\sigma \leftarrow \Pi\theta\sigma$ for any $i$, i.e., $M_P \not\models (\Lambda_1 \vee \cdots \vee \Lambda_n \leftarrow \Pi)\theta\sigma$. In other words $\eta\theta\sigma$ is a counterexample on a reference node.

(7) Let $\eta$ be a substitution which changes a clause on the reference node to the variant used in the transformation. We have two cases:

(a) $M_P \not\models (\Pi\theta, \Gamma_2 \vee \Gamma_3 \leftarrow \Delta)\sigma$. Obviously $\sigma$ is a counterexample.

(b) $M_P \models (\Pi\theta, \Gamma_2 \vee \Gamma_3 \leftarrow \Delta)\sigma$, i.e., $M_P \models \exists(\Pi\theta\sigma)$. It is easily shown that $M_P \not\models \exists(\Lambda\theta\sigma)$ from $M_P \models (\Pi\theta, \Gamma_2 \vee \Gamma_3 \leftarrow \Delta)\sigma$ and conditions on $\theta$. We have $M_p \not\models (\Lambda \leftarrow \Pi)\theta\sigma$. In other words, $\eta\theta\sigma$ is a counterexample on a reference node.

(8) By the equivalence of $\Lambda_1 \vee \cdots \vee \Lambda_n$ and $\Pi$, for some $i$ $M_P \models \exists((\Lambda_i\theta, \Delta_2)\sigma)$ Therefore we can find a ground substitution $\sigma''$ such that $M_P \models (\Lambda_i\theta, \Delta_2)\sigma\sigma''$ and $\sigma''$ does not replace any internal variables in $\Gamma$. Clearly $\sigma\sigma''$ is a counterexample on $\Gamma \leftarrow \Lambda_i\theta, \Delta_2$.

**Theorem 4.9 (propagation of an example)** *If there is an example on a node $N$ in a dependence graph, there is at least one successor node of $N$ on which there is an example.*

The proof is similar to that of Theorem 4.8, and is easily derived.

**Definition 4.10** *A directed closed path in a dependence graph is called a contraction path iff:*

*(1) for any node in the path there exists a well-founded order ($\succ$) among the examples of the extended definite clauses on the node, and*

*(2) for any example $\sigma$ on any node (whose clause is $\Gamma \leftarrow \Delta$) in the path and any example $\sigma'$ on the node obtained as a result of propagations of $\sigma$ along the path, $(\Gamma \leftarrow \Delta)\sigma \succ (\Gamma \leftarrow \Delta)\sigma'$ (strict inequality)*

**Definition 4.11** *When a well-founded order stated in Definition 4.10 is defined, we accordingly define a well-founded order among examples such that:*
$\sigma \succ \sigma'$ *iff* $(\Gamma \leftarrow \Delta)\sigma \succ (\Gamma \leftarrow \Delta)\sigma'$

The well-founded order required by Definition 4.10 may be defined differently on different nodes and on different paths. For example, we can define it for a predicate $p(s, t)$, or a conjunct $\Delta$ as:

(a) $p(s_1, t_1) \succ p(s_2, t_2)$ iff $s_2$ is smaller in structure than $s_1$

(b) using the weight $w$ defined by Tamaki and Sato [13], $\Delta\sigma \succ \Delta\sigma'$ iff $w(\Delta\sigma) > w(\Delta\sigma')$.

The latter is quite orthodox but it may be difficult in a real application, whereas the former is very easy to use but is limited. But if all the predicates are defined in $P$ in the way "primitive recursive functions" are defined, that is, the truth value of a predicate at $s(t)$ is defined by the truth value of the predicate at $t$, then we can always find an argument which serves as an argument $s$ in (a), which guarantees equivalence of (a) and (b). This simplifies a great deal of work to be done to check the proof-condition.

# 5. Justification of the Algorithm and the Conditions

In this section we show justification of the basic algorithm and the conditions, that is, if the proof-condition is satisfied then the target clause is modeled by $M_P$, and if the disproof-condition is satisfied then it is not.

**Theorem 5.1** *Let $N$ be a node and $N_1, \cdots, N_n$ be $N$'s sons in a transformation tree.*
*(1) If a transformation applied to $N$ is marked equivalence-preserved, then*
   $M_P \models N$ *iff* $M_P \models N_1, \cdots,$ *and* $M_P \models N_n$
*(2) If it is not marked equivalence-preserved and is neither cut-right nor cut-left, then*
   $M_P \models N$ *if* $M_P \models N_1, \cdots,$ *and* $M_P \models N_n$
*The proof is straightforward.*

**Theorem 5.2** *If a transformation tree satisfies the condition stated in Condition 4.1 (2) and there is a counterexample on a node in a transformation tree, then there is a counterexample on a leaf which is a result of propagations of the former counterexample.*

(proof) The proof is by induction on the construction of the tree.
Basis case: When the tree consists of a root node only, the statement is true.
Induction step:
(1) When the last transformation is other than cut, the statement is true by virtue of Theorem 5.1 and the induction hypothesis.
(2) When the last transformation is either cut-right or cut-left, supposing that there is a counterexample on the cut-node, we deduce that there is a counterexample on the resultant leaf, which is a result of propagations. Let $T$ be the transformation tree. The proof is by reductio ad absurdum.
   Let us suppose that we don't have counterexamples on the resultant node, whereas we have at least one on the cut node. Let $\sigma$ be the smallest among the counterexamples (use the order required by Definition 4.10). By the same argument as in the proof of Theorem 4.8 (cases (6) and (7)), there should be a counterexample $\sigma'$ on a reference node of the cut. By virtue of the induction hypothesis, for the transformation tree $T'$ which is the same as $T$ except for the resultant leaf (i.e. the tree just before the cut is applied), the statement holds. Therefore $\sigma'$ propagates to some leaf of $T'$. Since we are supposing that there is no counterexample on the leaves of $T$, the propagated counterexample $\sigma''$ inevitably comes to the cut node. Since $\sigma''$ is a result of propagations along a directed path, by the contraction property of the path $\sigma \succ \sigma''$. This contradicts the minimality of $\sigma$.

**Theorem 5.3** *Let $\Gamma \leftarrow \Delta$ be a clause on a root.*
*(1) If a proof-condition is satisfied, then $M_P \models \Gamma \leftarrow \Delta$.*
*(2) If a disproof-condition is satisfied, then $M_P \not\models \Gamma \leftarrow \Delta$.*
*(3) If a failure-condition is satisfied, then either of the above cases may happen.*

(proof)
(1) Let us suppose the contrary holds. By the hypothesis, there is a counterexample on a root node. By virtue of Theorem 5.2, there is a counterexample on a leaf. But by the proof-condition all the leaves (or more precisely all the nodes one branch up from the leaves) are obviously true (i.e., modeled by $M_P$). This is a contradiction.
(2)(3) Obvious by Theorem 5.1.

## 6. Discussion

Among interesting topics which we have not discussed in this paper are:

(1) how to reduce the degree of non-determinism occurring in the algorithm

(2) the relation between the algorithm we proposed and the inductionless-induction method adopting the Knuth-Bendix completion algorithm.

(3) what procedures are to be added to augment capability of the algorithm

Concerning the first item, we are currently investigating two ways. One is to introduce an order between conjuncts, and allow on a transformation tree only clauses reduced according to this order. The other is to implement a strategy to find the most appropriate action to take, which, observing that unless cut or replacement is used non-trivial simplification or delete can not be applied, incorporates a way to find appropriate unfold sequences and appropriate lemma.

For the second item, we have three things worth mentioning.

· To simulate the Knuth-Bendix algorithm, we have to:

   (i) add some procedures to imitate the whole capability of superpositions

   (ii) modify procedures to use a simplification order

   (iii) make some modifications to utilize the functionality of the predicates

· Even without those modifications, the proposed algorithm has capabilities almost matching the Knuth-Bendix algorithm. Note that "delete" procedure is a powerful tool, which has no counterpart in the Knuth-Bendix algorithm.

· The proposed method is advantageous on the following points

   (i) it proves "implication"

   (ii) it knows which clauses must be proved, and which clauses are just prospective lemma that do not need to be proved.

   (iii) it does not rely on a structure-induced order of terms. In the Knuth-Bendix algorithm it is almost always necessary to make the equality relation directed.

For the last item, we are studying two approaches: procedures to utilize nice properties of system predicates; and restrictions on transformations (1), (3) and (10), so that equivalence can be proved by one root node.

## 7. Acknowledgement

We would like to express our thanks to Mr. Yutaka Takuma, general manager of Naka Works, Hitachi Ltd.; to Dr. Eiichi Maruyama, general manager of the Advanced Research Laboratory, Hitachi Ltd.; and to Mr. Masahiro Mori, manager of the System and Software Design Department of Naka Works, Hitachi Ltd. for their giving us the chance to conduct this research. We also thank Mrs. Mariko Sakurai for her encouragement and fine typing.

## References

[1] Apt, K.R. and van Emden, M.H.: Contribution to the theory of logic programming, J. ACM **29** (1982) 841–862

[2] Boyer, R.S. and Moore, J.S.: Proving Theorems About LISP Functions, J. ACM **22** (1975) 129–144

[3] van Emden, M.H. and Kowalski, R.A.: The semantics of predicate logic as a programming language, J. ACM **23** (1976) 733–742

[4] Hsiang, J.: Refutational Theorem Proving using Term-Rewriting System, *Artificial Intelligence* **25** (1985) 255–300

[5] Hsiang, J. and Srivas, M.: Automatic Inductive Theorem Proving using Prolog, *Theoretical Computer Science* **54** (1987) 3–28

[6] Huet, G. and Hullot, J-M.: Proofs by Induction in Equational Theories with Constructors, *Comput. Syst. Sci.* **25** (1982) 239–266

[7] Kanamori, T. and Fujita, H.: Formulation of induction formulas in verification of Prolog programs, *ICOT Technical Report TR-094* (1984)

[8] Kapur, D. and Musser, D.R.: Proof by Consistency, *Artificial Intelligence* **31** (1987) 125–157

[9] Lassez, J.-L. and Maher, M.J.: Closures and fairness in the semantics of programming logic, *Theoretical Computer Science* **29** (1984) 167–184

[10] Lloyd, J.W.: Foundations of Logic Programming, Springer-Verlag (1984)

[11] Paul, E.: On solving the Equality Problem in Theories Defined by Horn Clauses, *Theoretical Computer Science* **44** (1986) 127–153

[12] Sakurai, A. and Motoda, H.: Inductionless Induction Method in Prolog, *Proc. 4th Conference Proceedings of Japan Society of Software Science and Technology* (1987) 231–234

[13] Tamaki, H. and Sato, T.: Unfold/fold transformation of logic programs, *Proc. 2nd International Logic Programming Conference* (1984) 127–138

## Appendix A. Examples

In this section some examples of application of the proposed algorithm are presented. The program under consideration is as follows.

Note that in definite clauses on transformation trees, the variables appearing on both sides are considered universally quantified, and those appearing on only one side are considered existentially quantified.

$$rev([\,],[\,]). \tag{p1}$$
$$rev([A|X],Z) \leftarrow rev(X,Y), lins(A,Y,Z). \tag{p2}$$
$$lins(A,[\,],[A]). \tag{p3}$$
$$lins(A,[B|Y],[B|Z]) \leftarrow lins(A,Y,Z). \tag{p4}$$
$$mem(A,[A|X]). \tag{p5}$$
$$mem(A,[B|X]) \leftarrow mem(A,X). \tag{p6}$$
$$perm([\,],[\,]). \tag{p7}$$
$$perm([A|X],Z) \leftarrow perm(X,Y), ins(A,Y,Z). \tag{p8}$$
$$ins(A,X,[A|X]). \tag{p9}$$
$$ins(A,[B|Y],[B|Z]) \leftarrow ins(A,Y,Z). \tag{p10}$$

### A.1 Rev–rev Problem

The first example is the "rev-rev" problem [2] stated in Prolog [7]. The problem is to show the validity of $rev(Z,X) \leftarrow rev(X,Z)$. The stem of a complete tree resulted in a proof tree is created as follows.

$$rev(Z, X) \leftarrow rev(X, Z). \tag{r1}$$

$$\Downarrow \text{ unfold-right. cases for (p1) omitted}$$

$$rev(Z, [A|X]) \leftarrow rev(X, Y), lins(A, Y, Z). \tag{r2}$$

$$\Downarrow \text{ cut-right with (r1).}$$

$$rev(Z, [A|X]) \leftarrow rev(Y, X), lins(A, Y, Z). \tag{r3}$$

$$\Downarrow \text{ unfold-right. cases for (p1) omitted}$$

$$rev(Z, [A|X]) \leftarrow rev(Y, U), lins(B, U, X), lins(A, [B|Y], Z). \tag{r4}$$

$$\Downarrow \text{ unfold-right.}$$

$$rev([B|Z], [A|X]) \leftarrow rev(Y, U), lins(B, U, X), lins(A, Y, Z). \tag{r5}$$

$$\Downarrow \text{ unfold-left.}$$

$$rev(Z, V), lins(B, V, [A|X]) \leftarrow rev(Y, U), lins(B, U, X), lins(A, Y, Z). \tag{r6}$$

$$\Downarrow \text{ unfold-left.}$$

$$rev(Z, [A|V]), lins(B, V, X) \leftarrow rev(Y, U), lins(B, U, X), lins(A, Y, Z). \tag{r7}$$

$$\Downarrow \text{ cut-left with (r3).}$$

$$rev(Y', V), lins(A, Y', Z), lins(B, V, X)$$
$$\leftarrow rev(Y, U), lins(B, U, X), lins(A, Y, Z). \tag{r8}$$

$$\Downarrow \ Y' \leftarrow Y, \ V \leftarrow U.$$

$$\square$$

Before going to the next example, we show two (stems of) different transformation trees based on two different formalizations of the "rev-rev" problem. The first one is as follows:

$$X = Z \leftarrow rev(X, Y), rev(Y, Z). \tag{s1}$$

$$\Downarrow \text{ unfold-right. cases for (p1) omitted}$$

$$[A|X] = Z \leftarrow rev(X, U), lins(A, U, Y), rev(Y, Z). \tag{s2}$$

$$\Downarrow \text{ unfold-left.}$$

$$X = Z', [A|Z'] = Z \leftarrow rev(X, U), lins(A, U, Y), rev(Y, Z). \tag{s3}$$

$$\Downarrow \text{ cut-left with (s1)}$$

$$rev(X, Y'), rev(Y', Z'), [A|Z'] = Z \leftarrow rev(X, U), lins(A, U, Y), rev(Y, Z). \tag{s4}$$

$$\Downarrow \ Y' \leftarrow U \text{ and delete}$$

$$rev(U, Z'), [A|Z'] = Z \leftarrow lins(A, U, Y), rev(Y, Z). \tag{s5}$$

$$\Downarrow \text{ unfold-right. cases for (p3) omitted}$$

$$rev([B|U], Z'), [A|Z'] = Z \leftarrow lins(A, U, Y), rev([B|Y], Z). \tag{s6}$$

$$\Downarrow \text{ unfold-right.}$$

$$rev([B|U], Z'), [A|Z'] = Z \leftarrow lins(A, U, Y), rev(Y, W), lins(B, W, Z). \tag{s7}$$

$$\Downarrow \text{ unfold-left.}$$

$$rev(U, V), lins(B, V, Z'), [A|Z'] = Z$$
$$\leftarrow lins(A, U, Y), rev(Y, W), lins(B, W, Z). \tag{s8}$$

$$\Downarrow \text{ cut-right with (s5).}$$

$$rev(U, V), lins(B, V, Z'), [A|Z'] = Z$$
$$\leftarrow rev(U, W'), [A|W'] = W, lins(B, W, Z). \tag{s9}$$

$$\Downarrow \text{ equality elimination.}$$

$$rev(U, V), lins(B, V, Z'), [A|Z'] = Z \leftarrow rev(U, W'), lins(B, [A|W'], Z). \tag{s10}$$

$$\Downarrow \text{ unfold-right.}$$

$$rev(U, V), lins(B, V, Z'), [A|Z'] = [A|Z] \leftarrow rev(U, W'), lins(B, W', Z). \tag{s11}$$

$$\Downarrow \ Z' \leftarrow Z, \ V \leftarrow W' \text{ etc.}$$

$$\square$$

We now show the second formalization of the problem. In the following, a predicate $list(X)$ is defined by $list([\,])$. $list([A|X]) \leftarrow list(X)$.

$$rev(X,Y), rev(Y,X) \leftarrow list(X). \tag{t1}$$

$\Downarrow$ unfold-right.

$$rev([A|X],Y), rev(Y,[A|X]) \leftarrow list(X). \tag{t2}$$

$\Downarrow$ unfold-left.

$$rev(X,Y'), lins(A,Y',Y), rev(Y,[A|X]) \leftarrow list(X). \tag{t3}$$

$\Downarrow$ cut-right with (t1)

$$rev(X,Y'), lins(A,Y',Y), rev(Y,[A|X]) \leftarrow rev(X,U), rev(U,X). \tag{t4}$$

$\Downarrow$ $Y' \leftarrow U$ and delete

$$lins(A,U,Y), rev(Y,[A|X]) \leftarrow rev(U,X). \tag{t5}$$

$\Downarrow$ unfold-right. cases for (p1) omitted

$$lins(A,[B|U],Y), rev(Y,[A|X]) \leftarrow rev(U,V), lins(B,V,X). \tag{t6}$$

$\Downarrow$ unfold-left.

$$lins(A,U,Y), rev([B|Y],[A|X]) \leftarrow rev(U,V), lins(B,V,X). \tag{t7}$$

$\Downarrow$ unfold-left.

$$lins(A,U,Y), rev(Y,W), lins(B,W,[A|X]) \leftarrow rev(U,V), lins(B,V,X). \tag{t8}$$

$\Downarrow$ unfold-left and $\lor$-delete.

$$lins(A,U,Y), rev(Y,[A|W]), lins(B,W,X) \leftarrow rev(U,V), lins(B,V,X). \tag{t9}$$

$\Downarrow$ cut-right with (t5).

$$lins(A,U,Y), rev(Y,[A|W]), lins(B,W,X)$$
$$\leftarrow lins(A,U,Y'), rev(Y',[A|V]), lins(B,V,X). \tag{t10}$$

$\Downarrow$ $Y \leftarrow Y'$, $W \leftarrow V$

$\square$

## A.2 Last-is-a-member Problem

The "last-is-a-member" is an example of a problem where we have to use many heuristics for without knowing the proposed algorithm [7]. The problem is to show the validity of

$$\forall A, X, Z \; mem(A,X) \leftarrow rev(X,[A|Z]).$$

One transformation tree is:

$$mem(A,X) \leftarrow rev(X,[A|Z]). \tag{m1}$$

$\Downarrow$ unfold-right.

$$mem(A,[B|X]) \leftarrow rev(X,U), lins(B,U,[A|Z]). \tag{m2}$$

$\Downarrow$ unfold-right. cases for (p3) omitted

$$mem(A,[B|X]) \leftarrow rev(X,[A|U]), lins(B,U,Z). \tag{m3}$$

$\Downarrow$ unfold-left.

$$mem(A,X) \leftarrow rev(X,[A|U]), lins(B,U,Z). \tag{m4}$$

$\Downarrow$ cut-left with (m1).

$$rev(X,[A|Z']) \leftarrow rev(X,[A|U]), lins(B,U,Z). \tag{m5}$$

$\Downarrow$ $Z' \leftarrow U$.

$\square$

## A.3 Perm-perm Problem

Show that if a list $Z$ is a permutation of a permutation of a list $X$, then $Z$ is a permutation of $X$. The problem seems very trivial if we understand the abstract meaning of 'permutation', but if we refer only to the formal definition of the predicate "perm", then it is quite complicated. Readers who have the opposite opinion are challenged to solve it without using the proposed algorithm.

$$perm(X, Z) \leftarrow perm(X, Y), perm(Y, Z). \tag{pm1}$$

$\Downarrow$ unfold-right. cases only for (p8)

$$perm([A|X], Z) \leftarrow perm(X, U), ins(A, U, Y), perm(Y, Z). \tag{pm2}$$

$\Downarrow$ unfold-left.

$$perm(X, V), ins(A, V, Z) \leftarrow perm(X, U), ins(A, U, Y), perm(Y, Z). \tag{pm3}$$

$\Downarrow$ cut-left with (pm1).

$$perm(X, W), perm(W, V), ins(A, V, Z) \leftarrow$$
$$perm(X, U), ins(A, U, Y), perm(Y, Z). \tag{pm4}$$

$\Downarrow$ $W \leftarrow U$ and delete

$$perm(U, V), ins(A, V, Z) \leftarrow ins(A, U, Y), perm(Y, Z). \tag{pm5}$$

$\Downarrow$ unfold-right. cases only for (p10)

$$perm([B|U], V), ins(A, V, Z) \leftarrow ins(A, U, Y), perm([B|Y], Z). \tag{pm6}$$

$\Downarrow$ unfold-right.

$$perm([B|U], V), ins(A, V, Z) \leftarrow ins(A, U, Y), perm(Y, W), ins(B, W, Z). \tag{pm7}$$

$\Downarrow$ unfold-left

$$perm(U, V'), ins(B, V', V), ins(A, V, Z) \leftarrow$$
$$ins(A, U, Y), perm(Y, W), ins(B, W, Z). \tag{pm8}$$

$\Downarrow$ cut-right with (pm5)

$$perm(U, V'), ins(B, V', V), ins(A, V, Z) \leftarrow$$
$$perm(U, Y), ins(A, Y, W), ins(B, W, Z). \tag{pm9}$$

$\Downarrow$ $V' \leftarrow Y$ and delete

$$ins(B, Y, V), ins(A, V, Z) \leftarrow ins(A, Y, W), ins(B, W, Z). \tag{pm10}$$

$\Downarrow$ unfold-right. cases only for (p10)

$$ins(B, [C|Y], V), ins(A, V, Z) \leftarrow ins(A, Y, W), ins(B, [C|W], Z). \tag{pm11}$$

$\Downarrow$ unfold-right. cases only for (p10)

$$ins(B, [C|Y], V), ins(A, V, [C|Z]) \leftarrow ins(A, Y, W), ins(B, W, Z). \tag{pm12}$$

$\Downarrow$ unfold-left and v-delete.

$$ins(B, Y, V), ins(A, [C|V], [C|Z]) \leftarrow ins(A, Y, W), ins(B, W, Z). \tag{pm13}$$

$\Downarrow$ unfold-left and v-delete.

$$ins(B, Y, V), ins(A, V, Z) \leftarrow ins(A, Y, W), ins(B, W, Z). \tag{pm14}$$

$\Downarrow$ cut-right with (pm10)

$$ins(B, Y, V), ins(A, V, Z) \leftarrow ins(B, Y, W), ins(A, W, Z). \tag{pm15}$$

$\Downarrow$ $V \leftarrow W$

$\square$

Readers may be interested in what is happening in side branches. One branch stemmed from (pm11) is as follows.

$$ins(B, [C|Y], V), ins(A, V, Z) \leftarrow ins(A, Y, W), ins(B, [C|W], Z). \qquad \text{(pm11)}$$

$\Downarrow$ unfold-right. cases only for (p9)

$$ins(B, [C|Y], V), ins(A, V, [B, C|W]) \leftarrow ins(A, Y, W). \qquad \text{(pm12}'\text{)}$$

$\Downarrow$ unfold-left and V-delete.

$$ins(B, [C|Y], [B|V]), ins(A, V, [C|W]) \leftarrow ins(A, Y, W). \qquad \text{(pm13}'\text{)}$$

$\Downarrow$ unfold-left and V-delete.

$$ins(B, [C|Y], [B, C|V]), ins(A, V, W) \leftarrow ins(A, Y, W). \qquad \text{(pm14}'\text{)}$$

$\Downarrow$ unfold-left and V-delete.

$$ins(A, Y, W) \leftarrow ins(A, Y, W). \qquad \text{(pm15}'\text{)}$$

$\Downarrow$

$\square$

## Appendix B. Inequality

This example is intended to show some key ideas of the proposed algorithm. In this example, an inequality is proved using an algorithm based on the same principle as ours for Prolog. Similar applications may be found in other fields.

Suppose you know only three things: arithmetic of non-negative integers, inequality relations between integers, and the fact that you may deduce an identical term from both sides of an inequality.

How do you prove $(n+1)^2 \geq 4n$ when $n \geq 1$?

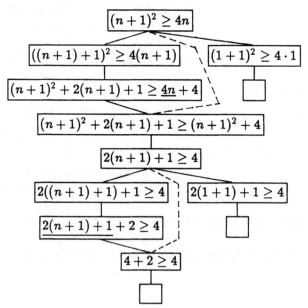

# Pseudo Extension in Default Reasoning

# and

# Belief Revision by Model Inference

Hiroko Yuasa* and Setsuo Arikawa

Department of Information Systems,

Kyushu University 39, Kasuga 816, Japan

Mailing address: S. Arikawa, Research Institute of Fundamental Information Science,

Kyushu University 33, Fukuoka 812, Japan

### Abstract

This paper is concerned with extension and belief revision in Reiter's default reasoning. First we introduce a new notion of pseudo extension which is successively constructed from a given default theory. We show that the set of pseudo extensions contains the set of extensions, so that we can get some reasonable candidates of extension in a constructive way. This should be a first step towards computerization of the default reasoning. We also discuss the belief revision problem from the viewpoint of Shapiro's inductive inference of models.

## 1. Introduction

Reasoning we use in our daily problem solving is not always from complete information unlike mathematical reasoning. One of the main goals of artificial intelligence research is to computerize our reasoning. Hence much attention has been paid to such reasoning and formulations have been proposed by many authors. Reiter's default reasoning is one such formulation. He used the notion of default and formulated incomplete knowledge about a world as a pair : a set of true but incomplete knowledge and a set of special inference rules called *defaults*. He enlarged the incomplete knowledge to describe the world as completely as possible. The enlarged knowledge is called an *extension*, which is the set of knowledge that seems true as a result of reasoning from incomplete knowledge and is a possible world at that time. Thus the extension is not definite knowledge but just a belief about the world, and hence it needs to be modified when new facts are found.

In the Reiter's default theory we can reason from incomplete knowledge in a very natural way. However, the extension can not successively be constructed, because it is defined by using itself in applying the defaults.

In the present paper, we first try to solve this difficulty. We define a successively constructable set

---

*   Presently at Hitachi Central Research Laboratory, Hitachi Ltd.

of knowledge, which we call a *pseudo extension*, and discuss the relationship between Reiter's extensions and ours. We also show that our extension is a natural generalization of Reiter's.

Unlike the reasoning in classical logic, the reasoning from incomplete knowledge is necessarily non-monotonic. Hence we sometimes must modify the belief, i.e. the knowledge derived by such reasoning. In the present paper we take this problem of belief revision as that of extension modification. Then we can see that the process of belief revision is very similar to Shapiro's model inference. We also discuss the belief revision from this viewpoint.

## 2. Reiter's Default Reasoning

We start with recalling the definitions and important results on default reasoning according to [1, 2].

Let $L$ be a first order language. Then a *default* is a rule of the form

$$\frac{\alpha(x) : M\beta_1(x), \ldots, M\beta_m(x)}{\omega(x)},$$

where $\alpha(x), \beta_1(x), \cdots, \beta_m(x), \omega(x)$ are well-formed formulas (wff, for short) in $L$, and $x$ denotes a sequence of free variables. We call $\alpha(x)$ a *prerequisite*, $\beta_1(x), \ldots, \beta_m(x)$ *justifications*, and $\omega(x)$ a *consequence*.

The M is a special symbol to be read as "it is consistent to assume". Hence the default means that if it is consistent to assume $\beta_1(x), \ldots, \beta_m(x)$ we may infer $\alpha(x) \to \omega(x)$. Note that "it is consistent to assume $\beta_i(x)$" means that there is not sufficient information to conclude $\neg\beta_i(x)$. The prerequisite $\alpha(x)$ may possibly be empty, that is,

$$\frac{: M\beta_1(x), \ldots, M\beta_m(x)}{\omega(x)}$$

is also a default to mean that if it is consistent to assume $\beta_1(x), \ldots, \beta_m(x)$ then $\omega(x)$ can be concluded.

If $\alpha(x), \beta_1(x), \ldots, \beta_m(x), \omega(x)$ have no free variables, the rule is called a *closed default* and denoted

$$\frac{\alpha : M\beta_1, \ldots, M\beta_m}{\omega}.$$

A default of the form

$$\frac{\alpha(x) : M\beta(x)}{\beta(x)}$$

is called a *normal default*.

Now let $D$ be a set of defaults, and $W$ be a set of closed wffs. Then $\Delta = (D, W)$ is called a *default theory*. A default theory $\Delta$ is *closed* if every default in $D$ is closed, and $\Delta$ is *normal* if every default in $D$ is normal.

For a set $D$ of default rules, we define $Cons(D)$ by

$$Cons(D) = \left\{ \omega(x) \ \middle| \ \frac{\alpha(x) : M\beta_1(x), \ldots, M\beta_m(x)}{\omega(x)} \in D \right\}$$

Thus $Cons(D)$ is the set of all consequences of defaults in $D$.

For a set $S$ of closed wffs and a closed wff $\omega$, we write $S \vdash \omega$ to denote that $\omega$ is derived from $S$, and $S \not\vdash \omega$ to denote that $\omega$ is not derived from $S$. We also define a set $Th(S)$ by

$$Th(S) = \{\omega \,|\, \omega \text{ is a closed wff and } S \vdash \omega\}.$$

Let $\Delta = (D, W)$ be a closed default theory, $S \subseteq L$ be a set of closed wffs, and $\Gamma(S)$ be the smallest set satisfying the following three properties:

(1) $W \subseteq \Gamma(S)$.

(2) $Th(\Gamma(S)) = \Gamma(S)$.

(3) If $\dfrac{\alpha : M\beta_1, \ldots, M\beta_m}{\omega} \in D$, $\alpha \in \Gamma(S)$, $\neg\beta_1, \ldots, \neg\beta_m \notin S$ then $\omega \in \Gamma(S)$ .

A set $E \subseteq L$ satisfying $\Gamma(E) = E$ is an *extension* of $\Delta$. An intuitive characterization of the extensions is given by the following theorem :

**Theorem 1** (Reiter [1])   Let $E \subseteq L$ be a set of closed wffs, $\Delta = (D, W)$ be a closed default theory, and $E_0, E_1, \ldots$ be the following sequence of sets of closed wffs:

$$E_0 = W$$

$$E_{i+1} = Th(E_i) \cup \left\{ \omega(x) \;\middle|\; \begin{array}{l} \dfrac{\alpha : M\beta_1, \ldots, M\beta_m}{\omega} \in D \\ E_i \vdash \alpha \\ E \not\vdash \neg\beta_1, \ldots, E \not\vdash \neg\beta_m \end{array} \right\}$$

Then $E$ is an extension of $\Delta$ if and only if

$$E = \bigcup_{i=0}^{\infty} Ei \;.$$

The expression of $E_{i+1}$ in Theorem 1 is slightly different from the original one. Reiter [1] used conditions $\alpha \in E_1, \neg\beta_1, \ldots, \neg\beta_m \notin E$ instead of $E_i \vdash \alpha, E \not\vdash \neg\beta_1, \ldots, E \not\vdash \neg\beta_m$, respectively. These expressions are essentially the same. In order to check $\alpha \in E_1, \neg\beta_1, \ldots, \neg\beta_m \in E$, we need to check whether they are derivable or not. So we have adopted our expression, which should be more intuitive.

For a closed default theory there may exist two or more extensions or none at all. The existence of many extensions means the possibility of many worlds at that time. Selecting a correct extension and constructing an extension are different things. The correctness will gradually become clear as new facts about the world are known. We say that a closed default theory has an *inconsistent extension* if one of its extensions is the set of all closed wffs of $L$.

**Corollary 2** (Reiter [1])   A closed default theory $(D, W)$ has an inconsistent extension if and only if $W$ is inconsistent.

**Corollary 3** (Reiter [1])   If a closed default theory $\Delta$ has an inconsistent extension then it is only the extension of $\Delta$.

Since a closed default theory with an inconsistent $W$ has only inconsistent extensions, hereafter we restrict our discussions to default theories with consistent $W$'s, unless otherwise stated. Default theory may not have extensions, but we know the following :

**Theorem 4** (Reiter [1])   Every closed normal default theory has at least one extension.

## 3.   Pseudo Extensions and Their Properties

In defining extension $E$, Reiter used $E$ itself (Theorem 1). Hence it is a self-recursive definition. We can use Theorem 1 just to confirm for a given set of closed wffs to be an extension, but can not use it to construct extensions from a given closed default theory.

This section proposes a new kind of extensions which can successively be constructed from a closed default theory.

**Definition**   Let $\Delta = (D, W)$ be a closed default theory and let $F_i$ $(i \geq 0)$ be sets of closed wffs defined as follows:
$$F_0 = W$$

$$F_{i+1} = Th(F_i) \cup Cons(D_{F_i}) \quad (i \geq 0),$$
where $D_{F_i}$ is a subset of

$$\left\{ \delta = \frac{\alpha : M\beta_1, \ldots, M\beta_m}{\omega} \;\middle|\; \begin{array}{l} \delta \in D, \omega \notin Cons(\bigcup_{k=1}^{i-1} D_{F_k}) \\ F_i \vdash \alpha \\ F_i \not\vdash \neg\beta_1, \ldots, F_i \not\vdash \neg\beta_m \end{array} \right\}$$

such that $D_{F_i} \neq \emptyset$ if the above set is not empty. Then we call

$$F = \bigcup_{i=0}^{\infty} F_i$$

a *pseudo extension* of the theory $\Delta$.

The condition $F_i \not\vdash \neg\beta_1, \ldots, F_i \not\vdash \beta_m$ in applying a default with $M\beta_1, \ldots, M\beta_m$ is diffrent from Reiter's. Now we can successively construct the pseudo extensions. Moreover in constructing $F_{i+1}$ we can use an appropriate subset of defaults instead of the whole. A relation between Reiter's extension and ours is given as follows :

**Theorem 5**   Let $\tilde{E}$ be the set of all extensions of a closed default theory $\Delta$, and let $\tilde{F}$ be the set of all pseudo extensions of $\Delta$. Then

$$\tilde{E} \subseteq \tilde{F}.$$

Therefore every extension is also a pseudo extension.

**Proof**   Let $E = \bigcup_{i=1}^{\infty} E_i$ be any extension, and $D_i$ be the set of defaults used in defining $E_i$. Then we have

$$E_i = Th(E_{i-1}) \cup Cons(D_i).$$

For a default

$$\delta = \frac{\alpha : M\beta_1, \ldots, M\beta_m}{\omega} \in D_i,$$

we easily have

$$E_i \vdash \alpha$$

$$E \not\vdash \neg\beta_1, \ldots, E \not\vdash \neg\beta m .$$

By putting

$$D_i' = \{\delta \mid \delta \in D_i, \; Cons(\delta) \notin F_{i-1}\},$$

we construct sets of closed wffs $F_1, F_2, \ldots$ as follows :

$$F_0 = W$$

$$F_1 = Th(F_0) \cup Cons(D_1')$$

$$\vdots$$

$$F_i = Th(F_{i-1}) \cup Cons(D_i')$$

$$\vdots$$

Then, since $E_i = F_i$ for each $i$ ($\geq 0$), we have

$$E = \bigcup_{i=0}^{\infty} E_i = \bigcup_{i=1}^{\infty} F_i .$$

Now let us show that $D_i'$ satisfies the condition of $D_{F_i}$ in the definition of pseudo extensions. First assume that for some $j$ and for any $k (\geq j)$ a default satisfies the condition but $D_k' = \emptyset$. That is, assume that the set

$$\left\{ \delta = \frac{\alpha : M\beta_1, \ldots, M\beta_m}{\omega} \; \middle| \; \begin{array}{l} \delta \in D, \; \omega \notin Cons(\bigcup_{k=1}^{i-1} D_k') \\ F_i \vdash \alpha \\ F_i \not\vdash \neg\beta_1, \ldots, F_i \not\vdash \neg\beta_m \end{array} \right\}$$

is not empty but $D_k'$ is empty. Then by definition of $D_i'$ and $D_k' = \emptyset$, we have

$$D_{j-1} = D_j = D_{j+1} = \ldots$$

Hence we have

$$E_j = E_{j+1} = E_{j+2} = \ldots$$

From the assumption there exists a default

$$\delta = \frac{\alpha : M\beta_1, \ldots, M\beta_m}{\omega} \in D ,$$

which satisfies

$$\omega \notin Cons(\bigcup_{k=1}^{j-1} D_k')$$

$$F_j \vdash \alpha$$

$$F_j \not\vdash \neg\beta_1, \ldots, F_j \not\vdash \neg\beta_m.$$

By $E_j = F_j$, obviously

$$E_j \vdash \alpha$$

$$E_j \not\vdash \neg\beta_1, \ldots, E_j \not\vdash \neg\beta_m.$$

Also by

$$\omega \notin Cons(\bigcup_{i=1}^{\infty} D_i') \subseteq Cons(\bigcup_{i=1}^{\infty} D_i),$$

there exists at least one $k$ $(1 \le k \le m)$ such that

$$E \vdash \neg\beta_k.$$

Since $E = \bigcup_{i=0}^{\infty} E_i$, there exists an $i$ such that $E_i \vdash \neg\beta_k$. This $i$ must be $i > j$, because $E_i \not\vdash \neg\beta_k$ for $i \le j$. Since $E_i = E_j$ for such $i, j$, we have

$$E_j \vdash \neg\beta_k.$$

Also by $E_j = F_j$, we have

$$F_j \vdash \neg\beta_k,$$

which contradicts

$$F_j \not\vdash \neg\beta_1, \ldots, F_j \not\vdash \neg\beta_m.$$

Therefore $D_i'$ satisfies the condition of $D_{F_i}$, and hence $F = \bigcup_{i=0}^{\infty} F_i$ is a pseudo extension. Thus we have

$$E = \bigcup_{i=0}^{\infty} E_i = \bigcup_{i=0}^{\infty} F_i = F \in \tilde{F}.$$

Hence $\tilde{E} \subseteq \tilde{F}$. □

**Theorem 6**   In a closed normal default theory, any pseudo extension which is not an extension is inconsistent.

**Proof**   Let $F$ be a set of closed wffs such that $F \in \tilde{F}$ and $F \notin \tilde{E}$. Let $D_{F_i}$ be the set of defaults which is used in constructing $F_i$ of $F = \bigcup_{i=0}^{\infty} F_i$. Then by the assumption there exist an i and a default

$$\delta = \frac{\alpha : M\beta}{\beta}$$

such that $\delta \in D_{F_i}, F \vdash \alpha, F_i \not\vdash \neg\beta, F \vdash \beta$. By $\delta \in D, F \vdash \alpha, F_i \not\vdash \neg\beta$, we have

$$\beta \in F_{i+1} \subseteq F.$$

Hence $F \vdash \neg\beta$ and $F \vdash \beta$, which means $F$ is inconsistent.□

**Remark**   Theorem 6 is not valid if the default theory is not normal. In fact, there exists a default theory whose pseudo extension is neither an extension nor an inconsistent set. An example follows.

Let $\Delta = (D, W)$ be a default theory with

$$D = \left\{ \frac{: MA}{B}, \quad \frac{: M\neg B}{C}, \quad \frac{B \wedge C : MA}{A} \right\}$$

$$W = \emptyset .$$

Then $F = Th(\{A, B, C\})$ is a pseudo extension of $\Delta$, but neither an extension of $\Delta$ nor an inconsistent set.

From the discussions above we can conclude the following :

(1) Pseudo extensions can successively be constructed from a given default theory.

(2) Extensions are always pseudo extensions.

(3) In a closed normal default theory, every pseudo extension is an extension if it is not inconsistent.

(4) If $W$ in $\Delta = (D, W)$ is inconsistent then $\Delta$ has a unique pseudo extension, which is inconsistent and coincides with the extension. This result immediately follows from Corollaries 2, 3 and the definition.

## 4.  Extension Revision by Model Inference

Default reasoning is non-monotonic in the sense that an increase in facts does not always mean an increase in knowledge. Thus the extension is not a definite knowledge, but may need to be revised, because some defaults used in constructing it become inapplicable when new facts are found. Reiter has defined the belief as a subset of the extension and has discussed revising it. In this section we define the belief as the whole set of extensions, and the belief revision as constructing an extension as similar as possible to the world to be described by the default theory. Thus we identify belief revision with extension revision. Let us consider the world for the theory to describe as an unknown model in a first order language. Then we can formalize the problem of extension revision in the framework of Shapiro's model inference [3, 4]. Hereafter we assume readers are familiar with the model inference. Our problem can be expressed as follows:

Given a first order language $L$, an observational language

$$L_o = \{\text{ground unit clauses of } L\},$$

a hypothesis language $L_h = L$, and an oracle for an $h$-easy unknown model $K$ which satisfies the closed default theory $\Delta = (D, W)$, to find a finite $L_o$-complete axiomatization of $K$.

We say that the model $K$ *satisfies* a closed default theory $\Delta = (D, W)$ if it satisfies the following three conditions:

(1) $K \models W$

which means $K$ satisfies $W$.

(2) For a default

$$\frac{\alpha : \mathrm{M}\beta_1, \ldots, \mathrm{M}\beta_m}{\omega} \in D$$

if $K \models \alpha$ and $K \not\models \neg\beta_1, \ldots, K \not\models \neg\beta_m$ then $K \models \omega$.

(3) Let $D'$ be a subset of $D$ such that $W \cup Cons(D')$ is consistent. Then

$$W \cup Cons(D') \not\vdash u \implies M \not\models u$$

for any clause $u$ which is not a ground unit.

The condition above restricts the unknown model $K$ in Shapiro's model inference.

A closed default theory $\Delta = (D, W)$ with finite $D$ and $W$ is called a *finite closed default theory*. For such a theory the following theorem holds :

**Theorem 7**  Let $\Delta = (D, W)$ be a finite closed default theory and $E$ be an extension of $\Delta$. Then there exists a finite $L_o$-complete axiomatization of $E$.

**Proof**  It suffices to show $E \models T$ and $T \models L_o^E$ for some finite subset $T$ of $L$. By Theorem 1 any extension $E$ can be written as $E = \bigcup_{i=0}^{\infty} E_i$.

Let $D_i$ $(i \geq 1)$ be the set of defaults which are used in defining $E_i$. Then $D_i \subseteq D$ and

$$E_0 = W$$

$$E_i = Th(E_{i-1}) \cup Cons(D_i) \quad (i \geq 1).$$

Since $D$ is finite, there exists an $N$ such that $D_n = D_{n-1}$ for any $n > N$. Hence we have

$$E_0 \subseteq E_1 \subseteq \ldots \subseteq E_{N-1} \subseteq E_N = E_{N+1} = \ldots$$

and

$$E = \bigcup_{i=0}^{\infty} E_i = E_N .$$

We also have

$$
\begin{aligned}
E_N &= Th(E_{N-1}) \\
&= Th(Th(E_{N-2}) \cup Cons(D_{N-1})) \\
&= Th(Th(Th(E_{N-3}) \cup Cons(D_{N-2})) \cup Cons(D_{N-1})) \\
&= Th(Th(E_{N-3}) \cup Cons(D_{N-2}) \cup Cons(D_{N-1})) \\
&\ \ \vdots \\
&= Th(Th(Th(E_0) \cup Cons(D_1)) \cup \textstyle\bigcup_{i=2}^{N-1} Cons(D_i)) \\
&= Th(Th(W) \cup \textstyle\bigcup_{i=1}^{N-1} Cons(D_i)) \\
&= Th(W \cup \textstyle\bigcup_{i=1}^{N-1} Cons(D_i)) .
\end{aligned}
$$

Then

$$T = W \cup \bigcup_{i=1}^{N-1} Cons(D_i)$$

is finite because so are $W, D$, and obviously $E \models T$ and $T \vdash L_o^E$. Therefore there exists a finite $L_o$-complete axiomatization of $E$. $\square$

**Theorem 8**  Let $K$ be an $h$-easy unknown model which satisfies a finite closed default theory $\Delta = (D, W)$. If Shapiro's enumerative model inference algorithm identifies $K$ in the limit and produces a guess $T$ as the output, then $Th(T)$ is an extension of a default theory $\Delta' = (D, W \cup W')$, where $W'$ is a set of clauses.

**Proof** Put

$$W' = \{\, u \mid T \vdash u,\, W \cup Cons(D') \not\vdash u \,\} \cup \{f_i \mid 1 \le i \le k\}\,,$$

where $u$ is a ground unit clause and $f_i$ is defined by

$$f_i = \begin{cases} \alpha_i & \text{if } V_i = \text{true} \\ \neg\alpha_i & \text{if } V_i = \text{false} \end{cases}$$

when a fact $< \alpha_i, V_i >$, a pair of ground atom and its truth value, is given as input to the algorithm.

In order to show that $Th(T)$ is an extension of $\Delta' = (D, W \cup W')$, it suffices to show $Th(T) = \Gamma(Th(T))$. From the definition of $W'$ and $K \models W$, obviously $T \vdash W \cup W'$. Hence we have

$$W \cup W' \subseteq Th(T)$$

$$Th(Th(T)) = Th(T).$$

Since $K$ satisfies $\Delta$, there exists a default

$$\delta = \frac{\alpha : M\beta_1, \ldots, M\beta_m}{\omega} \in D$$

such that $K \models \alpha$ and $K \not\models \neg\beta_1, \ldots, K \not\models \neg\beta_b$ imply $K \models \omega$. Namely for a $\delta \in D$ if $Th(T) \vdash \alpha$ and $Th(T) \not\vdash \neg\beta_1, \ldots, Th(T) \not\vdash \neg\beta_m$ then $\omega \in Th(T)$. Hence $Th(T)$ satisfies the three conditions on $\Gamma(S)$. Therefore from the minimality of $\Gamma(S)$, we have

$$\Gamma(Th(T)) \subseteq Th(T).$$

We now show the converse. Let $v \in Th(T)$. There are four cases to be considered.

*Case* 1.  $v \in W \cup W'$ : $v \in \Gamma(Th(T))$ by $W \cup W' \subseteq \Gamma(Th(T))$.

*Case* 2.  A default

$$\delta = \frac{\alpha : M\beta_1, \ldots, M\beta_m}{v} \in D$$

exists and $K \models \alpha, K \not\models \neg\beta, \ldots, K \not\models \beta_m$ : Clearly

$$Th(T) \vdash \alpha$$

$$Th(T) \not\vdash \neg\beta_1, \ldots, Th(T) \not\vdash \neg\beta_m$$

$$Th(T) \subseteq \Gamma(Th(T))\,.$$

Hence $\Gamma(Th(T)) \vdash \alpha$ and $v \in \Gamma(Th(T))$.

*Case* 3.  $W \cup W' \cup Cons(D'') \vdash v$ for the set $D''$ of all defaults

$$\delta = \frac{\alpha : M\beta_1, \ldots, M\beta_m}{\omega} \in D$$

such that $K \models \alpha, K \not\models \neg\beta_1, \ldots, K \not\models \neg\beta_m$ : We have

$$v \in Th(W \cup W' \cup Cons(D''))$$

$$\subseteq Th(\Gamma(Th(T)))$$

$$= \Gamma(Th(T))\,.$$

*Case* 4.   $v \in Th(T)$ satisfies none of (1), (2), (3) : If $v$ is not a ground unit then $K \not\models v$ since $K$ satisfies $\Delta$. This contradicts that $L_o$ has an evidence to show the falsity of $T$. If $v$ is a ground unit then obviously

$$v \in W' \subseteq \Gamma(Th(T)) . \square$$

Theorem 7 asserts that an $L_o$-complete axiomatization exists for any extension of finite closed default theory. Hence the extension appears in the enumeration $Th(T_1), Th(T_2), \ldots$, where $T_1, T_2, \ldots$ is the enumeration of all subsets of $L_h$. On the other hand Theorem 8 asserts that if we restrict the objects of the inference to the unknown models which are $h$-easy and satisfy finite closed default theories, then the models identified by the enumerative model inference algorithm are extensions of some closed default theories. The $\Delta'$ in Theorem 8 is finite, and hence it has at most finite number of extensions. Therefore if for a finite closed default theory there exist two or more extensions in which the unknown model $K$ is included, the algorithm will find it in the search space of all extensions. Moreover if all the pseudo extensions of a finite closed default theory can be enumerated, the algorithm will find an extension for the unknown model by deleting guesses which are pseudo extensions but not extensions or contradict newly given facts.

## 5.   Discussions

There are some problems in Reiter's default theories. The extensions can not be constructed successively and even their existence is not guaranteed with exception of the closed normal cases. Many efforts to attack the problems have been made by many researchers. Reiter and Criscuolo [5] have introduced seminormal defaults. The seminormal default theories can describe some natural examples which the normal default theories can not, but still the existence of extensions is not guaranteed. Lukaszewicz [6] has studied a default theory of propositional logic and introduced another definition of extensions, for which the existence is guaranteed. Murakami et al. [7] have constructed a set of knowledge called a modified extensions, which is, in a sense, a generalization of Reiter's extension, and guaranteed the existence. [6, 7] have thus guaranteed the existence for any default theory, but still their extensions can not be constructed successively from $W$. Murakami et al. [8] have dealt with this problem independently. They have defined sets of knowledge called a nonrecursive extensions for closed normal default theories. The nonrecursive extension can be uniquely determined.

In case the closed normal default theory $\Delta = (D, W)$ has an inconsistent extension, that is, $W$ is inconsistent, the nonrecursive extension is also inconsistent and equal to the extension of $\Delta$. However, the inconsistency of the nonrecursive extension does not mean that of $W$. In other words, if $\Delta$ has two or more extensions, the nonrecursive extension is inconsistent or equal to some of the extensions. If $\Delta$ has just one extension, the nonrecursive extension coincides with it.

On the other hand, our pseudo extensions may include non-extensions but include all the extensions.

The extensions should be candidates for possible worlds. In this regard, our approach is better than the others.

We have introduced the notion of pseudo extensions which can be constructed successively and made a step towards the computerization of default reasoning. However, it is still not computable, because the condition $E_i \nvdash \neg\beta_1, \ldots, E_i \nvdash \beta_m$ for applying defaults is not even semi-computable. This aspect is common to all other approaches. To solve the problem we need some concept like the $h$-easiness.

# References

[1] Reiter, R. : A Logic for Default Reasoning, *Artificial Intelligence*, **13**, 41-72 (1980).

[2] Shinmura, T. : On the Inconsistency in Non-monotonic Logic, Master's Thesis, Dept. of Information Systems, Kyushu Univ. (1986) (in Japanese).

[3] Shapiro, E.Y. : Inductive Inference of Theories From Facts, TR-192, Dept. Compt. Sci., Yale Univ. (1981).

[4] Ishizaka, H. : Model Inference Incorporating Least Generalization, Master's Thesis, Dept. Information Systems, Kyushu Univ. (1986) (in Japanese). To appear in *J. Inf. Processing Soc. Japan.*

[5] Reiter, R., Criscuolo, G. : On Interacting Defaults, *Proc. 8th IJCAI*, 270-276 (1983).

[6] Lukaszewicz, W. : Considerations on Default Logic, *Proc. AAAI Non-monotonic Reasoning Workshop*, 165-193 (1984).

[7] Murakami, K., Aibara, T., Shitanda, H. : Modified Extension and Its Properties in Default Reasoning, *Trans. Inf. Processing Soc. Japan*, **12**, 1280-1287 (1987) (in Japanese).

[8] Murakami, K. Aibara, T., Shitanda, H. : Nonrecursive Extension and Its Properties in Default Reasoning, *J. Japanese Soc. Artificial. Intelligence*, **3**, 359-367 (1988) (in Japanese).

[9] Yuasa, H.: Pseudo Extensions in Default Reasoning and Belief Revision Using Model Inference, Master's Thesis, Dept. Information Systems, Kyushu Univ. (1988) (in Japanese).

# An Approach to Nonmonotonic Inference Mechanism in Production System KORE/IE

Toramatsu Shintani
IIAS-SIS FUJITSU LIMITED,
140 Miyamoto, Numazu-shi, Shizuoka 410-03, Japan
E-mail: tora%iias.fujitsu.junet@uunet.uu.net

## Abstract

In this paper, we propose a method for constructing a mechanism for nonmonotonic inference in KORE/IE which is a Prolog based forward-chaining production system. In the implementation, we utilize the form of default reasoning proposed by Reiter, and introduce the framework of TMS(Truth Maintenance System) for resolving contradictions. Relational information such as data dependencies is independently managed by KORE/EDEN, a network-based knowledge management system, for improving dependency-directed backtracking in TMS. Resolving contradictions is achieved by undoing the inference. The mechanism for resolving a contradiction can be realized by extending the inference steppers in KORE/IE along the framework of TMS. As an example of the mechanism, we show a maintenance mechanism for pairwise comparisons. Consistency of the comparisons is effectively maintained by using the mechanism.

## 1. Introduction

KORE/IE(Shintani 1988) is a fast production system on Prolog. Its inference mechanism implements a recognize-act cycle in a manner similar to OPS5(Forgy 1981) whose type of reasoning is forward chaining.

Generally, inferences of production systems are monotonic. Namely, consistency among facts in WM (working memory) is ignored, since WM is only used as a global data base for rules. However, if we want to treat inexact knowledge effectively, we need to create a mechanism for nonmonotonic reasoning (Matsumoto 1987) that can maintain consistency. This mechanism will be useful for improving the quality of knowledge representation for heuristics (or expertise) and constructing rule-based applications.

This paper describes a method that supports nonmonotonic inferences in KORE/IE. In the method, data dependencies are independently managed to improve efficiency of the inferences. The data dependencies are supervised by

KORE/EDEN (Shintani 1986,1986b) which provides functions for presenting and managing many relationships between knowledge in a knowledge base.

This paper consists of five sections. In Section 2, we present a basic architecture in KORE/IE for nonmonotonic inferences. In Section 3, details of the mechanism for the inferences are presented. In Section 4, an application implemented by utilizing the mechanism is described. In Section 5, some concluding remarks are presented.

## 2. The basic architecture

Inexact knowledge is a useful part of flexible problem solving. It can be classified into the following two types; (1)knowledge for choosing alternatives, generally needed for problem solving such as diagnosing; (2)knowledge for common sense information, needed for problem solving such as scheduling. The knowledge of type (1) usually has numerical values which indicate uncertainty. Consistency within the knowledge does not have to be maintained. Knowledge of type (2) requires consistency maintenance. In order to maintain the consistency, a problem solver needs to revise a part of past problem solving. In KORE/IE, we realize a nonmonotonic inference mechanism for managing the knowledge of the latter type. Its inference is based on default reasoning(Reiter 1980) which provides frameworks for managing the knowledge. We use the framework of TMS(Doyle 79) which is used as a mechanism for dissolving contradictions between knowledge. In order to effectively construct the mechanism of TMS, we utilize functions of inference steppers of KORE/IE, and make a new mechanism for managing default knowledge.

### 2.1 Utilizing inference steppers

In KORE/IE, when an inference is performed by executing a recognize-act cycle, cancellation of the inference is achieved by putting back the cycle. The recognize-act cycle can be illustrated as shown in Fig.1, which is a basic control mechanism for an inference engine. The cycle is a sequence of operations, which are (1)matching, (2)conflict resolution, and (3)an act process. In order to put back the cycle effectively, we record changes to WM(working memory) and the conflict set instead of recording every WM and conflict set. The elements are called WM elements and instantiations, respectively. Recording the changes is necessary for efficient memory use. An instantiation is a consistent set of bindings for a rule. Putting back the cycle by one step corresponds to changing the current state to a previous state. The state is determined by specifying WM and the conflict set.

KORE/IE provides inference steppers for controlling the recognize-act cycle, which are the "run" and "back" commands. The "run" command is used for performing inferences in forward chaining. In contrast, the "back command" is used for undoing effects of the inferences (or rule firings) by using the record of changes made while tuning to undo the changes, restoring the WM and conflict set to a previous state. Each of the commands takes a positive number argument which represents number of repetitions of the cycle.

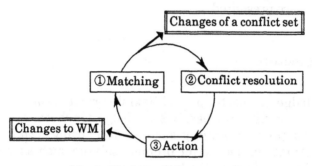

Fig.1. The recognize-act cycle

In order to record the changes, KORE/IE asserts a Prolog fact (or assertion) for every forward-running cycle. We call the assertion back data. The back data is expressed as follows;

back_data(Step, Flag, Instantiation, WM_list)

where the first argument "Step" represents a step number of a recognize-act cycle which corresponds to an inference step. The larger the step number, the more recently the back data was asserted. The second argument "Flag" represents a status which is used for nonmonotonic inferences. Details will be discussed in Section 3.2. The third argument "Instantiation" represents an instantiation which is selected in a conflict resolution process. The fourth argument "WM_list" represents a list which keeps input-output information of WM elements. By using a Prolog term, the input information which indicates WM elements added to WM is described in the list as follows;

in_wm(WM_ELEMENTS)

where "WM_ELEMENTS" represents the WM elements. The output information which indicates WM elements removed from WM can also be described in the list as follows;

out_wm(WM_ELEMENTS).

Fig.2 is given to clarify the description, which illustrates the internal mechanisms of the run command and the back commands. In Fig.2, the "run(5)" is an example of the run command which runs 5 steps of the recognize-act cycle forward. The "back(2)" is an example of the back command which undoes the effects of the 2 previous recognize-act cycles. By using information of the back data in reverse order and restoring current WM to a previous state, the inferences are undone. In the example, for undoing the inferences, the back data for Step 5 is applied first, and then the back data for Step 4 is applied. Keeping the back data is started by the command "ie_debug". The end of keeping the back data is specified by the command "ie_no_debug". These commands are used for avoiding needless recording of back data and for improving the efficiency of the inferences. The back data are only needed for debugging a rule base and enabling nonmonotonic inference.

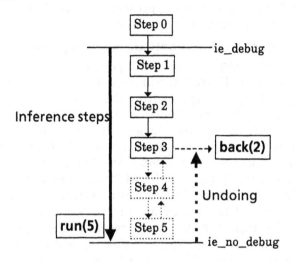

Fig.2. An internal mechanism of the run and back commands

## 2.2. Representation for default knowledge and contradiction

Default reasoning is reasoning based on inexact knowledge. "Default knowledge" is used as long as no contradictory evidence is present. In a default rule(Reiter 1980), the knowledge can be represented by attaching a modal operator M as follows;

$$\frac{\alpha(x): M\ \beta(x)}{\gamma(x)}$$

where $\beta(x)$ corresponds to the default knowledge. This default rule is interpreted as saying "For all individuals x, if $\alpha(x)$ is valid and if $\beta(x)$ is consistent with our beliefs, then $\gamma(x)$ may be believed". If a contradiction is detected by adding new knowledge to a knowledge base, an inference engine for default reasoning needs to correct the default knowledge which causes the contradiction and undo results of inferences which depend on the default knowledge. Namely, a contradiction is due to the default knowledge. The correction of the default knowledge is achieved by asserting its negation, because the validity of the knowledge is assumed as long as the negation of the knowledge is not proved.

In KORE/IE, a mechanism for resolving the contradiction is implemented using a method for maintaining consistency adopted in TMS(Doyle 1979). When a contradiction is detected, TMS evokes its own reasoning mechanism, dependency-directed backtracking, to resolve the contradiction by altering a minimal set of beliefs. In TMS, the backtracking uses data dependencies(McDermott 1983) kept in each TMS node, and is inefficient. In KORE/IE, the dependencies are recorded independently for improving the efficiency of the backtracking (for further details, see Section 3.1).

We use two flags in WM elements for representing default knowledge. An internal expression for a WM element can be shown as follows;

$$\text{Class\_name(Time\_tag,Default,Not\_Contradicted,Value}_1,...\text{Value}_n)$$

where the first argument "Time_tag", the second argument "Default", and the third argument "Not_Contradicted" are built-in arguments. The second and third arguments are used as flags for representing the default knowledge. If the value of the second argument is true, the WM element represents default knowledge; otherwise it is not default knowledge. If the value of the third argument is "nil", it represents a negative element; otherwise it represents an affirmative element. If values for the second and third arguments are unknown, the values automatically take "nil" and "true", respectively. The first argument is a time tag which is a unique number determined automatically by the system. It is used by an inference engine for conflict resolution. The larger the time tag, the more recently the element was entered or modified. The rest of the arguments "$\text{Value}_1$, ..., $\text{Value}_n$" are values defined by a user. The functor name "Class_name" is a class name for a WM element defined by the user.

A WM element can be matched by a user by using a pattern description. The pattern description consists of (1)a class name and (2)some number of slot descriptions which are attribute-value pairs. In KORE/IE, the pattern description is expressed as follows;

$$\text{Class\_name(Slot}_1 = \text{Value}_1, ... , \text{Slot}_n = \text{Value}_n)$$

where $\text{Slot}_n$ and $\text{Value}_n$ are a slot name and its value, respectively. There are three prereserved slots which are "time_tag", "default", and "not_contradicted". These slots are used for representing the "Time_tag", "Default", and "Not_Contradicted" arguments in the internal expression mentioned above, respectively.

By using "make" command a default knowledge can be added to WM as follows;

$$\text{make(man(default = true,name = taro,weight = 80))}$$

where the argument is a pattern description which represents the knowledge. The "man" is a class name. The "default" slot is the prereserved slot. The "name" and "weight" are slot names defined by a user. For user's convenience, the "make_assumption" command can be used for making the same default knowledge as follows:

$$\text{make\_assumption(man(name = taro,weight = 80)).}$$

The order in which slot descriptions are specified is not significant. Thus the knowledge can also be made as follows;

$$\text{make\_assumption(man(weight = 80,name = taro)).}$$

The pattern description compiled into the internal expression as follows;

man(12,true,true,taro,80)

where the first and third arguments are a time tag and the value of the "not_contradicted" slot taken by the system, respectively. The second, fourth and fifth arguments are the value of the default slot, the name slot and the weight slot, respectively. The order of the arguments except the built-in arguments are determined by "literalize" command as follows;

literalize(man,[name,weight])

where the first argument defines the class name of the pattern. The second argument is a list in which the order mentioned above is defined by arranging the slot names.

## 3. The mechanism for a nonmonotonic inference

In KORE/IE, TMS is used as a mechanism for maintaining consistency among WM elements. In order to implement the mechanism, we need the following functions: (1)recording inference chains, (2)backtracking based on the chains, and (3)resolving a contradiction for checking and denying default knowledge which causes the contradiction.

### 3.1. Recording inference chains

If a rule is fired, an inference chain is recorded by keeping the relationship between WM elements which matched LHS patterns in its LHS(left-hand side) and new WM elements made by its RHS(right-hand side) actions. In order to record the relationship, we use time tags for those WM elements. The records for the relationships are managed by KORE/EDEN as shown in Fig.3.

For example, consider following rules;

```
ex1: if a(slot = 1) & b(slot = 1) then modify(1,slot = 2).
ex2: if a(slot = 2) then make(b(slot = 2)).
```

where a rule consists of (1)the name of the rule (such as "ex1" and "ex2"), (2)the symbol ":", (3)the symbol "if", (4)the LHS which has some LHS patterns (such as "a(slot=1)", "b(slot=1)", and "a(slot=2)"), (5)the symbol "then", (6)the RHS which has some RHS actions (such as "modify" and "make"), and (7)the symbol ".". The symbol "&" is a delimiter. The "make" command is used to create a new WM element. The "modify" command is used to modify one or more slot values of a WM element, in which the first argument indicates which WM element to modify. After the following commands (that is, Prolog goals);

```
?- make_assumption(a(slot = 1)),
    make(b(slot = 1)).
```

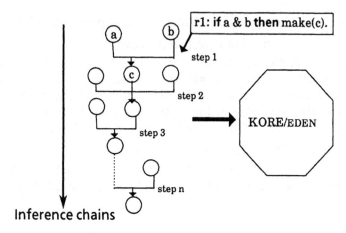

**Fig.3. Recording inference chains by KORE/EDEN**

then, the following WM elements are generated;

2: b(slot = 1)
1: a(slot = 1)*

where the numbers before the symbol ":" represent time tags. The symbol "*" indicates that the WM element to which the symbol is attached is default knowledge. The representation is used for displaying WM in KORE/IE. If the WM elements are created, the rules mentioned above can be fired successively and generate the inference chains as shown in Fig.4.

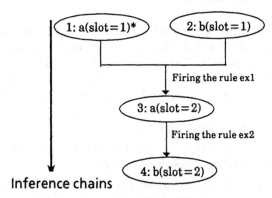

**Fig.4. An example of inference chains**

The inference chains can be kept by executing the following "add_to" commands of KORE/EDEN;

add_to((3,a,fact),[(1,a,assumption),(2,b,fact)],example).
add_to((4,b,fact),[(3,a,fact)],example).

where the first, the second, and the third argument represent a node, a list of parent nodes of the node, and a name of the chains, respectively. In Fig.4, the node is illustrated by the WM element encircled by an ellipse. The representation for nodes can be shown as follows;

(Time_tag, Class_name, Type)

where the first, second, and third argument represent a time tag, a class name, and a type of the node. If the type is "assumption", then the node is default knowledge; otherwise the node is not default knowledge. KORE/EDEN provides basic functions (such as searching, deleting, appending relationships, and etc.) to manage the relationships. For example, in Fig.4, we can retrieve the default knowledge on which the node for the time tag 4 depends by achieving next Prolog goals;

```
?- supers((4,Class,Type),Result,example),
      bagof(Tag, C^member((Tag,C,assumption),Result),Answer).
```

where the "supers" is a KORE/EDEN command for searching reachable nodes in the direction of parents from a node which is given the first argument. The result returns to the second argument "Result". The third argument is the name of the chains mentioned above. In the second goal which is a built-in Prolog predicate, the default knowledge is bound to the third argument "Answer". For the convenience and improving the efficiency, the "assumption_super" command can be used, which is exactly the same as the "super" command except that the result will contain only nodes whose type are assumptions.

## 3.2. Controlling the TMS backtracking

In KORE/IE, the backtracking mechanism for TMS uses the inference stepper mentioned in Section 2.1. The back data includes information for finding and revising default knowledge which caused a contradiction. A flag kept in each back data is used to prevent loops while attempting to resolve contradiction. The flag takes on values of "real", "unreal", or "contradiction". The "real" flag is used when the back data is kept during usual recognize-act cycles. The "unreal" flag is used when the back data is kept during recognize-act cycles under applying a procedure for resolving a contradiction. The "contradiction" flag is used for marking back data which become the objects of backtracking. The flags are needed for resolving a given contradiction by revising one of current default knowledge WM elements. While resolving the contradiction, the flags are used to avoid entering the same procedure recursively when a new contradiction is found. If a new contradiction is found, the procedure needs to check the rest of the default knowledge instead of trying to resolve the new contradiction. Fig.5 is given to clarify the description.

Fig.5 illustrates the mechanism for using the flags when a contradiction is detected, in which the default A and B represent default knowledge. It shows the current inference steps by asserting negation of the default A in order to resolve the contradiction. When the system backtracks to the step

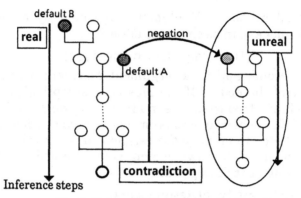

**Fig.5. Using the flags in back data**

which includes the default A, the flags of the back data which depend on the default are changed to "contradiction". The backtracking is realized by using the back command in KORE/IE. These back data are used for undoing the backtracking when the contradiction is not resolved by the assertion. By asserting the negation, when new inference steps are done, the flags of the newly recorded back data are set to "unreal". The flag "unreal" used for indicating temporary back data. If the negation causes a new contradiction, the system checks the rest of the default knowledge (such as the default B) by undoing the inference steps which depend on the negation. The back data with the flag "unreal" are used for undoing the inference steps. If the negation does not cause a new contradiction, resolving the contradiction is achieved by removing the back data with the flag "contradiction" and changing the flag "unreal" of the back data to the flag "real".

### 3.3. The procedure for resolving contradictions

In order to maintain consistency among WM elements, a procedure is used in KORE/IE. It is called the "contradiction", and provides a mechanism which corresponds to that of TMS. In KORE/IE, for example, the procedure is used as an RHS action in RHS as follows;

cry: if cry(name = X, for = Toy) then contradiction.

where the "contradiction" in the RHS is the procedure. This rule means that it is inconsistent if there exists a WM element which matches the LHS pattern. If the rule is fired, the procedure is applied and resolves the contradiction by finding and revising a default knowledge which causes the contradiction. The procedure is achieved by performing following steps:

**Step 1:** Get a list L of default knowledge on which a contradiction depends. Go to Step 2.

The elements of the list L are arranged in the order of decreasing time. The time can be determined by using the time tags. The list L consists of nodes which can be obtained by using the "assumption_supers" command mentioned in Section 3.1.

> **Step 2**: If the list L is empty then stop the procedure and the procedure fails; otherwise go to Step 3.

The procedure fails in the same manner as TMS when a contradiction needs to be resolved by negating two or more assumptions together, since it only looks for one at a time. If the procedure fails, the system helps us to resolve the contradiction by showing the all default knowledge and inference chains checked by the system. Then, for resolving the contradiction, we need to undo and redo some inference steps by revising some default knowledge or some rules.

> **Step 3**: Get a default knowledge from the list L, which is the first element (that is, $L_{head}$) of the list L (that is, $L = [L_{head}|L_{tail}]$ ), and backtrack to the inference step which includes the default knowledge by using the back command. Then, assert a negation of the default knowledge. Go to Step 4.

When default knowledge was used multiple times, the procedure backtrack to the step which includes the earliest default knowledge. As mentioned in Section 2.2, the negation can be generated by modifying the value of the "not_contradicted" slot to "nil" in the pattern (i.e. WM element) which represents the default knowledge. This modification can be achieved by using the "modify" command in KORE/IE.

> **Step 4**: If a new contradiction is detected, then undo the result of Step 3, let $L = L_{tail}$ , and go to Step 2; otherwise go to Step 5.

In order to undo the result, the procedure removes the back data which have the "unreal" flags, and return the current state to the previous sate in which Step 3 is not yet applied by using the back data which have the "contradiction" flags.

> **Step 5**: Change the "unreal" flags to the "real" flags, stop the procedure, and the procedure succeeds.

In the procedure, removing the back data and changing the flag of the back data are simply realized by using built-in Prolog predicates such as "assert" and "retract" in which backtracking mechanism of Prolog can be utilized effectively.


## 3.4. Other details

In order to resolve a contradiction, TMS changes statuses (i.e. IN or OUT) of all the nodes which depend on the assumption node causing the contradiction. The process is performed in a bottom up manner by using dependency-directed backtracking. The statuses need to be changed for maintaining consistency of belief for a data base (or a knowledge base). In this approach, for representing and maintaining the belief, it needs to record data dependencies in each node. The data dependencies are information for dependency-directed backtracking. In our approach, the procedure "contradiction" resolves the contradiction in a top down manner. Namely, in the process, default knowledge which correspond to the assumption nodes are found first by KORE/EDEN. Then, the default knowledge are successively tested and revised for resolving the contradiction. Since the belief is managed dynamically by performing inferences, it need not record the data dependencies in WM elements, which correspond to nodes of TMS. The information for backtracking, which corresponds to dependency-directed backtracking in TMS, is kept independently by using KORE/EDEN as mentioned in Section 3.1.

An assumption node in TMS must have a IN list which is an empty list. In KORE/IE, a default knowledge does not have such a constraint. Namely, the default knowledge can depend on knowledge which is not default knowledge. For example, a rule can be described as follows;

ex3: if a(slot = 3) & b(slot = 1) then make_assumption(c(slot = 1)).

where a default knowledge is generated by achieving the RHS action. The rule can be fired if the following WM elements are made:

2: a(slot = 3)
1: b(slot = 1)

By firing the rule, a new WM element (that is, a default knowledge) is added to the WM as follows;

3: c(slot = 1)*
2: a(slot = 3)
1: b(slot = 1)

where the default knowledge which has the time tag 3 depends on the two WM elements which have time tag 1 and 2. In order to resolve the contradiction which depends on the default knowledge, the procedure "contradiction" needs to modify not only the default knowledge but also the rule. In our approach, the RHS of the rule is modified as follows;

ex3: if a(slot = 3) & b(slot = 1) then make_assumption(\c(slot = 1)).

where the pattern used in the make_assumption command is modified. The pattern is obtained by changing the value of the not_contradicted slot to "nil". In KORE/IE, the pattern for representing such negation can be simply expressed by adding the symbol "\" to the pattern.

In KORE/IE, there are no cyclic inference chains because the relationship between knowledge is generated by using time tags. Namely, patterns are classified and kept if they have different time tags. An aim of TMS is to realize logical deduction for belief revision. The aim of our approach is to realize a mechanism for nonmonotonic inference on a forward-chaining production system such as KORE/IE,OPS5, etc. The main difference between TMS and our approach is that the purpose of TMS is to maintain the validity status of nodes, and that of our approach is to maintain the validity of inference steps.

## 4. An application

We have implemented an application to see how flexibly and effectively the nonmonotonic inference mechanism can be used. The application is called KORE/CDSS(Choice Decision Support System). KORE/CDSS helps decision makers to make a reasonable choice from alternatives. Two processes are used. One is a process which clarifies attributes used for estimating the alternatives. The other is a process which determines the priorities of the alternatives by estimating the attributes. In this section, we sketch the mechanism for the estimation processes by using the nonmonotonic inference in KORE/IE.

In the estimation, a pairwise comparison method based on AHP(Analytic Hierarchy Process; Saaty 1980) is used. AHP is one of the weighting methods, and has an advantage of being able to treat subjective judgments of a decision maker. However, in the method, it is difficult to maintain consistency of the judgments. In AHP, the consistency can be checked by using the consistency index (C.I.) which can be represented as follows;

$$(\lambda_{max} - n)/(n - 1)$$

where $\lambda_{max}$ and $n$ are the maximum eigenvalue and the dimension of a pairwise comparison matrix, respectively. The matrix is a square matrix whose rows (or columns) consist of alternatives used for the comparisons. Elements of the matrix are weighting numbers for the comparisons, where if the value V for element $a_{ij}$ is determined then the reciprocal value 1/V is automatically entered in the $a_{ji}$. The value V takes a positive integer no greater than 9. The larger the number, the more importantly the judgment is agreed upon. If C.I. is less than 0.1, the consistency of a matrix is considered acceptable; otherwise it is inconsistent. If the inconsistency has occurred, we need to revise a few pairwise comparisons for maintaining consistency by finding inadequate comparisons which are the comparisons causing the inconsistency . However, it is difficult to find them. In the worst case, it forces us to revise all the comparisons.

KORE/CDSS provides a mechanism for maintaining the consistency of the pairwise comparisons automatically. It uses the nonmonotonic inference mechanism in KORE/IE. In the mechanism, we can group weighting numbers into two classes such as (1)temporary numbers and (2)reliable numbers, which can be generated by using the "make_assumption" and the "make" command, respectively. If inconsistency has occurred, the temporary numbers are checked and revised first for maintaining consistency. Fig.6 illustrates the process. In Fig.6, the symbol in a square represents the name

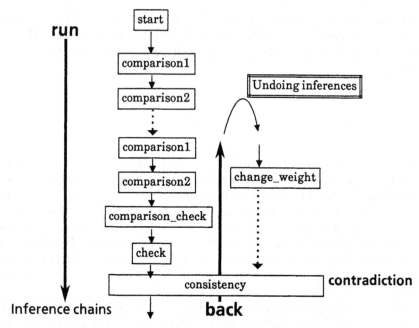

**Fig.6. Maintaining consistency of pairwise comparisons**

of a rule. The rule "start" is used for initializing pairwise comparisons and does the "ie_debug" command described in Section 2.1. The rules "comparison1" and "comparison2" are used for obtaining a pairwise comparison matrix. By the rule "comparison1", weighting numbers are entered and grouped into the matrix. The rule "comparison2" determines and enters their reciprocal values into the matrix. The rule "comparison_check" checks whether the matrix is filled or not. The rule "check" is used for computing the C.I. of the matrix. The rule "consistency" is used for achieving the procedure "contradiction" if the C.I. is not less than 0.1. The rule can be described as follows:

consistency: if matrix(ci > 0.1) then contradiction.

The rule "change_weight" is used for revising the inadequate pairwise comparison, which can be described as follows;

```
change_weight:
    if \matrix_element(name = X,column = C,row = R,weight = W)
    then
        remove(1) &
        new_weight(W,W2) &
        make(matrix_element(name = X,column = C,row = R,weight = W2).
```

where the LHS pattern corresponds to the negation of the inadequate comparison which needs to be revised. The negation is generated by the procedure "contradiction" if the procedure finds the inadequate comparison as a default knowledge. By firing the rule "change_weight", the inadequate comparison is revised. In order to revise the comparison, the RHS action "new_weight" is used. The action changes the old weighting value "W" to the new weighting value "W2" which decreases the C.I. of the matrix. The range of the change is $\pm 2$ because we assume that the old value is not so inadequate for maintaining the consistency. If the C.I. becomes less than 0.1, the procedure "contradiction" is stopped and the consistency is automatically maintained. If the system can not resolve the contradiction by using the procedure "contradiction", the system try to change several temporary numbers at once. The temporary numbers to change are determined systematically in which the numbers reduce $\lambda_{max}$ effectively.

## 5. Conclusions

In KORE/IE, in order to realize a nonmonotonic inference, we introduce the framework of the mechanism in TMS. Belief is managed dynamically by performing inferences in the system. The mechanism for resolving contradictions is simply implemented by utilizing and extending inference steppers such as the run and back commands. The main features of our approach can be described as follows: (1)The mechanism for the nonmonotonic inference can be effectively realized without drastically changing the architecture of KORE/IE. The method for implementing the inference is generally applicable to forward-chaining production systems; (2)In order to improve the dependency-directed backtracking used in TMS, the information for relationship (such as data dependencies) is independently managed by using KORE/EDEN; (3)The mechanism for checking the contradiction can be implemented without using meta programming which is usually used as an easy method for the mechanism in Prolog. The mechanism used in KORE/IE contributes to speeding up the nonmonotonic inference in Prolog.

In Section 4, we have shown an example for using the mechanism in KORE/IE. In the example, in order to maintain the consistency of pairwise comparisons, we utilize the mechanism. By using the mechanism, the consistency is effectively maintained with simple rule programming in KORE/IE.

## Acknowledgment

The author would like to acknowledge the continuing guidance and encouragement of Dr. Tosio Kitagawa, the president of IIAS- SIS, and Dr. Hajime Enomoto, the director of IIAS-SIS. The author is deeply grateful to Dr. Mitsuhiko Toda, IIAS-SIS, for reading the draft of this paper and giving him many valuable comments. Also many thanks to Mr. Yoshinori Katayama and Mr.Kunihiko Hiraishi, IIAS-SIS, for their useful comments.

This research has been carried out as a part of Fifth Generation Computer Project.

# References

[Doyle 79] J.Doyle: Truth Maintenance System, Artificial Intelligence Vol.12, pp.231-272(1979)

[Forgy 81] C.L.Forgy: OPS5 User's Manual, CMU-CS-81-135,July(1981)

[Matsumoto 87]Y.Matsumoto: Nonmonotonic Reasoning and Its Application, The Journal of Institute of Electronics, Information and Communication Engineers, pp.804-807(19887) (in Japanese)

[McDermott 83]D.McDermott: Contexts and Data Dependencies: A Synthesis, IEEE Trans., Vol.PAMI-5, NO.3, pp237-246(1983)

[Reiter 80]R.Reiter: A Logic for Default Reasoning, Artificial Intelligence Vol.13, pp.81-132(1980)

[Saaty 80]T.L.Saaty: The Analytic Hierarchy Process, McGraw Hill(1980)

[Shintani 86]T.Shintani, Y.Katayama, K.Hiraishi, and M.Toda: KORE:A Hybrid Knowledge Programming Environment for Decision Support based on a Logic Programming Language, Lecture Notes in Computer Science 264, Logic Programming '86, pp.22-33(1986)

[Shintani 86b]T.Shintani: Knowledge Table: An Approach to Knowledge Utilization Mechanism for Knowledge base, IIAS-SIS FUJITSU LIMITED Research Report No.70, p38(1986)

[Shintani 88]T.Shintani: A Fast Prolog-based Production System KORE/IE, Logic Programming: Proc. of the Fifth International Conference and Symposium (edited by R.A.Kowalski and K.A.Bowen), MIT Press(1988),pp.26-41(1988)

# Nonmonotonic Parallel Inheritance Network

Chiaki Sakama and Akira Okumura

Institute for New Generation Computer Technology
Mita Kokusai Bldg. 21F, 1-4-28, Mita, Minato-ku
Tokyo 108, Japan

## Abstract

This paper discusses a theory of nonmonotonic inheritance reasoning in a semantic network and presents a parallel inheritance algorithm based on this approach.

## 1 Background

First, consider such an inheritance hierarchy in a semantic network.

*Elephants are gray.*

*African elephants are elephants.*

*Clyde is an African elephant.*

This hierarchy is represented by a set of first order formulae as follows.

$$W = \{\forall x Elephant(x) \supset Gray(x),$$
$$\forall x AfricanElephant(x) \supset Elephant(x),$$
$$AfricanElephant(clyde)\}$$

In this case, $Gray(clyde)$ is deducible from $W$. That is, inheritance is realized by the repeated application of modus ponens.

However, when there are exceptions in the hierarchy, the case becomes somewhat more complicated. Consider the following hierarchy.

*Elephants are normally gray.*

*Royal elephants are elephants, but are not gray.*

*Clyde is a royal elephant.*

This hierarchy can be represented by a set of first order formulae as follows.

$$W = \{\forall x RoyalElephant(x) \supset Elephant(x),$$

$\forall x\, RoyalElephant(x) \supset \neg Gray(x),$

$\forall x\, Elephant(x) \wedge \neg RoyalElephant(x) \supset Gray(x),$

$RoyalElephant(clyde)\}$

Suppose we add the fact, $Elephant(taro)$, to $W$. When $taro$ is not a royal elephant, the fact, $\neg RoyalElephant(taro)$, also has to be represented explicitly in $W$ to deduce $Gray(taro)$. Thus, to represent such an inheritance hierarchy in first order formulae, all the negative information has to be represented explicitly.

[ER83,Eth87a] represented such an inheritance hierarchy by Reiter's *default logic* [Rei80]. For example, the above hierarchy is represented as:

$$W \;=\; \{\forall x\, RoyalElephant(x) \supset Elephant(x),$$
$$RoyalElephant(clyde)\}$$

$$D \;=\; \{\frac{Elephant(x) : Gray(x) \wedge \neg RoyalElephant(x)}{Gray(x)}\}$$

$D$ is a set of defaults and read as: "when $Elephant(x)$ holds, and $Gray(x)\wedge \neg RoyalElephant(x)$ is consistent with this, then infer $Gray(x)$." As a result, $Elephant(clyde)$ is deduced from $W$, but $RoyalElephant(clyde)$ in $W$ blocks the derivation of $Gray(clyde)$ from the default $D$. Besides, when $Elephant(taro)$ is added to $W$ and $taro$ is not a royal elephant, $Gray(taro)$ can be deduced from $D$ without $\neg RoyalElephant(taro)$. Such an inheritance hierarchy is called a *nonmonotonic inheritance hierarchy*, and it enables us to treat exceptions implicitly.

This formulation, however, seems to have some drawbacks since it requires as many inheritance rules as exceptions in a hierarchy. Moreover, update of such a hierarchy requires modification of all the affected default rules as well as the corresponding first order statements. It will become increasingly complex as the network grows, and does not make the most of default reasoning.

The following sections present the formalization of nonmonotonic inheritance reasoning by default logic in a different manner from Etherington, and also give a parallel algorithm based on this approach.

## 2 Theory of Nonmonotonic Inheritance Reasoning

First, two predicates are introduced.

1. $IS\_A(x, y)$: an acyclic relation between an individual $x$ and a class $y$, or a subclass $x$ and a superclass $y$; that is, $IS\_A(x, y)$ $iff$ $x \in y$, or $x \subseteq y$.

2. $Property(x, y)$ (*resp.* $\neg Property(x, y)$): a class or an individual $x$ has (*resp.* has not) a property $y$.

Now a nonmonotonic inheritance network is defined.

**Definition 2.1** A *nonmonotonic inheritance network* $\Delta = (W, D)$ is defined as follows.

$W$ : *a consistent set of ground instances of either $IS\_A(x, y), Property(z, w)$,*

   *or $\neg Property(u, v)$.*

$$D = \{ \frac{IS\_A(x, y) \wedge Property(y, z) : Property(x, z)}{Property(x, z)},$$
$$\frac{IS\_A(x, y) \wedge \neg Property(y, z) : \neg Property(x, z)}{\neg Property(x, z)} \} \quad \square$$

**Example 2.1** Suppose the following classical hierarchy.

   *Molluscs are normally shellbearers.*

   *Cephalopods are molluscs but are not normally shellbearers.*

   *Nautili are cephalopods but are shellbearers.*

   *Fred is a nautilus.*

In this hierarchy, cephalopods become an exception to molluscs with respect to shellbearers, and nautili also become an exception to cephalopods with respect to shellbearers.

Such a hierarchy is represented by $\Delta = (W, D)$, where

$W = \{IS\_A(cephalopod, mollusc),$

$IS\_A(nautilus, cephalopod),$

$IS\_A(fred, nautilus),$

$Property(mollusc, has\_shell),$

$\neg Property(cephalopod, has\_shell),$

$Property(nautilus, has\_shell)\}$

As a result, the extension of $\Delta$ becomes:

$E = W \cup \{Property(fred, has\_shell)\}.$

(Informally, an extension denotes a set of logical consequences of a default theory.) $\quad \square$

The same hierarchy is represented by [ER83,Eth87a] as:[1]

$$W = \{\forall x Cephalopod(x) \supset Mollusc(x),$$
$$\forall x Nautilus(x) \supset Cephalopod(x),$$
$$\forall x Nautilus(x) \supset Shellbearer(x),$$
$$Nautilus(fred)\}$$

$$D = \{\frac{Mollusc(x) : Shellbearer(x) \wedge \neg Cephalopod(x)}{Shellbearer(x)},$$
$$\frac{Cephalopod(x) : \neg Shellbearer(x) \wedge \neg Nautilus(x)}{\neg Shellbearer(x)}\}$$

Compairing these two formulations, our approach describes the data in the network, $W$, apart from the inheritance rules, $D$. This provides a simple description of inheritance hierarchies, since default rules are independent of the network. It also facilitates updation of the network, since it requires changing only the corresponding data in $W$ and does not need to modify defaults.

Such a system, which consists of a set of classes and a set of inheritable properties associated with each class, is called a *class/property inheritance system* [Tou86]. Our approach defines exceptions as nonmonotonic properties of classes, while $IS\_A$ hierarchy defines a monotonic relation between classes. In the $IS\_A$ hierarchy, transitivity is not assumed since it generates a redundant link. For example, $IS\_A(fred, cephalopod)$ is deduced using transitivity in Example 2.1, then it leads to an extension which contains $\neg Property(fred, has\_shell)$, which is an undesired result. To derive a transitive class-subclass relation, it is necesarry to add, for example, $Property(nautilus, upper(cephalopod))$ to $W$, to derive $Property(fred, upper(cephalopod))$.

$\Delta$ is called a *normal default theory* and has at least one consistent extension for every consistent $W$ [Rei80]. Nonmonotonic inheritance networks are classified by the number of their extensions.

**Definition 2.2** A nonmonotonic inheritance network $\Delta$ is *definite* iff it has only one extension. □

Example 2.1 is a definite case. However, there is a network with multiple extensions which are inconsistent with each other. Consider the notorious example of *Nixon diamond*. The problem is: *Nixon is both a Quaker and a Republican, and Quakers are typically pacifists,*

---

[1][Eth87b] employs a different manner of representation, based on Touretzky's approach.

*while Republicans are typically not. Then, whether Nixon is a pacifist or not?*

This hierarchy is represented in $\Delta$ with $W$:

$$W = \{IS\_A(nixon, quaker),$$
$$IS\_A(nixon, republican),$$
$$Property(quaker, pacifist),$$
$$\neg Property(republican, pacifist)\}.$$

In this case, there exists the following two extensions which are inconsistent with each other.

$$E_1 = W \cup \{Property(nixon, pacifist)\}$$
$$E_2 = W \cup \{\neg Property(nixon, pacifist)\}$$

Such a network which has more than one extension is called *indefinite*, and there are two attitudes for treating such an indefinite network [THT87]. A *skeptical reasoner* draws no conclusion from ambiguous information, and hence offers no conclusion as to whether Nixon is a pacifist or not. A *credulous reasoner*, on the other hand, tries to draw as many conclusions as possible, and hence offers two alternatives: Nixon is a pacifist in one case, and is not in the other.

From an algorithmic point of view, a skeptical reasoner always generates a unique extension, then its algorithm seems to be simpler and more efficient than that of the credulous one, which generates multiple possible extensions that grow exponentially as ambiguity increases. The credulous attitude, on the other hand, seems to be more expressive than the skeptical attitude, since the explicit representation of ambiguities suggests that there is some disagreement in the network structure.

To take advantage of each attitude, an algorithm which can treat ambiguities but does not generate multiple extensions is considered. The next section discusses such an inheritance algorithm and its parallel execution.

## 3   Parallel Inheritance Algorithm

Inheritance algorithms combined with parallelism have been studied over the past few years. NETL [Fah79] is a pioneering semantic network system. In NETL, inheritance is performed by *parallel marker propagation* over nodes in a network. However, as is pointed out by [ER83,Eth87a], NETL does not treat nonmonotonic cases correctly.

[Tou86] has proposed some inheritance algorithms for a nonmonotonic inheritance system. Those algorithms are based on the choice of inference paths in multiple inheritance and limited parallelism is achieved. They offer a credulous inference system and also a skeptical version is discussed in [HTT87]. These methods, however, require each derived path to contain its entire derivation history and seem to become overloaded as the size of the network increases.

[ER83,Eth87a] have shown a parallel algorithm based on their formalization and proved its correctness, that is, all inferences lie within a single extension. However, this algorithm is not complete in general; there might be some extensions which do not come out of the algorithm. Related to this work, [Cot85] has shown a parallel *connectionist* architecture, but there is no assurance of correctness.

The remainder of this section shows a $\pi$ *(parallel inheritance) algorithm* for the nonmonotonic inheritance network presented in the previous section. First, notation in the algorithm corresponding to $\Delta$ is given:

(a) $property(class, \emptyset)$ iff $\forall cprop, Property(class, cprop) \notin W$ and $\neg Property(class, cprop) \notin W$.

Otherwise, $property(class, CProps)$ iff $\forall cprop \in CProps, Property(class, cprop) \in W$, and $\forall not(cprop) \in CProps, \neg Property(class, cprop) \in W$.

(b) $is\_a(class, \emptyset)$ iff $\forall upper, IS\_A(class, upper) \notin W$.

Otherwise, $is\_a(class, Uppers)$ iff $\forall upper \in Uppers, IS\_A(class, upper) \in W$.

Here, $\emptyset$ denotes an empty set and notation which begins with a capital letter denotes a set. Now, the $\pi$ algorithm is presented below.

```
procedure π(input : class, output : Props);
  begin
    call property(class, CProps);
    call is_a(class, Uppers);
    Temp ← ∅;
    while Uppers ≠ ∅ do
      begin
        select upper from Uppers;
        call π(upper, UProps);
        Temp ← Temp ∪ UProps;
```

$$Uppers \leftarrow Uppers - \{upper\}$$

  end

  call $reverse(CProps, RevCProps)$;

  $Props \leftarrow CProps \cup (Temp - RevCProps)$

 end

 procedure $reverse(input : CProps, output : RevCProps)$;

  begin

  $RevCProps = \emptyset$;

  while $CProps \neq \emptyset$ do

   begin

   select $cprop$ from $CProps$;

   if $cprop = not(prop)$ then

   $RevCProps \leftarrow RevCProps \cup \{prop\}$

   else $RevCProps \leftarrow RevCProps \cup \{not(cprop)\}$;

   $CProps \leftarrow CProps - \{cprop\}$

   end

  end

**Example 3.1** In Example 2.1, $\pi(fred, \{has\_shell\})$ where

 $property(mollusc, \{has\_shell\})$,  $property(cephalopod, \{not(has\_shell)\})$,

 $property(nautilus, \{has\_shell\})$,  $property(fred, \emptyset)$,  $is\_a(mollusc, \emptyset)$,

 $is\_a(cephalopod, \{mollusc\})$,  $is\_a(nautilus, \{cephalopod\})$, and $is\_a(fred, \{nautilus\})$.

In Nixon Diamond, $\pi(nixon, \{pacifist, not(pacifist)\})$ where

 $property(quaker, \{pacifist\})$,  $property(republican, \{not(pacifist)\})$,  $property(nixon, \emptyset)$,

 $is\_a(quaker, \emptyset)$,  $is\_a(republican, \emptyset)$, and $is\_a(nixon, \{quaker, republican\})$.  □

The procedure $\pi$ produces a set of inheritable properties for an input class downwards from upper classes to their subclasses. Nonmonotonic inheritance is achieved through overriding higher properties by conflicting lower ones. When there is more than one upper class at $is\_a(class, Uppers)$, each upper class calls the recursive $\pi$ procedure independently. This process will be executed in parallel on a massively parallel architecture, where each processor will have cost proportional to the length of the inheritance path. The $\pi$ algorithm is implemented in the parallel logic programming language GHC (Guarded Horn Clauses) [Ued86], and is shown in Appendix A.

The next proposition assures the soundness and completeness of the $\pi$ procedure with respect to a nonmonotonic inheritance network $\Delta$.

**Proposition 3.1** Suppose a nonmonotonic inheritance network $\Delta$ then

$\forall class, \pi(class, Props)$ *iff*

$Props = \{prop \mid \exists E_i, Property(class, prop) \in E_i\}$

$\cup \{not(prop) \mid \exists E_j, \neg Property(class, prop) \in E_j\},$

where $E_i$ and $E_j$ are extensions of $\Delta$.

**Proof**  See Appendix B.  $\square$

## 4  Discussion

The previous sections presented a formalization of the nonmonotonic inheritance network and its parallel execution algorithm. Our approach enables us to define inheritance rules apart from data in a network, and simplifies description and maintenance of the network. The problem is, as is mentioned in an earlier section, a redundant $IS\_A$ link often causes some ambiguities in the network.

The $\pi$ algorithm produces a set of inheritable properties for an input class, and parallel execution is achieved in multiple inheritance. When a network is definite, the properties generated by the algorithm are included in an extension, while in the case of an indefinite network, it collects ambiguous information from multiple extensions. Note that the output of the algorithm is not an extension itself, thus there is no problem of logical inconsistency in the indefinite case. It may seem that such ambiguities give us no information, but they suggest the problem in the network structure and help us to reconstruct it.

In general, however, it is not straightforward to decide whether an inheritance network is definite or not. Let us consider an example from [San86] (Figure (a)).

[San86] has defined some basic structure types for inheritance networks and given sound inference rules for these structures. According to his inheritance system, Clyde is not gray in the above network. Whereas Touretzky's system [Tou86] yields two alternatives; Clyde is gray in one case and is not in the other, and our system also returns gray and not(gray) for an input class Clyde. This shows that the above network is interpreted as definite in Sandewall's system, and indefinite in Touretzky's and ours. In this example, it seems to be more intuitive

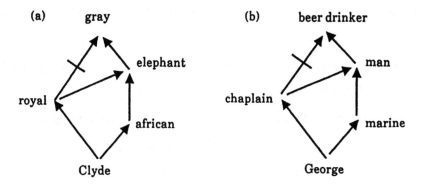

to infer that Clyde is not gray. However, as in shown in [THT87], there is a counter-example which has the the same structure with (a), but the Sandewall's inference seems to be doubtful (Figure (b)). In this case, whether George drinks beer or not is not clear and it depends on the rate of beer drinking among marines.

These examples suggest that it is difficult to infer the intended meaning of the network from its structure alone.

## Acknowledgment

We would like to thank David W. Etherington for his comments for improving earlier drafts of this paper. We are also grateful to the colleagues at ICOT for useful discussions and comments.

## References

[Cot85] Cottrell,G.W.: "Parallelism in Inheritance Hierarchies with Exception", *IJCAI'85*, pp.194-202, 1985.

[ER83] Etherington,D.W. and Reiter,R.: "On Inheritance Hierarchies with Exceptions", *AAAI'83*, pp.104-108, 1983.

[Eth87a] Etherington,D.W.: "Formalizing Nonmonotonic Reasoning Systems", *Artificial Intelligence 31*, pp.41-85, 1987.

[Eth87b] Etherington,D.W.: "More on Inheritance Hierarchies with Exceptions", *AAAI'87*, pp.352-357, 1987.

[Fah79] Fahlman,S.E.: "NETL: A System for Representing and Using Real-World Knowledge", *MIT Press*, Cambridge, MA, 1979.

[HTT87] Horty,J.F., Thomason,R.H. and Touretzky,D.S.: "A Skeptical Theory of Inheritance", *AAAI'87*, pp.358-363, 1987.

[Rei80] Reiter,R.: "A Logic for Default Reasoning", *Artificial Intelligence 13*, pp.81-132, 1980.

[San86] Sandewall,E.: "Nonmonotonic Inference Rules for Multiple Inheritance with Exceptions", *Proc. of IEEE*, vol.74, pp.1345-1353, 1986.

[Tou86] Touretzky,D.S.: "The Mathematics of Inheritance Systems", *Research Notes in Artificial Intelligence*, Pitman, London, 1986.

[THT87] Touretzky,D.S., Horty,J.F. and Thomason,R.H.: "A Clash of Intuitions", *IJCAI'87*, pp.476-482, 1987.

[Ued86] Ueda,K.: "Guarded Horn Clauses", *Lecture Notes in Computer Sciences 221*, Springer-Verlag, Berlin, 1986.

## Appendix A

Here, we show an implementation of the $\pi$ algorithm in GHC. GHC is the parallel logic programming language developed as the kernel language of fifth generation project at ICOT.

The syntax of a clause in GHC is in the following form:

$$H :- G_1, G_2, ..., G_m \mid B_1, B_2, ..., B_n.$$

where the part preceding '|' is called a guard, and the part succeeding it is called a body. A clause with an empty guard is a goal clause. The declarative meaning of the clause is the same as Prolog.

The execution of a GHC program proceeds by reducing a given goal clause to the empty clause as follows.

(a) The guard of a clause cannot export any bindings to the caller of that clause.

(b) The body of a clause cannot export any bindings to the guard of that clause before commitment.

(c) When there are several candidate clauses for invocation, the clause whose guard first succeeds is selected for commitment.

Under these conditions, the execution of goal reduction is done in parallel. Now the procedure is shown with an example of shellbearers.

```
/*** Nonmonotonic Parallel Inheritance Network in GHC ***/
%%% inheritance procedure %%%
  pi(Class,Props,Tail):- true |
                         property(Class,Props,Temp),
                         is_a(Class,Uppers),
                         has_property(Uppers,UProps,Res),
                         filter(Props,UProps,Res,Temp,Tail).
  has_property([UClass|Rest],UProps,Tail):- true |
                         pi(UClass,UProps,Temp),
                         has_property(Rest,Temp,Tail).
  has_property([], UProps,Tail):- true | UProps=Tail.
  filter([CProp|Rest], In,Tail1,Out,Tail2):- CProp\=not(_) |
                         filter2(not(CProp),In,Tail1,Temp,Tail3),
                         filter(Rest,Temp,Tail3,Out,Tail2).
  filter([not(CProp)|Rest],In,Tail1,Out,Tail2):- true |
                         filter2(CProp,In,Tail1,Temp,Tail3),
                         filter(Rest,Temp,Tail3,Out,Tail2).
  filter(Out, In,Tail1,Out,Tail2):- true |
                         In=Out,Tail1=Tail2.
  filter2(CProp,[P1|P2],Tail1,Temp,Tail2):- P1\=CProp |
                         Temp=[P1|Rest],
                         filter2(CProp,P2,Tail1,Rest,Tail2).
  filter2(CProp,[P1|P2],Tail1,Temp,Tail2):- P1=CProp |
                         filter2(CProp,P2,Tail1,Temp,Tail2).
  filter2(CProp,Tail1, Tail1,Temp,Tail2):- true |
                         Temp=Tail2.

%%% data %%%
  is_a(mollusc, Uppers):- true | Uppers=[].
  is_a(aquatic, Uppers):- true | Uppers=[].
  is_a(cephalopod, Uppers):- true | Uppers=[mollusc,aquatic].
```

```
is_a(nautilus, Uppers):- true | Uppers=[cephalopod].

is_a(fred, Uppers):- true | Uppers=[nautilus].

property(mollusc, CProps,Tail):- true | CProps=[soft_body,has_shell|Tail].

property(aquatic, CProps,Tail):- true | CProps=[swimming|Tail].

property(cephalopod,CProps,Tail):- true | CProps=[not(has_shell),has_legs|Tail].

property(nautilus, CProps,Tail):- true | CProps=[has_shell,not(swimming)|Tail].

property(fred, CProps,Tail):- true | CProps=[american|Tail].

%%% execution results %%%

| ?- ghc pi(fred,Props,[]).

21 msec.

Props = [american,has_shell,not(swimming),has_legs,soft_body]

yes
```

This GHC program is easily translated into a Prolog program, which performs sequential inheritance in a network.

## Appendix B

First, some notation used in the proof is given. For an $IS\_A(x,y)$, the closure of $x$ is defined as a set, $Upper_k(x)$ $(k \geq 0)$, as follows:

1. $x \in Upper_0(x)$

2. $z \in Upper_{k+1}(x)$ $iff$ $\exists y, y \in Upper_k(x)$ and $IS\_A(y,z)$.

Note that the $IS\_A$ hierarchy is acyclic, then $x \notin \bigcup_{k \geq 1} Upper_k(x)$. Now we show the proof of the proposition.

**Proposition 3.1** Suppose a nonmonotonic inheritance network $\Delta$ then

$\forall class, \pi(class, Props)$ $iff$

$Props = \{prop \mid \exists E_i, Property(class, prop) \in E_i\}$

$\qquad\qquad \cup \{not(prop) \mid \exists E_j, \neg Property(class, prop) \in E_j\}.$

where $E_i$ and $E_j$ are the extensions of $\Delta$.

**Proof** Suppose first that $\exists n, n+1, Upper_n(class) \neq \emptyset, Upper_{n+1}(class) = \emptyset$, then

$\forall c_n \in Upper_n(class)$ , $is\_a(c_n, \emptyset)$ holds.

Assume $\pi(c_n, Props_n)$ and $property(c_n, CProps_n)$ then

$$Props_n = CProps_n \cup (Temp_n - RevCProps_n)$$
$$= CProps_n \cup (\emptyset - RevCProps_n)$$
$$= CProps_n$$
$$= \{cprop \mid Property(c_n, cprop) \in W\} \cup \{not(cprop) \mid \neg Property(c_n, cprop) \in W\}.$$

Next assume $\forall c_k \in Upper_k(class)$ $(0 < k \leq n)$, $\pi(c_k, Props_k)$ where

$$Props_k = \{prop \mid \exists E_i, Property(c_k, prop) \in E_i\}$$
$$\cup \{not(prop) \mid \exists E_j, \neg Property(c_k, prop) \in E_j\} \text{ holds.}$$

Let $\forall c_{k-1} \in Upper_{k-1}(class)$, $\pi(c_{k-1}, Props_{k-1})$, then

$$Props_{k-1} = CProps_{k-1} \cup (Temp_{k-1} - RevCProps_{k-1})$$

where $property(c_{k-1}, CProps_{k-1})$.

(a) If $uprop \in CProps_{k-1}$ or $not(uprop) \in CProps_{k-1}$, then

$Property(c_{k-1}, uprop) \in W$ or $\neg Property(c_{k-1}, uprop) \in W$.

(b) Otherwise, $uprop \in Temp_{k-1} - RevCProps_{k-1}$

or $not(uprop) \in Temp_{k-1} - RevCProps_{k-1}$, then

$uprop \in Temp_{k-1}$ or $not(uprop) \in Temp_{k-1}$ where $Temp_{k-1} = Props_k$.

By the assumption, $\forall c_k \in Upper_k(class)$, then

$\exists E_i, Property(c_k, uprop) \in E_i$ or $\exists E_j, \neg Property(c_k, uprop) \in E_j$.

In case $uprop \in Temp_{k-1}$, clearly $uprop \notin RevCProps_{k-1}$, then

$\neg Property(c_{k-1}, uprop) \notin W$ and $\exists E_i, Property(c_{k-1}, uprop) \in E_i$.

In case $not(uprop) \in Temp_{k-1}$, clearly $not(uprop) \notin RevCProps_{k-1}$, then

$Property(c_{k-1}, uprop) \notin W$ and $\exists E_j, \neg Property(c_{k-1}, uprop) \in E_j$.

Therefore,

$$Props_{k-1} \subseteq \{prop \mid \exists E_i, Property(c_{k-1}, prop) \in E_i\}$$
$$\cup \{not(prop) \mid \exists E_j, \neg Property(c_{k-1}, prop) \in E_j\} \quad (*).$$

While, let $\forall c_{k-1} \in Upper_{k-1}(class)$, $\exists E_i, Property(c_{k-1}, uprop) \in E_i$,

or $\exists E_j, \neg Property(c_{k-1}, uprop) \in E_j$.

(a) If $Property(c_{k-1}, uprop) \in W$ or $\neg Property(c_{k-1}, uprop) \in W$, then

$uprop \in CProps_{k-1}$ or $not(uprop) \in CProps_{k-1}$.

(b) Otherwise, $\exists E_i, Property(c_k, uprop) \in E_i$, or $\exists E_j, \neg Property(c_k, uprop) \in E_j$.

By the assumption, $\forall c_k \in Upper_k(class)$, $uprop \in Props_k$,

or $not(uprop) \in Props_k$, where $\pi(c_k, Props_k)$.

In case $\exists E_i, Property(c_{k-1}, uprop) \in E_i, \neg Property(c_{k-1}, uprop) \notin W$ holds, then

$uprop \notin RevCProps_{k-1}$ and $uprop \in Props_k - RevCProps_{k-1}$.

So, $uprop \in CProps_{k-1} \cup (Temp_{k-1} - RevCProps_{k-1})$.

In case $\exists E_j, \neg Property(c_{k-1}, uprop) \in E_j, Property(c_{k-1}, uprop) \notin W$ holds, then

$not(uprop) \notin RevCProps_{k-1}$ and $not(uprop) \in Props_k - RevCProps_{k-1}$.

So, $not(uprop) \in CProps_{k-1} \cup (Temp_{k-1} - RevCProps_{k-1})$.

Hence $uprop \in Props_{k-1}$, or $not(uprop) \in Props_{k-1}$ holds, where $\pi(c_{k-1}, Props_{k-1})$.

Therefore,

$$Props_{k-1} \supseteq \{prop \mid \exists E_i, Property(c_{k-1}, prop) \in E_i\}$$
$$\cup \{not(prop) \mid \exists E_j, \neg Property(c_{k-1}, prop) \in E_j\} \quad (\dagger).$$

Together from $(*)$ and $(\dagger)$,

$$Props_{k-1} = \{prop \mid \exists E_i, Property(c_{k-1}, prop) \in E_i\}$$
$$\cup \{not(prop) \mid \exists E_j, \neg Property(c_{k-1}, prop) \in E_j\}.$$

By induction, we have the desired result. $\quad \square$

# Logic Programming Debugger
# Using Control Flow Specification

Hideo Tamura            Hideo Aiso
Keio University
Japan

In this paper , a control specification for logic programming and the Deterministic Trimming Method for bug detection are Proposed.

Using information from the control specification, the query complexity of our Deterministic Trimming Method is less than that of Shapiro's debugging system.

## §1   Introduction

Prolog is a popular language for programming prototypes of parallel language interpreters and natural language processors, and for knowledge representation. But it is said that it is difficult to show Prolog's execution flow explicitly, so one cannot understand another's programs. To reduce the programmer's load, many Prolog debugging systems have been proposed and used. They are classified into two groups.

① Programmer oriented
   Using debugger's facilities to detect bugs by programmer.
   [Byrd78] [Numao85]

② System oriented
   Debugging system asks programmer about a test program, analyses that information and detects bugs.
   [Shapiro83] [Pereira,L.M 86] [Lloyd87] [Maechi87]
   [Takahasi86]

If there were a program-specification that did not put additional load on programmer and did not let down the Prolog's abilities, it would be very useful and make Prolog more powerful. In this paper, a control specification is proposed, that is based on the Control Flow Model [Byrd78], very familier to Prolog users as the Box Model. This control specification can represent the programmer's intention of how the program is to perform.

We propose the Deterministic Trimming Method, which uses control specification information based on Shapiro's Algorithmic Program Debugging [Shapiro83].

## §2 Control Specification

If there are specifications of each goal's mode declarations, argument types and determinancy, it is easy to debug and maintain a program. Even a beginner will understand the program's meaning easily.

There is not a general Prolog program specification notation, even if there were a new one proposed, it probably would be difficult to get aquainted with, and programmer's load would increase linearly with the number of program steps.

Therefore a control specification based on the poppular control flow model is adopted and applied to this debugging system.

§2.1 Control flow specification

Whereas the control flow model represents the dynamic run time behavior of a program, control specification represents it a statically. Although control specification cannot represents a program's entire behavior, it can represent the programmer' practical intention.

In the following, control specification is described, and we indicate how the programmer's intention is represented and its relationship with the debugger.

The control specification mainly represents relations between goals of program text. In figure 2.1, its difference from the control flow model is an additional 'FAIL' line. This additional 'FAIL' line is used for 'cut fail', which means backtracking invoked after a 'cut' operation dose not affect goals before the 'cut' in the same clause.

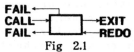

Fig 2.1

There are 5 patterns of control specification, which the programmer can use to express control flow.

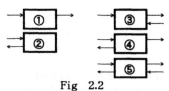

Fig 2.2

○ Goal ① succeeds deterministically does not allow back-tracking (deep backtrack).
○ Goal ② finitely fails.
○ Goal ③ always succeeds. If there is backtracking after the goal's success, there must be alternative solutions of the goal. There is never the case of no solution of the goal.
○ Goal ④ permits both success of failure. If the goal succeeds the goal does not allow backtracking (deep backtracking).

Examples of control specifications for some built-in predicates is shown in figure 2.3.

CUT            FAIL            REPEAT

Fig 2.3

## §2.2 The relation of goals

Control specification notation represents control flow
between goals, though it does not regulate the behavior
within the subgoals. It regulates control flow on the
clause level of the program text. Each subgoal's control
flow is regulated on the level of it's own clauses. A goal's
determinancy is not specified, therefore the goal may succeed even though it causes shallow backtracking. A control
specification box represents a goal's final behavior of
success or failure or backtracking.

Example 2.4

Goal ①②③ means it does not fail. Backtracking might
occur inside of the goal, but it must eventually succeed.
Goal ⑤⑥ have the posibility of backtracking, and eventually
it gets an alternative solution or fails. Cut operator ④
inhibits backtrack to th goal ③ from FAIL ⑤, and switches
the flow of control from REDO line to upper FAIL line.

Fig 2.4

Example of actual simple control specifications are fig
2.5 and fig 2.6. There are four types of 'append' usages,
type I being most common. The control specification in fig
2.5 allows type I, II and III but not type IV. In fig 2.6, all
types are allowed. In this way, control specification sets
constraints on goals, therefore reducing bugs.     If a
programmer wants 'append' to be used as type I and IV,
control specification must use type IV.

```
append( [ H|T ],L,[ H|Z ] ):- append( T,L,Z ).
append( [],L,L ).
```

```
         Fig 2.5                      Fig 2.6
I  append( +,+,- )
      ex   ?- append( [a,b,c],[d,e],Ans )
           Ans = [a,b,c,d,e]
II append( +,-,+ )
      ex   ?- append( [a,b],X,[a,b,c] )
           X = [c]
III append( -,-,+ )
      ex   ?- append( X,[b,c],[a,b,c] )
           X = [a]
IV append( -,-,+ )
     ex ?- append( H,T,[a,b,c,d] )
           H = [a,b,c,d]
           T = [];
           H = [a,b,c]
           T = [d];
           H = [a,b]
           T = [c,d];
           ....
```

§2.3 Clarify backtrack area by control specification

One of the reasons why another programmer's Prolog program is difficalt to understand is that there is no sign of where the backtrack area starts and ends in the program. How the backtrack area is represented in control specification is discussed as following.

The program in Fig 2.7 searches for multiples of three from numbers in the data base. If it finds one , it is saved in the database. The reagion of backtrack is between the 'generate' and 'test' goals, so there is a link between them with a FAIL and REDO line. The backtrack invocation goal is the last goal within a backtrack region, namely 'is'.

```
tripple:- generate(A),test(A),assert(tripple(A)).
generate(A):- num(A).
test(A):- 0 is A mod 3.
num(1).
num(2).
num(3).
num(4).
num(5).
```

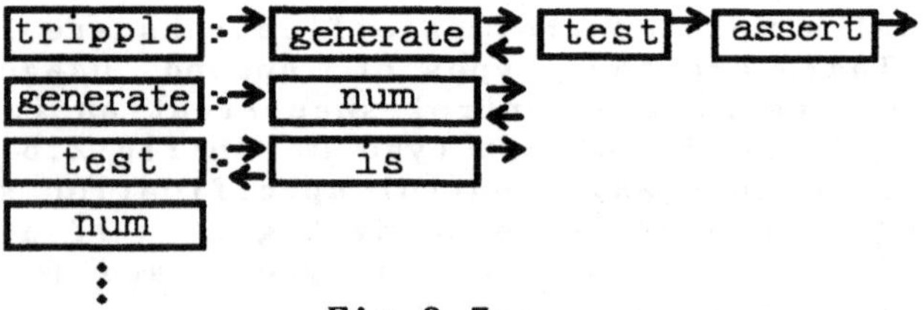

Fig 2.7

Example of quick sort control specification
```
sort( X,Y ):- qsort( X,Y-[] ).
qsort( [],R-R ):- !.
qsort( [Key|Other],B1-B2 ):-
     partition( Key,Other,Small,Large ),
     qsort( Small,B1-[Key|Tmp] ),
     qsort( Large,Tmp-B2 ).
partition( _,[],[],[] ):- !.
partition( Key,[ Top|Other ],[ Top|Small ],Large ):-
     Top =< Key,!,
     partition( Key,Other,Small,Large ).
partition( Key,[ Top|Other ],Small,[ Top|Large ] ):-
     Key < Top , !.
partition( Key,Other,Small,Large ).
```
            List 2.2   quick sort

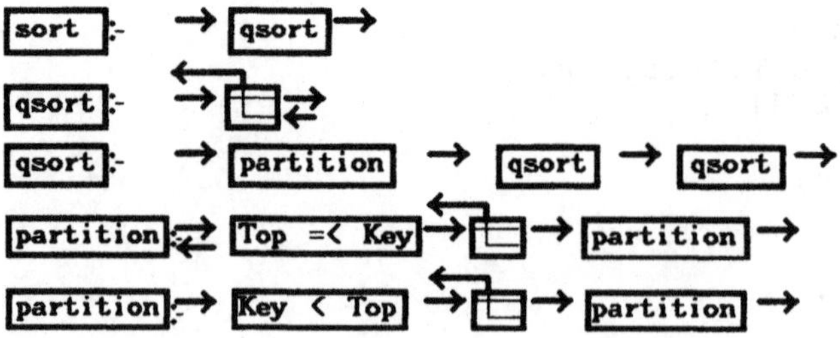

Fig 2.8

## §2.4 The relation of Control Specification and debugger

When a user begins to debug, the debugging system will show a default control specification for the user's program in order to reduce programmers load to construct all control specification. There may be many symptoms of bugs that affect default control specification, so the programmer may debug at this first stage.

At the next stage, the programmer must correct the erroneous control specification. This step proceeds with a control specification editor.

The debugging system needs the information below to analyse a bug.

    ○A goal's relations that can be known from control specification.
      ( Existence of backtrack region )
    ○The goals that violate the control specification.
      ( There is the case that the goal which should not fail actually does fail. )

## §3 Deterministic Trimming Method

The Deterministic Trimming Method is a bug detection algorithm that is based on Shapiro's devide-and-query algorithm, using the control specification. In processing this algorithm, the information below is required.

① Whether backtracking affects a particular branch; that is, which nodes fail or succeed.

② Whether a goal succeeds with a value that the programmer does not expect. Identification of a node includes that value.

Backtracking information ① is obtained from the control specification notation. For example, figure 3.1 shows that a subtree rooted at the goal 'a' has a possibility of changing its computation tree due to the result of a subtree rooted at the goal 'b'. However, a subtree rooted at the goal 'b' is not affected by a subtree rooted at the goal 'c'.

$$\rightarrow\boxed{a}\,\underset{\leftarrow}{\rightarrow}\,\boxed{b}\rightarrow\boxed{c}\rightarrow$$

Fig 3.1

The information ② about unexpected values is obtained from the user. The debugging system has facilities for managing information regarding binding values and nodes, and the system finds the position where an indicated argument value was produced.

For example, it will query the user about a goal that has an erroneous argument.
When 'qsort( [4;1,2,5,3],[3,1,2,4,5] )' succeeds, the system asks the programmer:

    Query
      qsort( [4,1,2,5,3],[3,1,2,4,5] ) (yes/no) ?n

The programmer responds "no".
The second argument is indicated and we call it 'false instance production node'.

## Deterministic Trimming Method

step 1 Call the root node 'R'.

step 2 Calculate the weight[*-1] of the node 'R', if it is 1
then report that there is a bug in the clause that
matched with this node.

step 3 Calculate the middle node of root 'R', call it 'Q'.
Query the programmer at the node 'Q' is true or not.

step 4 If the node 'Q' is true, then trim the subtree rooted
at the node 'Q', go to step 2.

step 5 If the node 'Q' is flase then indicate erroneous
value in the argument. ( The programmer may indicate
values in the argument ). The system will find nodes
that produce only indicated values, we call that set
of nodes as 'B'.

step 6 If there is at least one node of set 'B' outside of
the subtree rooted node 'Q', trim the branches that
have no possibility of backtracking on the path from
the node 'Q' to the node 'R'. Trim the subtree rooted
at the node 'Q' and go to step 2.

step 7 If all nodes of set 'B' are in the subtree rooted at
the node 'Q', trim the branches that have no
possibility of backtracking on the path from the old-
est node within the set 'B' to the node 'Q'. We
rename the node 'Q' as 'R' and go to step 2.

step 8 If there is no indication of a false term at step 5,
rename the node 'Q' as 'R' and go to step 2.

note *-1
To calculate weight, assume that
- a node of a built in predicate = 0
- a leaf node ( except for built in predicate ) = 1
- other node = $\Sigma$(weight of child node ) + 1

Example figure 3.2 represents step 7, Figure 3.3
represents step 7, These examples are assumed to be
non-backtracking case. In Shapiro's algorithm, region 'A'
can be trimmed from the search area at one query. In Determi
nistic trimming Method, region 'A' and 'B' can be trimmed
from the search area in one query.

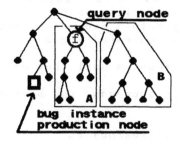

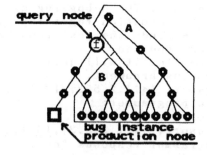

Fig 3.2 step 6                    Fig 3.3 step 7

## More detail of example step 7 and step 8

The case that there is a false instance node in a subtree rooted at the queried node ( figure 3.4, step 7 ).

We call the queried node 'Q',the false instance node 'B'. In this case, we find a false instance node 'Q' whose false value was actually produced by the node 'B', so there is a high probability that there is a bug on the path from 'B' to' Q'. ( There is also a possibility that the true bug is in another path ). Therefore the path from 'B' to 'Q' and the paths that affect it cannot be trimmed. Not only the 'B'~'Q' path but also the nodes that precede that path are bug affection nodes. The noticeable nodes are after the 'B'~'Q' path ( after the node 'B' ). If these nodes are reduced deterministically, there is no problem, but if backtrack occurs, the previously successful nodes are re-invoked in order to search for another solution. Therefore we cannot trim the nodes that invoked backtracking to the 'B'~'Q' path.

In the case of figure 3,4 , we cannot trim the node 'D' that invokes backtracking to the node 'C' ( this information is given by the control specification notation ). It does not affect the 'B'~'Q' path that the node 'F' invokes backtracking to the node 'E' and 'E' itself, so they are to be trimmed. Even if the node 'D' possibly invokes backtracking, the child nodes of 'D' are to be trimmed because of their determinancy.

Figure 3.5 and step 6 show tha case that a false instance production node is in the outside of a subtree rooted at the query node.

We assume queried node 'Q', a false instance production node 'B', and root node 'R'. Similar to the case of figure 3.4 , considering the nodes that may affect 'B'~'Q' path, the nodes in the 'Q'~'R' path are doubtful. We cannot trim the node 'D' that may invoke backtrack to the node 'C' on the 'Q'~'R' path, but any other node that is after 'Q'~'R' path except node 'D' can be trimmed.

## §4 Bug Detection Strategy

The features of this program diagnosis is follows.
①     The diagnosis of a successful procedure with bug uses the deterministic trimming method.
②     The step of diagnosing a failure procedure with bug is same as that of Shapiro's trace query algorism, but we improve the querying step by providing instances of unbound variables in order to make it easier step for the programmer. In a case that a goal has matched many clauses ( causing shallow backtracking ), programmer can select which clause must be matched, as this debugger uses a history of test program's execution.
③     If there is a goal for which execution is inhibited by the control specification, remove the execution history after that goal. Because this removed area is generated after production of a bug. If this is done before ① and ②, redundant query times can be reduced. For example, in figure 4.1 it is the case that the node 'J' behaves

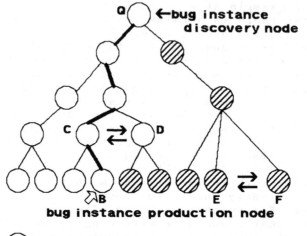

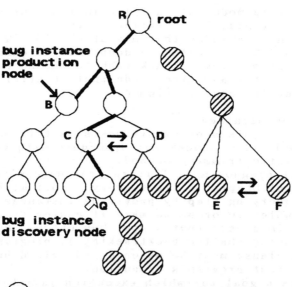

bug instance production node

○ node that possibly affects the above path

◐ node that does not affect the above path

━━ possibly buggy path

Fig 3.4

bug instance
discovery node

○ node that possibly affects the above path

◐ node that does not affect the above path

━━ possibly buggy path

Fig 3.5

illegaly with respect to the control specification, the
subtrees of node 'C' and node 'D' are very big. In the
dividing query algorism, when a query node is selected in
order to devide a search area in half, then the selection
is based to a big subtree, so the bug detection step
becomes roundabout. Given the control specification, we
can know that some bugs are in the nodes ('A','B','E','I',
'J') so irrelevant parts can be trimmed.

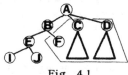

Fig 4.1

## Combination of Deterministic Trimming Method and trace query algorism

Practical diagnosis of a Prolog program has a case that
even if the program suceeds with bugs, it may include
subprograms that fail with bugs. For example, there are
clauses 'c1'c2' that may match with goal 'a'.

     clause c1    a:- g1,g2,g3,…….
     clause c2    a:- k1,k2,k3,…….

First of all, match goal 'a' to clause 'c1', but clause
'c1'is assumed to have bugs in its body and invoked backtrack.

Next, match goal 'a' to clause 'c2', goal 'k1','k2' are
executed successively. This program succeeds with bugs so
deterministic trimming method is adopted, but it cannot find
bugs in the successful path. Deterministic Trimming Method
only finds out that goal 'a' must not match with clause 'c2'.
In this case, trace query algorism must be applied to the
failed path in which goal 'a' is matched with clause 'c1'.
Therefore the system has to decide which clause to choose
and switch to the trace query algorism. If the system
applies all steps of the trace query algorism, a bug will be
found but many queries are necessary. In order to solve this
problem, we combine both algorisms.

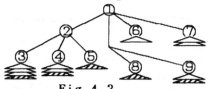

Fig 4.2

Figure 4.2 shows the execution history of a test program
using an execution tree representation ( hierarchical part
means 'OR' subtree of 'AND' tree ). Each triangle also
represents an execution tree. Oblique parts are successful
trees. If the bug search area is in a successful tree, the
system applies the Deterministic Trimming Method, otherwise
it applies the trace query algorism.

The bug search step in figure 4.2 is shown below.

First of all, the system applies the Deterministic Trimming Method because execution tree rooted at the node '1'. Since node '3' has four alternatives, the system urges the programmer to select a valid one. If the lowest layer of node '3' is selected, continue to apply the Deterministic Trimming Method, otherwise apply the trace query algorism.

If the programmer indicates that node '3' must not match with that fourth layer, the system will trim the subtree under node '3' when using Deterministic Trimming Method. It will report that the node '3' is a bug when using the trace query algorism.

### Bug search strategy related to an assert predicate

Features of an 'assert' predicate are

·Assert predicate always succeeds.

·Variables are not bound by an 'assert' predicate.

Therefore execution flow is not affected directly by an 'assert' predicate. A bug symptom will appear since a goal refers to a false instance produced by 'assert' predicate.

We will show an example of using 'assert' predicate. At position node ① 'assert( animal(cat) )' has done, then node ② picks up an instanced 'cat' to bind variable 'A' of 'animal( A )'. We assume that this step caused binding 'A' with 'cat'. All previous algorism diagnose this test program as that the node ② is bug, and it cannot diagnose before the node ①.

If a bug node that was obtained by the all previous algorism refered to the asserted term, then the system searches this 'assert' node , and calls this node 'Z'. The system switches the bug search space to the subtree rooted at the node that most recently queried an ancestor node of 'Z' ( if there is no such node, it will be a present root node ). Using all previous algorism, if the queried node is true, then trim its subtree. However, if there is node 'Z' in the trimmed area, the system begins to search for a bug in the subtree rooted at that query node.

## §5 Debugging Sequence

Debugging sequence of this system is shown below.

① Execute test program.
   ○Environment is almost like C-Prolog
② Modify control specification
   ○System shows test program's execution flow on a display
     with control specification. Some times a programmer
     notices a bug at this step.
   ○Modify control specification with a special editor.
③ Bug search step with query and respond.
   ○The system will indicate a clause that has bug.

We will show our debugger the diagnosis test program below. Underlined statements are inputed by a programmer and a pair of curly brackets means comments.

```
cat isort
isort( [ X|Xs ],Ys ):- isort( Xs,Zs ),insert( X,Zs,Ys ).
isort( [],[] ).
insert( X,[ Y|Ys ],[ Y|Zs ] ):- Y > X,insert( X,Ys,Zs ).
insert( X,[ Y|Ys ],[ X,Y|Ys ] ):- X ≦ Y.
insert( X,[],[ X ] ).

pgdb    { invoke the debugging system }
?- [+isort].
?- pgdb( isort( [2,3,1],Ans ) ).
Ans = [2,3,1]
yes
?- halt.
```

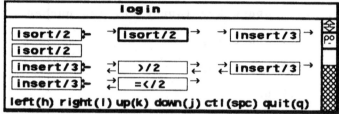

Fig 5.1 Modify mode of control specification
{ In Figure 5.1,you can move cursor of curved box by using
'h','j','k','l' keys( this is like 'vi' mode ). Each time
you push the space bar, the cursor's box control specification will change. '/2' and '/3' represent the number of
arguments in a goal. }

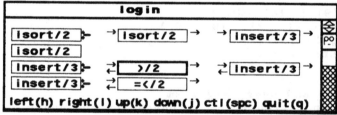

Fig 5.2 Modify mode of control specification
{ In Figure 5.2, there must not be 'REDO' control after the
'>' built-in predicate. The programmer can modify it with
the box cursor. }

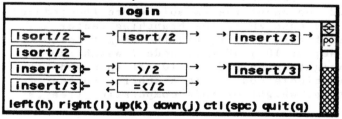

Fig 5.3 Modify mode of control specification
{ In Figure 5.3, predicate 'insert' should not fail, but
actually it did fail. So the programmer moves the cursor to
it and modifies its control specification. To end the
modification step, push 'q' }

{ Bug search mode with query and reply }

Input y(es) or n(o)
Query isort( [3],[3] ) success ? <u>y</u>

Input y(es) or n(o)
Query insert( 1,[3],[3,1] ) success ? <u>n</u>

select bug instance
space .. change scope, b.. bug,
q..end selection

```
insert( 1,[3],[3,1] )
          *              ...? space key {space bar was pushed}
insert( 1,[3],[3,1] )
          ***            ...? space key
insert( 1,[3],[3,1] )
          *              ...? space key
insert( 1,[3],[3,1] )
          *****    ...? b
insert( 1,[3],[3,1] )
          ***      ...? b
insert( 1,[3],[3,1] )
          *        ...? b
insert( 1,[3],[3,1] )
     *             ...? q
```

Bug clause is
insert( _21,[_18| _19],[_18| _20] ):-
     _18 > _21,insert( _21, _19, _20 ).
called by insert( 1,[3],[3,1] )
{ Bug clause was found. }

## §6 Evaluation
### §6.1 Shapiro's devide and query algorism
The weight of a computation tree is reduced by one query
as described below.

$$\frac{1}{2b} N \leq W \leq \{1- \frac{1}{2b} \}N \qquad (6.1)$$

'N' is length of computation tree
'b' is factor of branches

Figure 6.1 and 6.2 represent the example where the reduced
weight is not $1/2N$. The case where the branching factor
equals 2 is shown in figure 6.1. Within the weight below
the middle node ( weight 10 ) of root node ( weight 20 ),
the heaviest node weight is only 5 not 10. If this node is
true, and adopt this middle node, trim a subtree rooted
at this node. The total weight of this computation tree is

$$\{ 1 - \frac{1}{2b} \}N$$

If the middle node is false, trim outside of the subtree
rooted at that node. the total weight of this computation
tree is

$$\frac{1}{2b}N$$

In the divide and query algorism, the upper bound and lower bound of total weight depend on the branching factor 'b', shown in formula ( 6.1 ). Figure 6.2 shows the case where branching factor equals 3.

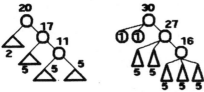

Fig 6.1          Fig 6.2

The lower bound of query times, $Q_L$, is represented by formula ( 6.2 ).

$$Q_L = \frac{-1}{\log_2(1/2b)} \times \log_2 N \qquad\qquad ( 6.2 )$$

The upper bound of query times, $Q_B$, is represented by formula ( 6.3 ).

$$Q_B = \frac{-1}{\log_2(1-1/2b)} \times \log_2 N \qquad\qquad ( 6.3 )$$

Proposal ( Deterministic trimming method )

The weight of computation tree is reduced by one query.

$$\frac{\alpha}{2b} N \leq W \leq \{ 1- \frac{1}{2b} \} \alpha N \qquad ( 6.4 )$$

The lower bound of query times, $Q_L$, is represented by formula ( 6.5 )

$$Q_L = \frac{-1}{\log_2( \alpha/2b)} \times \log_2(N-\beta) \qquad ( 6.5 )$$

The upper bound of query times $Q_B$ is represented by formula ( 6.6 )

$$Q_B = \frac{-1}{\log_2\{(1-1/2b)\alpha\}} \times \log_2(N-\beta) \qquad ( 6.6 )$$

Where $\alpha$ is the trimming factor , $0 < \alpha \leq 1$, and $\beta$ is the number of node that was trimmed due to illegal control flow.

Comparing upper bound $Q_B$

Comparing Shapiro's algorism with Deterministic Trimming Method is accomplished by comparing the coefficients of formula ( 6.6 ) for different values of $\alpha$. This comparison is given in figure 6.3.

Figure 6.3 shows that the upper bound of query times in Shapiro's algorism depends on the branching factor linearly, but the Deterministic Trimming Method shows the increase in query times by a percentage of the trimming factor.

Comparing lower bound $Q_L$.

As for the upper bound, comparing the lower bound $Q_L$ in both algorisms is the same as comparing coefficients in formula ( 6.8 ) for different values of $\alpha$. This comparison is shown in figure 6.4.

Figure 6.4 shows that Deterministic Trimming Method is not as powerful, but is lower, than Shapiro's method.

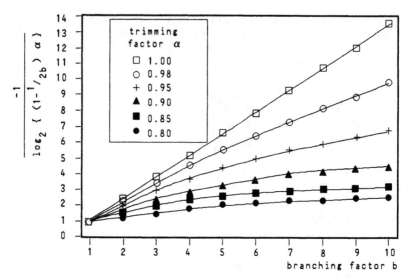

Fig 6.3   Upper bound of query times.

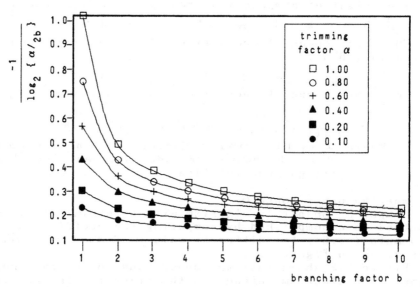

Fig 6.4   Lower bound of query times.

## System configuration

This debugging system consists of
- Execution block for test Prolog program,
  ( This block is based on C-Prolog source code )
- Editor for control specification notation,
- Bug search block.

They are invoked in sequentially, communicating by
intermediate files.

## Conclusion

The size of the intermediate files produced by the debugging system is 164 KBytes when the non-backtrack test program fills the local stack ( 128K Bytes ), so it has no practical problem.

We have implemented a system that support meta-predicates ( 'call', 'not' ). We are considering how to cope the 'assert' predicate. There are two types of bug the 'retract' predicate can cause:

① The case where variables are bound to the arguments of 'retract'.
② The case where a term is deleted by the 'retract' predicate.

This system can cope with the case ①, but not ②.

## Acknowledgement

This research, and the development of the debugging system, was supported by Aiso Laboratory at Keio University. The authors would like to thank Dr. Yang Rong, Mr. Show Ei Ken, and members of the Logic Programming Group.

## References

[Lloyd87]Lloyd,J.W.
  Declarative Error Diagnosis,
  New Generation Computing,5  1987  Springer-Verlag
[Maechi87]Machi MAEJI and Tadashi KANAMORI
  Top-down Zooming Diagnosis of Logic Programs,
  35th Conference of Information Processing Society of Japan,
  1987
shinichi MORISHITA and Masayuki NUMAO
  BPM-Visual prolog computation model and debugger PROEDIT2,
  Proc. of The Logic Programming Conference '86 , 1986
[Numao85]Masayuki NUMAO
  PROEDIT Screen oriented Prolog programming Environment,
  Proc. of the Logic Programming Conference '85, 1985
[Pereira,L.M 86] Pereira,Luis Moniz
  Rational debugging in logic programming,
  Lecture Note in Comp. Science 225, 1986 Springer-Verlag
[Shapiro83]Shapiro,E.
  Algorismic Debugging, M.I.T. Press, 1983
[Takahashi86]Hidehisa TAKAHASHI, Etsuya SHIBAYAMA
  PRESET - A Debugging Environment for Prolog,
  Lecture Note in Comp. Science 1986, Springer-Verlag
Naohisa TAKAHASHI, Satoshi ONO and Makoto AMAMIYA
  Parallel-processing-oriented Algorismic Bug-detection Method
  for Functional Programming Languages,
  Study of Basic Software,1984

# ALEX : The Logic Programming Language with Explicit Control and without Cut-Operators

Masaki Hoshida* and Mario Tokoro

Department of Electrical Engineering
Keio University
Yokohama 223, Japan

We propose a Prolog-like new programming language "ALEX". It is an extension of Prolog from the view point of procedural programming, keeping the merit of declarative feature of Prolog. In ALEX, the backtrack mechanism is divided into two categories : "Recall" and "Retry". "Recall" corresponds to "essential trial and error" and it appears rarely in the program, while "Retry" corresponds to "branch on condition" and it appears frequently. In ALEX, these actions are controlled by different methods, and "Recall" is restricted in default state. Control in ALEX is described as prefix of predicate. As a result, cut-operators are excluded, and we achieve easy debugging and higher readability.

## 1   INTRODUCTION

Prolog has a backtrack mechanism and enables declarative programming. Its drawbacks are that over-strong backtrack and cut-operators make the program difficult to write, read and debug. Prolog's mechanism has the following problems.

1) The way of controlling the backtrack mechanism seems unnatural to users.

> We want to use the backtrack mechanism for a limited part of the Prolog program. At the moment, cut-operators are used to control backtrack. They are inserted at the parts that the user wants to execute deterministically. However, since the deterministic part in a program is generally larger than the nondeterministic part, this way of controlling backtrack seems unnatural for users. It is also the major cause of bugs.

---

*Currently with ICOT on leave from Matsushita Electric Industrial Co.,Ltd.

2) Backtrack control cannot be described on the source code level on which that control is achieved.

> If we read just one clause of a Prolog program, we cannot tell which predicate may fail and which predicate may be reactivated by backtracking. To find out these things, we must read at a deeper level of the Prolog program. In other words, in the Prolog program, the source code level on which a backtrack is achieved cannot contain a description of which predicate is reactivated by backtracking. The description must be made at a deeper level to insert the cut-operators. This makes the program difficult to code, debug, and read.

> In any programming language, the control of the program should be described at the source code level on which the control is achieved. It is unnatural that the callee program describes the control of the caller program.

> In the hierarchy of the program, if the deeper level is related to the shallow level, and the modification or the bugs in the deeper level affect the shallow level, there is no point in making the program hierarchical.

3) Execution errors are not categorized

> In Prolog, "program execution error" and "failure in logical meaning" cannot be distinguished. Only "fail" appears and causes the backtrack. This makes it difficult to detect bugs; we have to scrutinize the program execution trace.

We think that the most important feature of a programming language is that the user can express what he wants to do easily and exactly. Even a programming language that has excellent theoretical features is impractical if it is difficult to write, read and debug. In order to make Prolog more practical and more useful, cut-operator should be scrapped.

Many Prolog debuggers have been tried, but we think that the control specification of Prolog itself should be re-examined. In this paper, we propose "ALEX" (Advanced pro-Log with Explicit eXpression), a programming language designed to improve the control specification of Prolog.

In ALEX, the problems we have just described are solved as follows.

Problem 1)

> In ALEX, the backtrack mechanism is divided into two categories. One of them corresponds to "branch on condition", and the other corresponds to "essential trial and error". And the latter is restricted.

Problem 2)

> In ALEX, control of backtrack can be described on the source code level on which that control is achieved. And that control is described explicitly.

Problem 3)

> In ALEX, the concepts "fail-possible-predicate" and "fail-impossible-predicate" are introduced.

# 2 BASIC CONCEPT OF ALEX

## 2.1 Recall and Retry

In ALEX, in order to restrict the backtrack, the backtrack is divided into two categories; Recall and Retry.

Recall:

> Recall is backtrack that the clause that finished execution is abandoned, and its alternative is re-selected.

$$\begin{array}{cc}
\begin{array}{l} \boxed{\phantom{x}} \downarrow \\ \text{---- P,Q ----} \end{array} &
\begin{array}{l} \boxed{\phantom{x}} \downarrow \\ \text{---- P,Q ----} \end{array} \\
\\
\begin{array}{l} \ulcorner \text{ P:-A,B. ---(1)} \\ \llcorner\!\!\rightarrow \text{P:-C,D. ---(2)} \end{array} &
\text{P:-A,B,C. ---(3)} \\
\\
& \begin{array}{l} \ulcorner \text{ B:-X. ---(4)} \\ \llcorner\!\!\rightarrow \text{B:-Y. ---(5)} \end{array} \\
\\
\text{(a)} & \text{(b)}
\end{array}$$

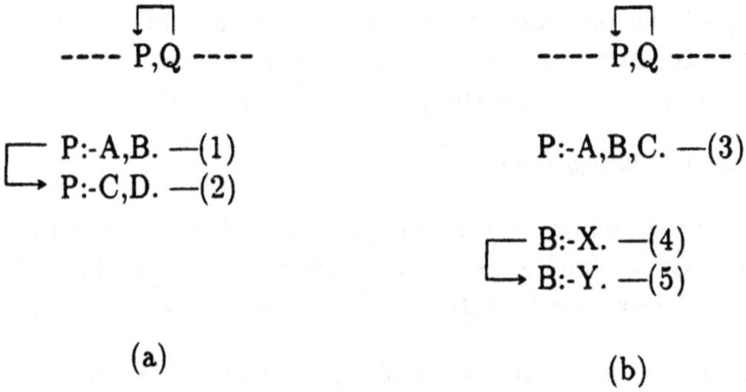

Fig 1 Example of Recall

(a) shows a case where predicate Q fails and predicate P is reactivated by backtracking, that is, the clause for the call P is re-selected. Suppose that when P was called, clause (1) was selected and the calls A,B were executed deterministically.

In this case, for the call P, clause (1) was selected and executed successfully. We named this kind of backtrack "Recall".

(b) shows a case where predicate Q fails and predicate B (called from P) is reactivated by backtracking. Suppose that when B was called, clause (4) was selected and the call C and the call X were executed deterministically. In this case, as in Fig 1, the clause that finished execution is abandoned, so this backtrack is categorized to "Recall".

Recall corresponds to "essential trial and error". Because the clause that finished execution is abandoned and its alternative is re-selected.

Retry:

> Retry is backtrack that, during the execution of a clause, the whole clause fails and its alternative is re-selected.

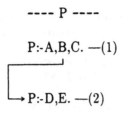

Fig 2 Example of Retry

Fig 2 shows a case where P was called, clause (1) was selected, A finished execution deterministically, the next B failed, and clause (2) was re-selected.

In this case, clause (1) has not finished execution. In other words, the clause for the call P has not been decided yet. In this sense, Retry corresponds to "branch on condition" like "if then else" or "case".

## 2.2 Basic Concept

As we said earlier, Recall corresponds to "essential trial and error", and Retry corresponds to "branch on condition". Generally, "branch on condition (Retry)" appears frequently in the program, while "essential trial and error (Recall)" appears rarely.

It is better to mark on the part which appears rarely. Because, if we mark on the part that appears frequently, it is easier for us to forget to put on marks.

In Prolog, we have to mark on the parts that appear frequently, deterministic part, by cut-operators. It seems unnatural. Further more, in Prolog, if we omit a cut-operator, it is hard to find out what we did wrong.

The reason why Prolog has such problems is that both Recall and Retry are controlled only by cut-operators. Cut-operators restrict both Recall and Retry at once.

In ALEX, the two categories "Recall and Retry" are controlled in different ways.

- Recall cannot be performed in default state; it can be performed only when it is explicitly permitted.

- Retry can be performed in default state; it can always be performed unless it is explicitly prohibited.

The prohibition of Recall in default state reduces the number of bugs caused by omission of cut-operators.

# 3 SYNTAX AND SEMANTICS OF ALEX

## 3.1 Abstract of Syntax and Semantics

Syntax:

An ALEX procedure is a set of horn clauses like Prolog. The pattern of horn clauses are same as Prolog, except for the following feature.

- A predicate in the head or the body of a clause can take a prefix such as "?", ":", "??", "::", "+". The prefix is used as control information.

- A clause can take control of a structure named "block". "Block" is a line of predicates which is clipped between "<" and ">".

- The head and body of a clause are divided by "<-".

Semantics:

An ALEX clause is executed "depth first, left to right" like Prolog. The unification mechanism and the pattern of atomic formulas are the same as in Prolog except for the backtrack mechanism.

## 3.2 Control on Recall (clause level)

In ALEX, when a clause finishes execution successfully in default state, its alternatives are prohibited from executing in the case of backtrack. In order to let its alternative execute in the event of backtrack, a prefix "+" must be added to the head of the clause.

$$P<-A,B,C.—(1)$$
$$+P<-D,E.—(2)$$
$$P<-F,G.—(3)$$

Fig 3 Control on Recall No.1

In Fig 3, if clause (1) finishes execution successfully, (2) and (3) (alternatives of (1)) cannot be executed in the event of a backtrack that reactivates the predicate P. If clause (2) finishes execution successfully, (2)'s alternatives (3) can be executed in the event of backtrack.

Retry can be performed in default state (in spite of the prefix "+"). In Fig 3, if predicate A fails, clauses (2) and (3) can be tried.

## 3.3 Control on Recall (predicate level)

In ALEX, the predicates in the body of a clause are mainly categorized into three classes as follows.

1) Predicate without Prefix

- Never fail.
- If it fails, ALEX interpreter halts with a error message.
- If it finishes execution successfully, it cannot accept "Recall".
  - Error message shows the functor of the failed predicate, the contents of the variable when the predicate was called, and the call number.

    – After the indication of the error message, the ALEX interpreter asks the user whether they want to continue the execution and regard the error as a failure or to make an abort.

2) Predicate with prefix "?"

- It can fail.
- If it fails, it causes Recall or Retry.
- If it finishes execution successfully, it cannot accept Recall.

3) Predicate with prefix ":"

- It can fail.
- If it fails, it causes Recall and Retry.
- If it finishes execution successfully, it can accept Recall.

    Note that the prefix "+" is necessary on the clause level to accept Recall, in addition to the prefix ":".

Table 1 Prefix and Control

|  | no prefix | "?" prefix | ":" prefix |
|---|---|---|---|
| possibility of failure | x | o | o |
| possibility of Recall | x | x | o |

Table 1 shows the essence of the control on Recall. In this table, "possibility of failure" cannot be described in Prolog. "Possibility of Recall" is expressed by using cut-operators in Prolog, but it is implicit from a view point of well-understandable programming. Because when we want to know the determinicity of a predicate, we have to read the deeper level of the program.

In ALEX, user can know "possibility of failure" and "possibility of Recall" of the predicate only to see the prefix of the predicate. So ALEX is easier to read.

Predicate that cannot fail or accept Recall are most often used in the program. Therefore in ALEX this kind of predicate is expressed as the predicate without prefix.

In this way, ALEX is designed to reduce the amount of the prefix for control in the source code so far as the necessary information is available. With ALEX, it is easy to detect bugs caused by the user omitting a prefix at a place where it was necessary.

P<- :A,B,:C,?D,?E,F.

Fig 4 Control on Recall No.2

In Fig 4, when ?D or ?E fails, only :B (inside :B) can accept Recall. C and ?D cannot accept Recall. If :B fails, P also fails as a result. In this case, if P has alternatives, the alternatives are tried. "Inside :B" means the predicates that are directly or indirectly called by :B.

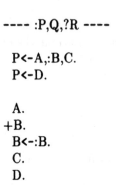

---- :P,Q,?R ----

P<-A,:B,C.
P<-D.

A.
+B.
  B<-:B.
C.
D.

Fig 5 Control on Recall No.3

Fig 5 shows the case in which :P and Q are executed successfully, and ?R fails. Then, as a result, :B is Recalled. In this case, the prefix ":" is necessary on both of P and B. And P is not reactivated by a failure of ?R. Because P does not have a prefix "+" at the head of the clause.

---- P,Q,?R ----

P<-A,:B,?C.

A.
+B.
  B<-:B.
C.

Fig 6 Control on Recall No.4

Fig 6 shows the modularity of the ALEX program. Suppose that the user wants to permit :B to accept Recall only from ?C. When programming in Prolog, in a case like this, the user has to insert the cut-operator behind ?C to protect :B from the backtrack from the upper level, (?R) in this example.

In ALEX, in this case, P has no prefix, so inside P is protected from Recall that is caused by a failure that occurs outside P.

If the user writes B for :B by mistake, when ?C fails, P fails and the error occurs as the result. Therefore the error is shut in a local part.

"Protection from Recall" and "Confinement of error" can achieve the easy debugging and the higher confidence of program. And the explicit expression of the backtrack control by the prefix of the predicate can achieve higher readability.

In Prolog, it is often difficult to see the reason why a cut-operator was inserted in a place. Unnecessary cut-operators are often inserted, too.

To make a failure unconditionally, an operator "?" (not a prefix) can be used. When this operator is executed, it makes a failure.

## 3.4   Control on Retry

Retry can be achieved in default state; and it is caused by the failure of the predicate with the prefixes "?" and ":". In order to prohibit Retry, the prefix "??" and "::" are used for "?" and ":".

The definition is shown as follows in addition to the section .

4) Predicate with prefix "??"

- It can fail.
- If it fails, its parent-predicate fails immediately.
- If it finishes execution successfully, it cannot accept Recall.

5) Predicate with prefix "::"

- It can fail.
- If it fails, its parent-predicate fails immediately.
- If it finishes execution successfully, it can accept Recall.

   "P's parent-predicate" means the predicate that calls P directly.

```
---- O,?P,Q ----

P<-?A,??B,C. —(1)
P<- D. —(2)
A.
B.
C.
D.
```

Fig 7 Control on Retry

In Fig 7, if ??B fails, ?P fails immediately. (2) is not tried. In ALEX, Retry can be prohibited in such a way. Note that Retry is prohibited very rarely, so these two prefixes are not often used.

To make the parent-predicate fail unconditionally, the operator "??" (not a prefix) can be used. When this operator is executed, the parent-predicate of this operator fails immediately.

## 3.5   Block

To restrict the area where Recall can be performed, the control structure "block" is introduced. "block" can protect an area from Recall. "block" is the sequence of the predicates clipped between "<" and ">".

   "block" has the following features.

- A failure that occurs outside "block" does not reactivate inside "block".

- If a whole "block" fails, the "block" makes an error, and the system halts with an error message.

- To give the possibility of failure to "block", it is necessary to put a prefix "?" or "??" at the head of the "block". "?" means mere fail, and "??" means the parent-predicate fails.

- "block" can be nested.

$$P<- A, ?<:B,C,?D>, ?E.$$

Fig 8 Block

In Fig 8, Recall can be performed from ?D to :B. Once ?D succeeds, :B cannot be reactivated any more.

# 4 PROGRAMMING IN ALEX

In this section, we show an example of ALEX program.

```
gps(S,[],S,[]).
gps(S,G,S,[])<-?subset(G,S).
gps(S,G,S3,ANS)<-
    sorting(G,GN),
    difference(S,GN,DIFLIST), —(1)
    :member(DIF,DIFLIST), —(2)
    operator(DIF,OPLIST), —(3)
    :member(OP,OPLIST), —(4)
    precondition(OP,PRECOND), —(5)
    ?gps(S,PRECOND,S1,ANS1), —(6)
    apply(OP,S1,S2), —(7)
    ?gps(S2,G,S3,ANS2), —(8)
    cat(ANS1,OP,ANS1,ANS). —(9)
difference(_,[],[]).
difference(S,[X|Y],R)<-
    ?member(X,S), —(10)
    difference(S,Y,R).
difference(S,[X|Y],[X|R])<-
    difference(S,Y,R).
+member(X,[X|_]).
member(X,[_|Y])<- :member(X,Y).
```

Fig 9 A Part of the GPS Program in ALEX

Fig 9 is a part of the GPS (General Problem Solver) program to resolve the monkey and banana problem.

The calling pattern at top-level is

```
?-gps(<initial state : input>,
    <goal state : input>,
    <final state : output>,
    <operator sequence : output>).
```

to be concrete

```
?-gps([at(monkey,banana,),at(box,b),empty],
    [hold(banana)],
    FS,
    ANS).
```

GPS calculates the difference between current state and goal state, –(1), and select the most important difference, –(2). Next, GPS lists all operators to reduce the difference, –(3), and select the most effective operator, –(4). Then, GPS applies the GPS algorithm itself recursively regarding the precondition of this operator as the new goal, –(5)(6). If this application succeeds, GPS applies the operator, –(7). Next, GPS regards that result as the new current state, and GPS applies the GPS algorithm recursively further, –(8).

At the end, the sequences of the operators are concatenated, –(9).

In this ALEX program, we can easily know the control from the prefixes as follows.

In the 3rd clause of gps/4, when ?gps/4 at (6) or (8) fails, :member/2 at (4) is reactivated by Recall, and if (4) has no alternative, :member/2 at (2) is reactivated next. All predicates in the 3rd clause of gps/4 except (2) and (4) cannot be reactivated by Recall.

Thus, in ALEX program, the control of a program can be expressed on the source-code level at which the control is achieved.

When we translate this program into a Prolog program, we have to insert the cut-operators inside sorting/2, different/3, apply/3. It is not natural.

When we read the Prolog program that corresponds to this program, we cannot know the control of the program only from the 3rd clause of gps/4. We have to read the deeper level.

Also, :member/2 at (2) and (4) has a different function from ?member/2 at (10) in spite of calling the same substance. :member/2 at (2) and (4) are used to generate some data repeatedly by Recall, so it is necessary to be nondeterministic. While ?member/2 at (10) is used only to test the data and it should not be reactivated by Recall, so it is necessary to be deterministic.

In ALEX, the use of the predicate is expressed in the caller side, so only one substance is necessary, and the use of the predicate can be clearly understood.

# 5  PROLOG AND ALEX

In this section, we try to categorize the use of cut-operator of Prolog from the point of view of how the programmer uses it. And we show how these categories are expressed in ALEX about each case.

- Here, the word "freeze" is used to mean fixing the choice of clause.
- The word "procedure P" means the clauses that have the P at their heads.

- 1) The case that a clause freezes itself

For using a procedure deterministically, prohibiting the reactivation of procedure can be achieved to insert cut-operators into clauses which construct the procedure.

An example of a Prolog program and an ALEX program that have the same function is shown below.

Prolog

    member(X,[X|_]):-!.
    member(X,[_|Y]):-member(X,Y).

ALEX

    member(X,[X|_]).
    member(X,[_|Y])<-?member(X,Y).

In this example, member/2 in Prolog freezes itself. This kind of use of cut-operator is usually called "Confirming the Choice of a Rule". Most cut-operators are used like this.

In ALEX, this determinicity is realized in default state, which is without prefix ":" and "+" .

That is, Recall can be achieved only when the following two conditions are satisfied at the same time.

- The prefix "+" is at the head of a clause, on the clause level.
- The prefix ":" is at the predicate, on the predicate level.

It means that ALEX has a twofold protection mechanism, so it is easy to find bugs. But in ALEX, it is necessary to put the prefix "?" at member/2 in the body. Because it may fail. If the programmer forget to put this "?" and member/2 fails, it becomes a bug. But this bug comes out as an execution error, so we can find it out easily. This is the essential difference between the bug caused by the lack of the prefix "?" and the bug caused by the lack of the cut-operator. In the latter case, we have to spend a lot of effort looking for bugs.

- 2) The case that a procedure, though it can freeze itself, is frozen by the other one

Prolog

```
member(X,[X|_]).
member(X,[_|Y]):-member(X,Y).

subset([X|Y],Z):-member(X,Z),!,subset(Y,Z).
subset([],_).
```

ALEX

```
member(X,[X|_]).
member(X,[_|Y])<-?member(X,Y).

subset([X|Y],Z)<-?member(X,Z),??subset(Y,Z).
subset([],_).
```

In case 1), member/2 freezes itself. In case 2), subset/2 freezes member/2, even though member/2 can freeze itself. In actual programming in Prolog, cases 1) and 2) are often used redundantly. It means, for instance, cut-operators are inserted into both member/2 and subset/2 in case 2). The larger a program becomes, the less we can rely on determinicity of the predicate on the lower level. So we insert more redundant cut-operators. We can also insert cut-operators to achieve higher readability, although we know they are redundant. In ALEX, by a twofold protection mechanism on the clause level and the predicate level, such determinicity is achieved in default state. cases 1) and 2) are the most often used cases of cut-operators. according to our experience, more than 80% of cut-operators are used in this way.

- 3) The case that a procedure cannot freeze itself, and is frozen by the other one

(Whether a procedure is frozen or not depends on the condition of its surroundings)

This is the case that a predicate is frozen when the test by the other predicate succeeds. It is often called "termination of generation and test". This case is essentially different from cases (1) and (2) because a predicate cannot freeze itself.

Prolog

```
member(X,[X|_]):-!.
member(X,[_|Y]):-member(X,Y).

moreThanFive(X,LIST):-
member(X,LIST),X>5,!.

?-moreThanFive(X,[2,3,5,7,11]). (call)
```

ALEX

```
member(X,[X|_]).
member(X,[_|Y])<-?member(X,Y).

moreThanFive(X,LIST)<-
?< :member(X,LIST), ?(X>5) >.

?-moreThanFive(X,[2,3,5,7,11]). (call)
```

In this example, moreThanFive/2 is defined as the predicate that returns a number, which is more than five and found first. member/2 generates the element, and "X¿5" tests it. member/2 cannot determine when it should be frozen. So member/2 cannot freeze itself. In ALEX, in such case, "block" is usually used. By using "block", when "?(X>5)" succeeds, :member/2 cannot be reactivated by Recall any more. And by using "block", it becomes clear that "generation and test" is achieved only between :member/2 and "?(X>5)". In this example, if the number more than five cannot be found, moreThanFive/2 fails. It is expressed by "?" at the head of the block.

If moreThanFive/2 is always called without the prefix ":", it is not necessary even to use "block".

- 4) The case that the special predicate "fail" forces "the parent goal" to fail

  This case is often called "cut-and-fail" or "negation". In ALEX, it corresponds to the operator "??". That is, "!,fail" has same function as "??".

Here, we tried to categorize the use of the cut-operator in Prolog. It is often ambiguous, for what kind of purpose a cut-operator is used. In ALEX, a prefix expresses the control explicit, so it is easier to read. The control of Recall can be expressed on the level on which it is achieved, so we can do natural programming.

# 6   CONCLUSION

We believe that the most important feature of a programming language is that it should be easy to write, debug, and read. Prolog has high potential, but it is inconvenient in above feature. Many extensions of Prolog have been developed. But if it takes more time to debug, the extension is not practical.

In ALEX, we suggests a way to improve the execution control of Prolog.

Backtrack mechanism is divided into two categories. One of them corresponds to "essential trial and error" and the other corresponds to "branch on condition". We named the former "Recall" and the latter "Retry". Generally, "branch on condition (Retry)" appears frequently in the program, while "essential trial and error (Recall)" appears rarely. So Recall cannot be achieved in default state in ALEX. This enables "Protection from Recall" and "Confinement of error", and it reduces the number of bugs by omission of cut-operators. As a result, easy debugging and higher confidence of program are achieved.

Control in ALEX is described with the prefix at the head of predicate. The predicates in the body are categorized into five categories. And a prefix shows the possibility-of-failure or possibility-of-backtrack of a predicate. By the prefix, the user can know the control of program on the source code level on which the control is achieved.

# References

[1] Clocksin,Merish "Programming in Prolog", Springer-Verlag(1981)
[2] Naish,L "PROLOG CONTROL RULES", IJCAI86(1986)
[3] Sawamura,H "The Determinacy of Prolog Predicate(Call)",
    Computer Software Vol.4 No.4,(1985) in Japanese
[4] Chikayama,T "Unique Features of ESP",FGCS84(1984)
[5] Chikayama,T "ESP Reference Manual", ICOT TR-044,(1984)
[6] Nakashima,H "Prolog/KR User's Manual" METR 82-4,
    Dept. of Mathematical Engineering, University of Tokyo(1983)

# LATTICE PROGRAMMING METHODOLOGY

Kouichi Fukunaga     Shinichi Morishita

IBM Research, Tokyo Research Laboratory

5-19 Sanban-cho, Chiyoda-ku, Tokyo 102 JAPAN

# 1   Basic idea

Logic programming gives us a way to look at conventional algorithms from a different viewpoint and to reorganize or classify them. The separation of the logical aspect of the problem from the procedural control for searching for a solution makes the comparison of algorithms easier. As a result, in some cases algorithm derivations become easier in logic programming.

For example, many sorting algorithms can be regarded as the specializations of the following naive algorithm.

$$sort(List, SortedList) \leftarrow permutation(List, SortedList) \ \& \ ordered(SortedList).$$

Since the logic and control of this program are separated, it is easy to understand what this program does. If we assume the depth-first search as the control strategy, it does generate-and-test by backtracking between *permutation* and *ordered*. In this case, its inefficiency comes from the excessive backtracking and the specializations are concerned with reducing unnecessary backtracking by incorporating the test function of *ordered* into *permutation*. This clarity of algorithm derivation is one of the advantages of logic programming.

However, logic programming has still disadvantages. Since it only provides syntactic unification, programmers have to invent the way to represent their data structures by using this unification. These problem specific inventions sometimes obscure the declarative clarity of logic programs. In these cases, we would rather prefer to directly represent objects and their properties of the problem domain.

We found a way to clearly represent some algorithms whose goal is to produce minimal (or maximal) objects under the given ordering. Examples of the category include sorting, minimum spanning tree, and shortest path finding, which we will explain later in this paper.

We conclude that all the advantages of logic programming come from one theorem : its declarative semantics coincides with its procedural semantics. If we look carefully at the proof of this theorem, we find it depends on a technique which is not specific to logic but more widely applicable. The technique is largely based on lattice theory. This observation suggests an extension of logic programming as follows.

- {true, false}   →   complete lattices

- implication  →  lattice order

- and  →  meet  →  functions over complete lattices

- or  →  join

As we will briefly explain in the later section, the above theorem still holds under some conditions on functions over complete lattices. Since lattice is the simplest algebraic structure which many algebras of data structures satisfy. Thus, this extension has the potential for representing some data structure producing algorithms in a natural way. We call this extension *lattice programming* and show its applications in the following sections.

## 2  Lattice valued programs

In lattice programming, we use lattice valued programs in which each atom has a complete lattice as a range and each clause is associated with a function over complete lattices.

A *complete lattice* $L$ is a partial ordered set which has least upper bound ($\sqcup S$) and greatest lower bound ($\sqcap S$) for every subset $S$ of $L$. The least upper bound and the greatest lower bound of $L$ itself are denoted by $\top_L$ and $\bot_L$ respectively.

In a lattice valued program $P$, atoms which have the same predicate symbol and the same arity are associated with the same complete lattice. Let $L_A$ denote the complete lattice for $A$. A *lattice valued program* $P$ is a finite set of clauses each of which is associated with a function over complete lattices. Suppose that a clause $A \leftarrow B_1, \cdots, B_n$ $(n \geq 0)$ is given, then it is associated with a function $f : L_{B_1} \times \cdots \times L_{B_n} \rightarrow L_A$. If a clause has the form $A \leftarrow$, then it is associated with a constant function, that is, an element of $L_A$. We will denote the pair constitutes of a clause $A \leftarrow B_1, \cdots, B_n$ and its function $f$ by $\langle A \leftarrow B_1, \cdots, B_n, f \rangle$ which we call *a clause pair*. We also associate a goal $\leftarrow A_1, \cdots, A_n$ with a function $F$ from $L_{A_1} \times \cdots \times L_{A_n}$ to any complete lattice $L$. We will denote the pair constituting of a goal $\leftarrow A_1, \cdots, A_n$ and $F$ by $\langle \leftarrow A_1, \cdots, A_n, F \rangle$ and call it *a goal pair*.

We assume that every function $F : L_1 \times \cdots \times L_n \rightarrow L$ in any program satisfies the following two properties:

- Elementwise least upper bound preserving :
  $F(a_1, \cdots, a_{i-1}, \sqcup S, a_{i+1}, \cdots, a_n) = \sqcup \{ F(a_1, \cdots, a_{i-1}, x, a_{i+1}, \cdots, a_n) \mid x \in S \}$
  holds for any subset $S \subseteq L_i (i = 1, \cdots, n)$ and for $\forall a_1 \in L_1, \cdots, \forall a_{i-1} \in L_{i-1}, a_{i+1} \in L_{i+1}, \cdots, \forall a_n \in L_n$

- Elementwise strict :
  $F(a_1, \cdots, a_n) = \bot_L$ whenever at least one $a_i = \bot_{L_i}$

We will refer this requirement on a program by $(\alpha)$. Note that an elementwise least upper bound preserving function is monotonic increasing.

Informally, the declarative meaning of a clause $\langle A \leftarrow B_1 \& \cdots \& B_n, f \rangle$ is that , for any ground substitution $\rho$, the value of $A\rho$ is greater than or equal to $f(b_1, \cdots, b_n)$ ($b_i$ is the value of $B_i\rho$). Let denote this fact by $A\rho \sqsupseteq f(B_1\rho, \cdots, B_n\rho)$. We also describe the value of a goal pair $\langle \leftarrow A_1\rho, \cdots, A_n\rho, F \rangle$ by $F(A_1\rho, \cdots, A_n\rho)$ for any ground substitution $\rho$.

Suppose that a goal pair $\langle \leftarrow A_1, \cdots, A_n, F \rangle$ is given and $\leftarrow A_1, \cdots, A_n$ is ground. We can restrict the value of $F(A_1, \cdots, A_n)$ as follows ; if $A_i$ is selected from $A_1, \cdots, A_n$ and $A_i$ and $A$ in $\langle A \leftarrow B_1, \cdots, B_m, f \rangle$ are unifiable by an mgu $\theta$. Since $A \sqsupseteq f(B_1, \cdots, B_m)$ holds and $F$ is monotonic increasing, we have

$$F(A_1, \cdots, A_i, \cdots, A_n) \sqsupseteq F(A_1\theta, \cdots, f(B_1\theta, \cdots, B_m\theta), \cdots, A_n\theta).$$

Suppose that we have the following sequence, after deriving goal pairs repeatedly.

$$F(A_1, \cdots, A_i, \cdots, A_n) \sqsupseteq F(A_1\theta, \cdots, f(B_1\theta, \cdots, B_m\theta), \cdots, A_n\theta) \sqsupseteq \cdots\cdots \sqsupseteq F'$$

Then this process is called *a derivation* and an equality $F(A_1, \cdots, A_n) \sqsupseteq F'$ is obtained.

By the way, in each step of deriving goals there are two choices, that is a choice of an atom to be selected and a choice of a clause. In our framework, we can fix one rule for selecting an atom (see section 5), however, there still exist a choice of a clause. Due to this choice in each step, we may have many derivations for the same goal pair.

These derivations can be made up into a tree structure like a SLD-tree in usual logic programming. See Fig 1. Such a tree is called *a derivation tree*. In a derivation tree, each branch from the root to a leaf corresponds to a derivation. Since we can regard a derivation as an inequality which gives a lower bound of the given goal pair, each leaf node gives a lower bound for the initial goal. For example, in Fig.1, the leaf $F'$ is a lower bound for $F(A_1, \cdots, A_n)$ ($F(A_1, \cdots, A_n) \sqsupseteq F'$). In this way, from a derivation tree, many lower bounds for the initial goal may be obtained.

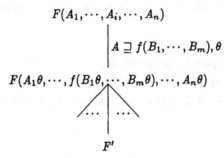

Fig.1   A Derivation Tree

In section 5, we show that the least upper bound of these lower bounds is equal to the solution. In this section, we discussed the declarative and procedural semantics informally. Its rigorous treatment is found in section 5.

# 3  Programming methodology

The steps of lattice programming proceeds as follows.

- Formulate the complete lattices to represent all of the potential data structures (including the problem solution) which may be handled by the program.

- Show the solution be restricted by a set of inequalities and represent them as clauses

- Show the least upper bound of the lower bounds derived from the inequalities is the solution.

The following example illustrates this process. Suppose we are given a problem of producing a sorted sequence out of a sequence of natural numbers (with $+\infty$). The first step is to construct a lattice of sequences of natural numbers $L_{seq}$. A sequence is denoted by $\langle x_1, \cdots, x_n \rangle$ $(n \geq 0)$. Let $L_{n,seq}$ be the set of sequences of the same length $n$. In $L_{n,seq}$, elements are ordered in lexicographic order $\sqsubseteq$.

$$\forall \langle x_1, x_2, \cdots, x_n \rangle, \langle y_1, y_2, \cdots, y_n \rangle \in L_{n,seq} \quad \langle x_1, x_2, \cdots, x_n \rangle \sqsubseteq \langle y_1, y_2, \cdots, y_n \rangle$$
$$\text{iff } x_1 > y_1 \text{ or } (x_1 = y_1 \text{ and } \langle x_2, \cdots, x_n \rangle \sqsubseteq \langle y_2, \cdots, y_n \rangle)$$

Note that $L_{n,seq}$ is totally ordered. The sequences of different lengths are unordered. The whole lattice $L_{seq}$ is obtained by taking the direct sum of $\{L_{n,seq} \mid n$ is a natural number $\}$ whose top ($\top_{seq}$) and bottom ($\bot_{seq}$) are newly introduced.

Next, consider a binary function % over $L_{seq}$. % concatenate two sequences. For $\top_{seq}$ and $\bot_{seq}$, the meaning of % is defined as follows:

$$\top_{seq} \mathbin{\%} s = \top_{seq}, \ s \mathbin{\%} \top_{seq} = \top_{seq}, \ \bot_{seq} \mathbin{\%} s = \bot_{seq}, \ s \mathbin{\%} \bot_{seq} = \bot_{seq} \text{ for any } s \text{ in } L_{seq}.$$

It can be easily shown that % satisfies requirement ($\alpha$).

Let $sequence(S)$ be an atom with which $L_{seq}$ is associated. Let $d\_union(S1, S2, S)$ be an atom expressing that $S$ is a disjoint union of $S1$ and $S2$. $d\_union(S1, S2, S)$ can be defined by a conventional logic program, and it is associated with {true, false}. The following discussion shows $sequence(S)$ defined below calculates the sorted sequence of $S$.

$\langle sequence(\{A\}) \leftarrow, \langle A \rangle \rangle$    for each element $A$

$\langle sequence(S) \leftarrow d\_union(S1, S2, S), sequence(S1), sequence(S2), f \rangle$

$f(X1, X2, X3) \overset{\text{def}}{=}$ if $X1 = true$ then $X2 \% X3$ else $\perp_{seq}$

Since $\%$ satisfies requirement $(\alpha)$, it is obvious that $f$ also satisfies $(\alpha)$. To clarify the declarative meaning of this program, we will replace $\leftarrow$ and $\&$ with $\sqsupseteq$ and $\%$ respectively. Furthermore we will use $+$ as a syntax sugar for $d\_union$. Then we get the following inequalities which $sequence(S)$ satisfies.

$sequence(\{A\}) \sqsupseteq \langle A \rangle$    for each element $A$

$sequence(S1 + S2) \sqsupseteq sequence(S1) \% sequence(S2)$    (1)

Now, let us execute a sample goal pair, for example, $\langle \leftarrow sequence(\{4, 3, 1, 2\}), I \rangle$, where $I$ is the identity function over $L_{seq}$. This goal pair is intended to calculate the value of $sequence(\{4, 3, 1, 2\})$ itself. After searching exhaustively (see Fig.2), we get the set of inequalities from the derivation tree.

$\{ sequence(\{4, 3, 2, 1,\}) \sqsupseteq X \mid X$ is a permutation of $\langle 4, 3, 1, 2 \rangle \}$    (2)

$sequence(\{4, 3, 1, 2\})$

$sequence(\{4, 3\}) \% sequence(\{1, 2\})$

$(sequence(\{4\}) \% sequence(\{3\})) \% (sequence(\{1\}) \% sequence(\{2\}))$

$((\langle 4 \rangle \% \langle 3 \rangle) \% (\langle 1 \rangle \% \langle 2 \rangle))$

$( = \langle 4, 3 \rangle \% \langle 1, 2 \rangle = \langle 4, 3, 1, 2 \rangle )$

Fig.2   (Case $\%$)   A Derivation Tree for $\langle \leftarrow sequence(\{4, 3, 1, 2\}), I \rangle$

Since the least upper bound of $\{X \mid X$ is a permutation $\}$ is $\langle 1, 2, 3, 4 \rangle$, the above set of inequalities is reduced to $sequence(\{4, 3, 1, 2\}) \sqsupseteq \langle 1, 2, 3, 4 \rangle$. Hence, $\langle 1, 2, 3, 4 \rangle$ becomes the solution of the given goal.

There is one problem in this program. The set (2) is quite large. This is caused by the naivety of concatenation. For example, during computation, we may be able to conclude that :

$sequence(\{4, 3\}) \sqsupseteq \langle 4, 3 \rangle$    $sequence(\{1, 2\}) \sqsupseteq \langle 1, 2 \rangle$

Then, the above program restricts $sequence(\{4,3,1,2\})$ by using the simple concatenation as follows.

$$sequence(\{4,3,1,2\}) \sqsupseteq sequence(\{4,3\}) \ \% \ sequence(\{1,2\}) \sqsupseteq \langle 4,3 \rangle \ \% \ \langle 1,2 \rangle \ = \ \langle 4,3,1,2 \rangle$$

If we use the *merge* operation $ defined below instead of %, we can restrict $sequence(\{4,3,2,1\})$ more strongly. Because $\langle 4,3 \rangle \$ \langle 1,2 \rangle \ = \ \langle 1,2,4,3 \rangle$ is much greater than $\langle 4,3,1,2 \rangle$. Moreover, we do not lose the solution $\langle 1,2,3,4 \rangle$ by this change. This observation suggests the following program which realizes the so-called *merge sort*.

$$sequence(\{A\}) \sqsupseteq \langle A \rangle \quad \text{for each element } A$$
$$sequence(S1 + S2) \sqsupseteq sequence(S1) \$ sequence(S2)$$
$$\top_{seq} \$ s = \top_{seq}, \ s \$ \top_{seq} = \top_{seq}, \ \bot_{seq} \$ s = \bot_{seq}, \ s \$ \bot_{seq} = \bot_{seq}$$
$$\langle a_1, a_2, \cdots, a_m \rangle \$ \langle b_1, b_2, \cdots, b_n \rangle \ \overset{\text{def}}{=}$$
$$\text{if } a_1 \leq b_1 \text{ then} \quad \langle a_1, \langle a_2, \cdots, a_m \rangle \$ \langle b_1, b_2, \cdots, b_n \rangle \rangle$$
$$\text{else} \quad \langle b_1, \langle a_1, a_2, \cdots, a_m \rangle \$ \langle b_2, \cdots, b_n \rangle \rangle \qquad (3)$$

'$' meets requirement ($\alpha$). It is easily shown that, given two sorted sequences, merge produces the sorted sequence of them. Hence, for the goal $\langle \leftarrow sequence(\{4,3,1,2\}), I \rangle$, we obtain the same lower bound $\langle 1,2,3,4 \rangle$ from any derivation of this goal, however $S$ is decomposed into $S1$ and $S2$ (see Fig.3).

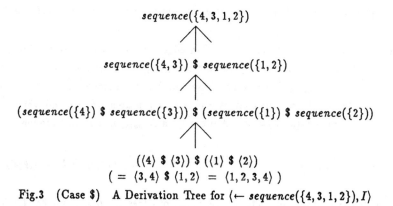

$$sequence(\{4,3,1,2\})$$

$$sequence(\{4,3\}) \$ sequence(\{1,2\})$$

$$(sequence(\{4\}) \$ sequence(\{3\})) \$ (sequence(\{1\}) \$ sequence(\{2\}))$$

$$((\langle 4 \rangle \$ \langle 3 \rangle) \$ (\langle 1 \rangle \$ \langle 2 \rangle)$$
$$( = \langle 3,4 \rangle \$ \langle 1,2 \rangle = \langle 1,2,3,4 \rangle )$$

Fig.3   (Case $) A Derivation Tree for $\langle \leftarrow sequence(\{4,3,1,2\}), I \rangle$

This gives the chance to reduce the complexity by fixing the method to decompose $S$. For example, if we decide $S2$ to be a singleton, we get the *insertion sort* as follows.

$$sequence(\{A\}) \sqsupseteq \langle A \rangle \quad \text{for each element } A$$
$$sequence(S1 + \{A\}) \sqsupseteq sequence(S1) \$ sequence(\{A\})$$

In this way, lattice programming give the following stepwise refinement method from naive algorithms to more efficient ones.

- Reduce the number of derived lower bounds for each goal by introducing new operations while retaining the solution.

- Incorporate an efficient search strategy into the program which utilizes the properties of the resulting set of lower bounds.

## 4   A further example

The above argument which clarifies the relation between algorithms by showing their algorithm derivations also applies to other problems. Due to the space limitation, we only show one example program which solves the single source shortest paths problem and its algorithm derivation from more naive versions is left to the reader.

Let $G = (V, E)$ be a directed graph which consists of a vertex set $V$ and a edge set $E$ each element of which has non-negative length. The length of an edge $e(v, w)$ from the vertex $v$ to the vertex $w$ is denoted by $\text{length}(e(v, w))$. A path from $v_1$ to $v_n$ is denoted by $e(v_1, v_2).e(v_2, v_3) \cdots e(v_{n-1}, v_n)$. The length of a path $p$ denoted by $\text{length}(p)$ is the sum of the lengths of the edges on $p$. The problem is :

*Given a source s, find a shortest path from a source s to every vertex in V*

(For simplicity, we assume that there exists an edge from a source $s$ to itself whose length is zero). First of all, we construct a complete lattice $L_{s,paths}$ whose elements are sets of paths from $s$. Every element $x$ in $L_{s,paths}$ is an array whose length is the number of vertices $V$. Each cell is indexed by a vertex $v \in V$, and its content $x[v]$ is a path $p$ from $s$ to $v$ or nil which means there is no path. We define $\text{length}(\text{nil}) = +\infty$. A order $\sqsubseteq$ in $L_{s,paths}$ is defined as follows.

$$\forall x, y \in L_{s,paths} \ : \ x \sqsubseteq y \ \overset{\text{def}}{\Longleftrightarrow} \ \forall v \in V, \ \text{length}(x[v]) \geq \text{length}(y[v])$$

Secondly we define another complete lattice $L_{edges}$ of edges $E$. $L_{edges}$ is a flat lattice in which all edges in $E$ are unordered and its top($\top_{edges}$) and bottom($\bot_{edges}$) are newly introduced. It can be proved that $L_{s,paths}$ and $L_{edges}$ are complete lattices.

Now we will give a function $f : L_{edges} \times L_{s,paths} \to L_{s,paths}$ which incrementally calculates path sets from $s$ by adding the effects of an edge. (By the way, to meet elementwise strictness, we will add $\bot_{s,paths}$ to $L_{s,paths}$, where $\bot_{s,paths}$ is less than every element in $L_{s,paths}$.)

$\forall x \in L_{s,paths}, \quad f(\bot_{edges}, x) = \bot_{s,paths}, \quad f(\top_{edges}, x) = x$

$\forall e \in L_{edges}, \quad f(e, \bot_{s,paths}) = \bot_{s,paths}$

$\forall x \in L_{s,paths} - \{\bot_{s,paths}\}, \quad \forall e(v_1, v_2) \in L_{edges} - \{\top_{edges}, \bot_{edges}\} \quad f(e(v_1, v_2), x) = y$ st.

if $(x[v_1] \neq$ nil and $x[v_2] =$ nil$)$

then $(y[v_2] = x[v_1].e(v_1, v_2)$ and $y[v] = x[v]$ for any $v \in V - \{v_2\})$ else $y = \bot_{s,paths}$

It is easily verified $f$ meets requirement $(\alpha)$. Then the following program calculates the shortest paths from $s$ to all vertices in $V$.

$paths(V + \{X, Y\}) \sqsupseteq f(edge(X, Y), paths(V + \{X\}))$

$paths(\{s\}) \sqsupseteq a$

$(a \in L_{s,paths}, \quad \forall v \in V - \{s\}, a[v] =$ nil, and $a[s] = e(s, s), \text{length}(e(s, s)) = 0)$

If we rewrite this top-down recursive program to a bottom-up iterative one and apply *branch and bound* strategy to the search, we get the non-deterministic version of the labeling algorithm of Ford [9]. Further, if we adopt the shortest first search as the special case for *branch and bound* strategy, we get the Dijkstra's shortest path algorithm ([8]). Note that if we change the lattice and the operation appropriately, the same program represents an algorithm which calculates the minimum spanning tree of $G$.

# 5 Theoretical Background

Now we give the declarative and procedural semantics special to our framework. The theoretical results are also presented, but the details of their proofs([1]) are omitted owing to the space limit.

## 5.1 declarative semantics

An *interpretation I* of a lattice valued program $P$ associates every ground atom $A$ with a value in $L_A$, which will be denoted by val$(A, I)$. The order in interpretations is introduced as follows : $I_1 \sqsubseteq I_2 \overset{\text{def}}{\Longleftrightarrow}$ val$(A, I_1) \sqsubseteq$ val$(A, I_2)$ for any ground atom $A$. Using this order, the set of interpretations of a program $P$ forms a complete lattice.

Some notations are useful for convenience and readability. Let $C$ be a clause $A \leftarrow B_1, \cdots, B_n$. $C^+$ denotes the head $A$ and $C^-$ denotes the body $B_1, \cdots, B_n$. Let $\langle A \leftarrow B_1, \cdots, B_n, f \rangle$ be a clause pair and $I$ be an interpretation. For example, $f(\text{val}(B_1, I), \cdots, \text{val}(B_n, I))$, can be denoted by VAL$(\langle B_1, \cdots, B_n, f \rangle, I)$.

Let $\langle C, f \rangle$ be a clause pair. The clause $C$ is *true* in an interpretation $I$ with respect to $f$ iff for every its ground instance $C'$, val$(C'^+, I) \sqsupseteq$ VAL$(\langle C'^-, f \rangle, I)$ holds. In this case, $I$ is called *model* for $\langle C, f \rangle$. An interpretation $M$ is called *model* of a program $P$ iff $M$ is a model for every clause pair in $P$. Let $M(P)$ denote the set of all models of a program $P$, then its greatest lower bound $\sqcap M(P)$ also becomes a model, which is called *the minimal model* of $P$.

In logic programming, van Emden and Kowalski [5] associate a program $P$ with a mapping $T_P$ over interpretations and show that models of $P$ are fixpoints of $T_P$. Furthermore, by virtue of mathematical results of $T_P$, $T_P$ can be used to discover properties of models and provides the link between declarative and procedural semantics. We also follows this method and define $T_P$ as follows. Let $P$ be a program, $A$ be an ground atom and $I$ be an interpretation.

$$\mathrm{val}(A, T_P(I))$$
$$= \sqcup\{\mathrm{VAL}(\langle C'^-, f \rangle, I) \mid C' \text{ is a ground instance of } C \text{ in } \langle C, f \rangle \text{ and } C'^+ = A\}$$
$$= \bot_{L_A} \text{ (if there exists no clause whose head and } A \text{ are unifiable)}$$

As in logic programming, it can be proved that $T_P$ is a monotone function over the complete lattice of interpretations and all models can be characterized in terms of $T_P$. Hence we can establish a useful connection between models and fixpoints, that is the least fixpoint of $T_P$ is equal to the minimal model of $P$. Furthermore, since $T_P$ is a continuous mapping, the least fixpoint of $T_P$ is equal to $T_P \uparrow \omega$. This is the very result that connect declarative and procedural semantics of lattice valued programs.

We will conclude this subsection by collecting the results.

**Theorem.**
Let $P$ be a program and $A$ be a ground atom. Then

$$\mathrm{val}(A, \sqcap M(P)) = \mathrm{val}(A, \mathrm{lfp}(T_P)) = \mathrm{val}(A, T_P \uparrow \omega)$$

## 5.2 procedural semantics

Now we give the procedural semantics, such as *a derivation, a derivation tree* and *a derived value*. Then we will show one result that combines declarative and procedural semantics.

Let $P$ be a program and $R$ be *a computation rule* which selects at least one atom from a goal if it is not an empty goal. A *derivation* of a goal pair $\langle G_0, F_0 \rangle$ via $R$ is a sequence of tuples $\langle \langle G_i, F_i \rangle, \langle C_i, f_i \rangle, \theta_i \rangle$ $(i = 0, 1, \cdots)$, in which a goal $\langle G_{i+1}, F_{i+1} \rangle$ is *derived* by a goal $\langle G_i, F_i \rangle$ and a clause $\langle C_i, f_i \rangle$ as follows. Let $G_i$ be $\leftarrow A_1, \cdots, A_k$, $F_i$ be $g(X_1, \cdots, X_k)$, $A_m$ be the atom selected by $R$, $C_i$ be $A \leftarrow B_1, \cdots, B_q$ whose head and $A_m$ are unifiable by an mgu $\theta_i$. Then

$$G_{i+1} = \leftarrow (A_1, \cdots, A_{m-1}, B_1, \cdots, B_q, A_{m+1}, \cdots, A_k)\theta_i$$
$$F_{i+1} = g(X_1, \cdots, X_{m-1}, f_i(Y_1, \cdots, Y_q), X_{m+1}, \cdots, X_k)$$

Especially, if $\langle C_i, f_i \rangle$ is $\langle A \leftarrow, f_i \rangle$ $(f_i \in L_A)$, then $G_{i+1}$ is $\leftarrow (A_1, \cdots, A_{m-1}, A_{m+1}, \cdots, A_k)\theta_i$ and $F_{i+1}$ is $g(X_1, \cdots, X_{m-1}, f_i, X_{m+1}, \cdots, X_k)$. Note that if the region of $F_0$ is $L$, then the region of each $F_i$ is also $L$.

A derivation can be *finite* or *infinite*. A finite derivation can be *successful* or *failed*. A successful derivation ends in a goal pair which has the form $\langle \leftarrow, F_n \rangle$. A failed derivation ends in a goal pair $\langle G_n, F_n \rangle$, where $G_n$ is not empty and the selected atom from $G_n$ does not unify with the head of the clause in any clause pair. Let $D$ be a derivation whose initial goal is $\langle G_0, F_0 \rangle$. The *derived value*, $\mathrm{der}(\langle G_0, F_0 \rangle, D)$, of $D$ is defined as follows:

- If $D$ is a successful derivation that ends in $\langle \leftarrow, F_n \rangle$, then $\mathrm{der}(\langle G_0, F_0 \rangle, D) = F_n$.

- If $D$ is failed or infinite, $\mathrm{der}(\langle G_0, F_0 \rangle, D) = \perp_L$, where $L$ is the region of $F_0$.

By the way, according to the definition of derivation, there are two choices in each step of deriving goals;

- Choice of computation rules which select an atom in a goal.

- Choice of a clause whose head and the selected atom are unifiable.

Due to these choices, we may have to consider a large number of derivations. Fortunately, however, since the independence of computation rules can be proved as in the usual logic programming [10] , we can enumerate derivations by a fixed computation rule. This fact really reduce the number of derivations. Furthermore, we can generate all derivations systematically and make up them into a tree, which we call *derivation tree*.

Let $P$ be a program, $\langle G, F \rangle$ be a goal pair and $R$ be a computation rule. The *derivation tree* for $\langle G, F \rangle$ via $R$ is defined as follows.

- Each node of the tree is a goal pair.

- The root node is $\langle G, F \rangle$.

- Let $\langle G', F' \rangle$ be a node of the tree and suppose that $A_m$ is selected from $G'$ by $R$. If there is no clause whose head and $A_m$ are unifiable, then this node is called *failure node* and it has no descendants. On the other hands, this node has a descendant for each clause pair $\langle C, f \rangle$ such that $C^+$ and $A_m$ are unifiable by an mgu $\theta$. The descendant node is the goal pair derived by $\langle G', F' \rangle$, $\langle C, f \rangle$, and $\theta$.

- If a node is $\langle \leftarrow, F' \rangle$, then this node is called *success node* and it has no descendants.

A derivation tree $T$ for a goal $\langle G, F \rangle$ contains all possible derived values. Each branch from the root to a leaf node can be regarded as a derivation. A branch to a success node is a successful derivation and a branch to a failure node is a failed derivation. We also define the derived value der($\langle G, F \rangle, T$) for a derivation tree $T$ : der($\langle G, F \rangle, T$) = $\sqcup\{$der($\langle G, F \rangle, D$) | $D$ is a derivation for $\langle G, F \rangle$ in $T\}$.

Now we give will our main result which connects the declarative and procedural semantics of lattice valued programs.

**Theorem.**
Let $A$ be a ground atom of a program $P$. If a derivation tree $T$ of a goal $\langle \leftarrow A, I \rangle$ ($I(X) = X$) via a computation rule is finite,

$$\text{val}(A, \sqcap M(P)) = \text{der}(\langle \leftarrow A, I \rangle, T).$$

# 6    Conclusion

From the programming viewpoint, the optimization process in the sorting example is similar to what is discussed as program transformation in Clark and Darlington [3] where the initial program is like:

$$sort(List, SortedList) \leftarrow permutation(List, SortedList) \ \& \ ordered(SortedList).$$

However, our algorithm derivation is much easier to understand than theirs, because lattice programming enables the explicit representation of the sequences and the separation of the ordering relation from the other aspects of the program. In lattice programming, as far as properly choosing the lattice of sequences and operations on sequences which satisfies requirement $(\alpha)$, the programmer can concentrate on reducing the computational complexity of *permutation* without paying attention to *ordered*. The system takes care of calculating the *ordered* solution. This property makes it easy to evaluate how much the program's computational complexity is reduced by each programming invention.

From the theoretical viewpoint, the notion of lattice valued programs is extended from a language **ProBoole** ([2]) which only considers free Boolean algebras as lattices. It is also a generalization of works done by van Emden([4]) and Sakakibara([6]) who tried to give meanings to logic programs with uncertainties. The interval [0,1] of uncertainties is one instance of complete lattices. O'Keefe([7]) proposed propositional Horn clauses over lattices having finite depths.

We are still in an early stage of the exploration of this new paradigm and much work is to be done before claiming its usefulness. The following list shows the part of the future research items.

- Accumulation of algorithm design experiences to refine the theory for the natural representation of various algorithms and to develop systematic programming methodologies.

- Design of a programming language which enables the declaration of lattices and functions of interest and facilitates the verification of their correctness.

- Implementation of a language processor which enables the execution of the primitive lattice operations in a fixed amount of time and storage.

# References

[1] S.Morishita , *Lattice-valued programs*, TRL Research Report, TR87-0041, 1988

[2] S.Morishita et al. , *Symbolical construction of truth value domain for logic program*, Proc. of 4th ICLP, 1987

[3] K.L. Clark and J. Darlington, *Algorithm classification through synthesis*, The Computer Journal, vol.23, 1980

[4] M.H. van Emden, *Quantitative Deduction and its fixpoint theory*, J. of Logic Programming, 1986

[5] M.H. van Emden and R.A. Kowalski, *The semantics of Logic as a Programming Language*, J.ACM, vol.23, pp733-742, 1976

[6] Y.Sakakibara, *On semantics of Logic Programs with Uncertainties*, ICOT Technical Report, 1987

[7] R.A. O'Keefe, *Finite fixed-point problems*, Proc. of 4th ICLP, MIT Press, 1987

[8] E.W. Dijkstra, *A note on two problems in connection with graphs* Numer.Math.,1, 1959

[9] L.R.Ford et al., *Flows in networks* Princeton Univ.Press, Princeton NJ, 1962

[10] J.W.Lloyd, *Foundations of logic programming*, Springer, 1984

# A Simple Programming System Written in GHC and Its Reflective Operations

Jiro Tanaka *

Institute for New Generation Computer Technology
4-28, Mita 1-chome, Minato-ku, Tokyo 108, JAPAN

## Abstract

A programming system can be defined as an environment where one can input and execute programs. In this paper, we try to describe a simple programming system written in GHC. We try to capture the function of the *metacall* first. Input/output problems in GHC are also considered. After describing the *shell,* we try to assemble these parts into a simple programming system, and discuss how to add new features such as *reflective* operations to the programming system. This paper assumes a basic knowledge of parallel logic languages such as PARLOG, Concurrent Prolog or GHC.

## 1. Introduction

The goal of Fifth Generation Computer Project exists in connecting knowledge information processing and parallel computer architecture [Fuchi 86]. Since we would like to realize everything in *logic,* it was quite natural for us to try to develop a logic-based machine and write an operating system in a logic programming language.

In the first stage of our project, ESP [Chikayama 84], which is the object-oriented dialect of Prolog, has been chosen as our tentative *Kernel Language.* Logic-based machine PSI [Taki 84] and logic-based operating system SIMPOS [Takagi 84] have been developed. However, SIMPOS was full of side effects. It might be an object-oriented system, but far from logic programming which we expected. What we have learned is that we need more elegant mechanisms which realize *logic* in natural way. Therefore, we next paid attention to *parallel logic languages* which are based on *and*-parallel execution of programs.

Various kinds of *parallel logic languages* have been proposed so far. PARLOG [Clark 85], Concurrent Prolog [Shapiro 83] and GHC [Ueda 85] [Tanaka 86] are examples of such languages. In these languages, we can create *processes* dynamically and express the *synchronization* between processes quite easily.

Therefore, it seems to be quite natural to try to describe an operating system in these languages. In fact, various proposals have been made for system programming from the very beginning of *parallel logic languages* [Clark 84] [Clark 85] [Shapiro 83] [Shapiro 84]. PPS (PARLOG Programming System) [Foster 86] [Clark 87] and Logix [Silverman 86] are the examples of such systems. However, they are kinds of empirical systems which consist of huge amounts of codes, and their overall structures are not clear enough.

---

*Authors current address: International Institute (IIAS-SIS), Fujitsu Limited, 1-17-25 Shinkamata, Ota-ku, Tokyo 144, e-mail: jiro%flab.fujitsu.junet@uunet.uu.net

In this paper, we try to describe a simple programming system written in GHC. Our objective is not building up a practical programming system like PPS or Logix. Rather, our interest exists in expressing a *simple* programming system more systematically. We would also like to test new features of a programming system such as *reflective* operations. We believe that our research will lead to the development of new programming techniques in parallel logic languages and prove the expressive power of GHC in the long run.

The organization of this paper is as follows. Section 2 describes *metacalls* which present the basic functions of our programming system. Section 3 discusses input and output handling in the programming system. Section 4 describes the UNIX-like *shell* and the overall structure of the simple programming system. Section 5 describes *reflective* operations in the programming system.

## 2. Metacalls and their descriptions

User programs can be executed on a programming system. However, the programming system must not fail even if a user program fails. Therefore, we need the *metacall* mechanism which protects the programming system from failure [Clark 84] [Foster 87]. This *metacall* predicate executes the given goal and reports the execution result.

### 2.1. Various metacalls

Various kinds of *metacalls* have already been discussed in [Clark 84]. Here, we briefly review how they work. The simplest metacall is the following single-argument metacall.

```
call(G)
```

This metacall simply executes goal *G*. However, this form of metacall does not help us much because it is too simple. Therefore, the following two-argument metacall has been proposed.

```
call(G,R)
```

This metacall executes goal *G* and returns the result by instantiating *R* to *success* when it succeeds and to *failure* when it fails.

The next extension is the following three-argument metacall, which has slightly been modified from [Clark 84].

```
call(G,In,Out)
```

Here, *In* is called *input stream* and used for communication from the system to the metacall. *Out* is called *output stream* and used for communication from the metacall. Goal execution can be suspended, resumed, or aborted by instantiating *In* to [susp|In'], [resume|In''] or [abort|In']. When the execution of the metacall finishes successfully, *Out* is instantiated to [success]. When it fails, *Out* is instantiated to [failure(R)], where *R* is instantiated to the message which shows the cause of the failure.

### 2.2. Metacall and meta-interpreter

The next problem is how to implement these metacalls. For efficiency, they should be implemented as a built-in predicate. Metacalls are prepared as primitives in [Clark 84].

Whereas, Shapiro takes the meta-interpreter and program transformation approach to keep flexibility [Silverman 86].

If we disregard efficiency, it is possible to express these *metacalls* as a *meta-interpreter*. The original notion of the *meta-interpreter* comes from the self-description of EVAL in Lisp. In Prolog, the following self-description is very famous [Bowen 83].

```
exec(true) :- !.
exec((P,Q)) :- !, exec(P), exec(Q).
exec(P) :- clause((P:-Body)), exec(Body).
exec(P) :- P.
```

This meta-interpreter simply executes the goal which is given as the argument of *exec*. You may notice that this meta-interpreter corresponds to the implementation of the single-argument metacall. The GHC version of this meta-interpreter can be written as follows:

```
exec(true) :-  true | true.
exec((P,Q)) :-  true | exec(P), exec(Q).
exec(P) :- not_sys(P) |
  reduce(P,Body), exec(Body).
exec(P) :- sys(P) | P.
```

This program is almost the same as the Prolog program except that every clause definition includes the | operator.

Two-argument metacalls can be written similarly by modifying the single-argument meta-interpreter.

```
exec(true,R) :-  true | R=success.
exec(false,R) :-  true | R=failure.
exec((P,Q),R) :-  true |
  exec(P,R1), exec(Q,R2),
  and_result(R1,R2,R).
exec(P,R) :- not_sys(P) |
  reduce(P,Body), exec(Body,R).
exec(P,R) :- sys(P) | sys_exe(P,R).
```

## 2.3. Three-argument metacall implementation

It has already been stated that metacalls should be implemented as a built-in predicate for efficiency. However, the three-argument metacall may be too complex to implement it in this way. Its specification also needs to be flexible. Therefore, we adopted a kind of hybrid approach. We split the metacall into two parts, the *exec* part which realizes the basic function of metacall and the *exec_server* part which is in charge of other services. The *exec* part should be implemented as a *built-in* predicate for execution efficiency and *exec_server* part should be implemented as a software to keep the system flexible. However, if we disregard efficiency, the *exec* can also be programmed as follows:

```
exec(true,In,Out) :- true |
  Out=[success].
exec(false(R),In,Out) :- true |
  Out=[failure(R)].
exec((A,B),In,Out) :- true |
  exec(A,In,O1), exec(B,In,O2),
  merge_result(O1,O2,Out).
exec(A,In,Out) :- sys(A),var(In) |
  sys_exe(A,In,Out).
exec(A,In,Out) :- is_io(A),var(In) |
  Out=[A].
exec(A,In,Out) :- not_sys(A),var(In) |
  reduce(A,In,Body,Out,NewOut),
  exec(Body,In,NewOut).
exec(A,[susp|In],Out) :- true |
  wait(A,In,Out).
exec(A,[abort|In],Out) :- true |
  Out=[aborted].

wait(A,[resume|In],Out) :- true |
  exec(A,In,Out).
wait(A,[abort|In],Out) :- true |
  Out=[aborted].
```

The unique features of this *exec* are *In* and *Out* which connect the object level and the metalevel. Note that I/O is handled as a message to the metalevel. Also, *var(In)* is the special predicate which checks the absence of messages in the argument variable.

The *exec_server* part which is in charge of other services can be expressed as follows:

```
exec_server(State,G,EI,[success|EO],In,Out) :-
  var(In) |
  Out=[output([success,goal=G])].
exec_server(State,G,EI,[failure(R)|EO],In,Out) :-
  var(In) |
  EI=[abort],
  Out=[output([failure,reason=R])].
exec_server(State,G,EI,[G1|EO],In,Out) :-
  var(In), is_io(G1)|
  Out=[G1|Out1],
  exec_server(State,G,EI,EO,In,Out1).
exec_server(State,G,EI,[undefined(G1)|EO],In,Out) :-
  var(In) |
  Out=[input([undefined_goal=G1,expected_result?],NG)|out1],
  G1=NG,
  exec_server(State,G,EI,EO,In,Out1).
exec_server(State,G,EI,EO,[C|In],Out) :-
  true |
```

```
control_receiver(C,State,G,EI,EO,In,Out).
```

This *exec_server* has six arguments. The first argument shows the internal state of the metacall. The second argument keeps the initial goal, *G*, and is used for printing computation result. The third and fourth arguments are connected to *exec*. The fifth and the sixth arguments are used for communication to the system. When the *exec_server* receives a success or failure message from *exec*, it transmits the message to the system by adding the appropriate message. I/O messages are also forwarded to the system. When an undefined goal *G1* appears in *exec*, the *exec_server* sends the message to the user and urges us to input the new goal, *NG*, which corresponds to the execution result. When the *exec_server* receives a control message from outside, it invokes *control_receiver*.

*exec* and *exec_server* can be connected as follows:

```
call(G,In,Out):- true|
   exec_server(run,G,EI,EO,In,Out),
   exec(G,EI,EO).
```

Note that the pair of *exec_server* and *exec* works as a metacall as a whole.

## 3. Input and output

Handling input and output in logic programming is an important problem. We assume virtual processes which correspond to the actual devices. We consider that there exists a single stream which connects these virtual processes to the system. These virtual processes are always *consuming* a stream. For output, we send a message in the form output(Message). The input message has the format input(Message_list, X). In this case, *Message_list* is printed first, then the user's input is instantiated to *X*. An other possibility is to assume two streams which correspond to input and output. However, the synchronization of input and output becomes difficult in this case.

In our approach, virtual processes can be created by the *create* predicate in a program. This predicate is a special one, which we can execute only once in our program for each virtual process.

### 3.1. Window

The window is usually created on a bitmap display and we can input and output messages from there. For example, a window is created when create(window,X) is executed. The input and output to the window are expressed as messages to stream *X*. (The actual input is completed when we move the cursor to the window and type in messages from the keyboard.) The virtual processes which correspond to devices are deleted by instantiating *X* to [].

### 3.2. Keyboard controller

As stated above, input and output are performed at the request of the program. That is, the system does not accept keyboard input without a request from the program. Therefore, we need to make a program which always generates this request. The keyboard controller acts as such a program in a programming system. It can be written as follows:

```
keyboard(Out,In) :- true|
  Out=[input([@],T)|Out1],
  keyboard(T,Out1,In).

keyboard(halt,Out,In) :- true|
  Out=[],
  In=[].

keyboard(T,Out,In) :- goal_or_command(T) |
  In=[T|In1],
  Out=[input([@],T1)|Out1],
  keyboard(T1,Out1,In1).
```

Here, the message input([@],T) outputs @ first, and user's input will be entered into T. Note that @ is used as a *prompt* for user input.

### 3.3. Database server

In the programming system, we need a database capability which can add, delete and check program definitions. The database capability is a kind of I/O in a broader sense. Therefore, we imagine a virtual process which corresponds to the database. Operations to the database can be realized by messages to the virtual process.

In fact, PPS tries to realize the database in this way [Clark 87]. However, every *exec* needs to carry the stream to the database in that case. This is very complicated and this may cause a database access bottleneck. Therefore, we have implemented *db_server* using a side effect as follows:

```
db_server([add(Code)|In],ready,Out):-true|
  add_definition(Code,Done,Out,Out1),
  db_server(In,Done,Out1).
db_server([delete(Name)|In],ready,Out):-true|
  delete_definition(Name,Done,Out,Out1),
  db_server(In,Done,Out1).
db_server([definition(Name)|In],ready,Out):-true|
  definition(Name,Done,Out,Out1),
  db_server(In,Done,Out1).
```

The *db_server* predicate has three arguments. The first is the input from the system. The second is used to sequentialize database access. The third is the output to the system.

## 4. Building a programming system

We have already discussed the description of *metacall* and the handling of I/O in the programming system. The next step is the construction of a programming system. In this section, we first describe the *shell* which plays the central role in the programming system. Then we try to assemble these parts into a simple programming system.

## 4.1. Shell

The shell creates the user task or enters the program to the database, depending on messages from the user. The following is a programming example for the *shell*.

```
shell([],Val,Db,Out):-true|
  Val=[],
  Db=[],
  Out=[].
shell([goal(Goal)|In],
  Val,Db,Out):-true|
  Val=[record_dict(Goal,NGoal)|Val1],
  create(Window,WOut),
  keyboard(KO,PI),
  exec_server(run,NGoal,EI,EO,PI,PO),
  exec(NGoal,EI,EO),
  shell(In,Val1,Db,Out),
  merge(KO,PO,WOut).
shell([db(Message)|In],
  Val,Db,Out):-true|
  Db=[Message|Db1],
  shell(In,Val,Db1,Out).
shell([binding(Message)|In],
  Val,Db,Out):-true|
  Val=[Message|Val1],
  shell(In,Val1,Db,Out).
```

The *shell* has four arguments; the first is the input stream, the second is the stream to the variable dictionary, the third is the stream to the database server, and the fourth is the output stream. This *shell* is connected to the variable dictionary where the user can freely define variables and their bindings. This variable dictionary is a kind of user interface and provides macro facilities. The *shell* program works as follows:

1. If the input stream is [], it means the end of input. All streams will be closed in this case.

2. If goal(Goal) is in the input stream, *Goal* is sent to the variable dictionary. The variable dictionary checks the bindings of every variable in *Goal* and creates *NGoal* where every variable is bound to the current bindings. A window, a keyboard controller, an *exec_server* and an *exec* are also created.

3. If a message to the *database_server* or the variable dictionary is received, the message is sent to the appropriate stream.

The function of the variable dictionary is to memorize the value of variables as its internal state. It works as a kind of user interface.

Figure 1 shows the snapshot where processes are created in accordance with the user input.

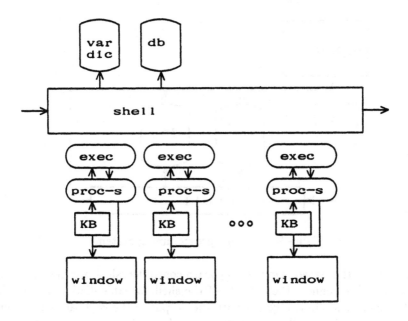

Figure 1  Creation of processes in the *shell*

Corresponding to the input goal, four processes, exec, exec-server, keyboard controller and window, are dynamically created.

Since the four processes each have their own window and keyboard, they can run independently from the *shell.* The keyboard controller always sends the read request to the window, and the user can input the control commands to the exec-server from the window.

## 4.2.  Example of a programming system
This section shows an example of a programming system by connecting the components described above.

```
create_world :- true|
  create(window,Out),
  keyboard(Out,In),
  shell(In,Va,Db,Out2),
  vr_dictionary(Va,[],Out3),
  db_server(Db,ready,Out4),
  merge4(Out1,Out2,Out3,Out4,Out).
```

This program can be illustrated as follows:

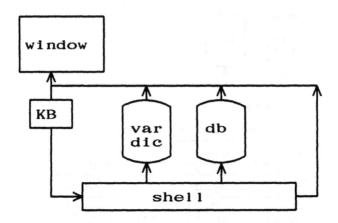

Figure 2  A simple programming system

Here, we create the system window, keyboard controller, shell, variable dictionary and database server. We connect the outputs of the shell, variable dictionary and database server to the system window, together with the output of the keyboard controller.

Since the keyboard controller always generates the read request to the system window, we can input goals from it. Commands to the database server or variable dictionary can also be entered.

Note that this shows just an example of a programming system. A more sophisticated programming system such as *distributed programming system* is also possible.

## 5.  Reflective operations in the programming system

Implementing various reflective operations, such as seen in [Weyhrauch 80] [Smith 84] [Maes 86] [Watanabe 88], is not too difficult, once we get the meta-interpreters.

We sometimes need to understand the current state of the system. We also need to be able to modify and return the state to the system. These kinds of *reflective* capabilities, seem to be very useful in the operating system. In 3-Lisp [Smith 84], we can easily obtain the current *continuation* and *environment* from the program. Smith used metacircular interpreters as a mechanism to obtain information from the program.

We extend our meta-interpreter in a similar way to Smith's approach. How do we extend the meta-interpreter? It depends on what kind of resources we want to control. We would like to control computation time, memories and processes in the programming system. Therefore, we introduce a *scheduling queue* explicitly in our meta-interpreter. Program *continuation* was explicit in the metacircular interpreter in 3-Lisp. We have thought that the *scheduling queue* acts as a *continuation* in GHC. We also introduce the *reduction count* to control computation resources. We assume that this *reduction count* corresponds to the *computation time* in conventional systems.

The three-argument *exec* in 2.3 becomes the following six-argument *exec* when we perform this modification.

```
exec(T,T,In,Out,MaxRC,RC) :- true |
  Out=[success(reduction_count=RC)].
```

```
exec([true|H],T,In,Out,MaxRC,RC) :-
  true |
  exec(H,T,In,Out,MaxRC,RC).
exec([false(R)|H],T,In,Out,MaxRC,RC) :-
  true |
  Out=[failure(R)].
exec([A|H],T,In,Out,MaxRC,RC) :-
  sys(A),var(In),MaxRC>RC |
  sys_exe(A,T,NT,RC,RC1,Out,NOut),
  exec(H,NT,In,NOut,MaxRC,RC1).
exec([A|H],T,In,Out,MaxRC,RC) :-
  is_io(A),var(In),MaxRC>RC |
  Out=[A|NOut],
  RC1=RC+1,
  exec(H,T,In,NOut,MaxRC,RC1).
exec([A|H],T,In,Out,MaxRC,RC) :-
  not_sys(A),var(In),MaxRC>RC |
  reduce(A,T,NT,RC,RC1,Out,NOut),
  exec(H,NT,In,NOut,MaxRC,RC1).
exec(H,T,In,Out,MaxRC,RC) :-
  MaxRC=<RC |
  Out=[count_over].
exec(H,T,[Mes|In],Out,MaxRC,RC) :- true |
  control_exec(Mes,H,T,In,Out,MaxRC,RC).
```

The first two arguments of *exec*, $H$ and $T$, express the scheduling queue in Difference list form. The use of Difference list for expressing scheduling queue was originally invented by Shapiro [Shapiro 83]. Goals are processed *sequentially* because we have introduced a scheduling queue. However, it does not mean that the whole world is sequential. It simply means that the world inside *exec* is sequential. The third and the fourth arguments are the same as before. The fifth argument, *MaxRC*, shows the limit of the reduction count allowed in that *exec*. The sixth argument, *RC*, shows the current reduction count.

There is no notion of job priority in this *exec*. We sometimes need to execute goals urgently. Therefore, we also introduce the *express queue* to execute *express goals* which have the form, *G@exp*. This can be realized by adding two more arguments, *EH* and *ET*, which correspond to the express queue, to the six-argument *exec*. The following two definitions describe the transition between the six-argument *exec* and eight-argument *exec*.

```
exec(In,Out,[G@exp|H],T,RC,MaxRC):-
  var(In)|
  exec([G|ET],ET,In,Out,H,T,RC,MaxRC).
exec(ET,ET,In,Out,H,T,RC,MaxRC):-
  var(In)|
  exec(In,Out,H,T,RC,MaxRC).
```

If we come across the express goal, we simply call the eight-argument *exec*. The eight-argument *exec* executes express goals first, and the reduced goals are also entered to the express queue. If the express queue becomes empty, we simply return to the six-argument *exec*.

The next thing is to realize the reflective operations. Here, we consider four kinds of reflective operations, *get_rc, put_rc, get_q, put_q*. These can be defined as follows:

```
exec([get_rc(Max,C)|EH],ET,In,Out,H,T,RC,MaxRC):- true|
  Max := MaxRC,are
  C := RC,
  RC1 := RC+1,
  exec(EH,ET,In,Out,H,T,RC1,MaxRC).
exec([put_rc(C)|EH],ET,In,Out,H,T,RC,MaxRC):- true|
  RC1 := RC+1,
  exec(EH,ET,In,Out,H,T,RC1,C).
exec([get_q(NH,NT)|EH],ET,In,Out,H,T,RC,MaxRC):- true|
  RC1 := RC+1,
  NH = H,
  NT = T,
  exec(EH,ET,In,Out,H,T,RC1,MaxRC).
exec([put_q(NH,NT)|EH],ET,In,Out,H,T,RC,MaxRC):- true|
  RC1 := RC+1,
  exec(EH,ET,In,Out,NH,NT,RC1,MaxRC).
```

*get_rc* gets *MaxRC* and *RC* from *exec*. *put_rc* resets *MaxRC* of *exec* to the given argument. *get_q* gets the current scheduling queue of *exec*. *put_q* resets the current scheduling queue to the given argument.

Here, we show an example which uses these reflective operations. This example shows how to define the *check_rc* predicate which checks the current reduction count of the system and changes it if allowed fewer than 100 reductions.

```
check_rc :- true |
  get_rc(MaxRC,RC),
  RestRC := MaxRC-RC,
  check(MaxRC,RestRC).

check(MaxRC,RestRC) :- 100>=RestRC |
  get_q(H,T),
  input([reduction_increment,@],AddRC),
  NRC := MaxRC+AddRC,
  put_rc(NRC),
  T=[check_rc@exp|NT],
  put_q(H,NT).
check(MaxRC,RestRC) :- 100<RestRC |
  get_q(H,T),
  T=[check_rc@exp|NT],
  put_q(H,NT).
```

In a sense, these *reflective* operations are very dangerous because we can easily access and change the internal state of the system. However, we can say that privileged users must have these capabilities for advanced system control. Our current interest exists in examining the reflective operations in a programming system. Thus, we assumed these it reflective operations in a very primitive manner. The more sophisticated handling of *reflective* operations can be seen in may [Tanaka 88].

## 6. Conclusion

In this paper, we discussed various factors in the programming system and showed an example of such a system. *Reflective* operations in the programming system were also considered.

You may have noticed that these program fragments are quite simple and declarative. Their simplicity mainly comes from the extensive use of streams, processes and meta-interpretation techniques. The clear separation of the meta from the object also makes the system very clean. Note that the program fragments shown here are the extremely simplified version. The more complete version, workable on DEC 2065, is available from the author.

We would like to answer the question of why we need to research the programming system now. Looking back on the history of parallel logic programming, we designed the language specification first. Then we made interpreters and compilers. Now we have started working on programming environments and applications for those languages.

It is clear that we can program easily in GHC. Techniques for parallel problem solving, such as in [Ohwada 87], are very similar to those of parallel programming systems. Research in parallel programming systems leads to research in parallel problem solving.

## 7. Acknowledgments

This research has been carried out as a part of the Fifth Generation Computer Project. I would like to express my thanks to Yukiko Ohta, Fujitsu Social Science Laboratory, for her useful comments. I am indebted to her for part of this research. I would also like to express my thanks to Koichi Furukawa, Deputy Director of ICOT, for his encouragement and giving me the opportunity to pursue this research.

# References

[Bowen 83]  D.L. Bowen et al., DECsystem-10 Prolog User's Manual, University of Edinburgh, 1983

[Chikayama 84] T. Chikayama, Unique Features of ESP, in Proceedings of the International Conference on Fifth Generation Computer Systems 1984, pp.292-298, ICOT, 1984

[Clark 84]  K. Clark and S. Gregory, Notes on Systems Programming in Parlog, in Proceedings of the International Conference on Fifth Generation Computer Systems 1984, pp.299-306, ICOT, 1984

[Clark 85]  K. Clark and S. Gregory, PARLOG, Parallel Programming in Logic, Research Report DOC 84/4, Dept. of Computing, Imperial College of Science and Technology, Revised 1985

[Clark 87]      K. Clark and I. Foster, A Declarative Environment for Concurrent Logic Programming, Lecture Notes in Computer Science 250, TAPSOFT'87, pp.212-242, 1987

[Foster 86]     I. Foster; The Parlog Programming System (PPS), Version 0.2, Imperial College of Science and Technology, 1986

[Foster 87]     I. Foster; Logic Operating Systems, Design Issues, in Proceedings of the Fourth International Conference on Logic Programming, Vol.2, pp.910-926, MIT Press, May 1987

[Fuchi 86]      K. Fuchi and K. Furukawa; The Role of Logic Programming in the Fifth Generation Computer Project, in Proceedings of the Third International Conference on Logic Programming, Lecture Notes in Computer Science 225, pp.1-24, Springer Verlag, July 1986

[Maes 86]       P. Maes; Reflection in an Object-Oriented Language, in Preprints of the Workshop on Metalevel Architectures and Reflection, Alghero-Sardinia, October 1986

[Ohwada 87]     H. Ohwada and F. Mizoguchi; Managing Search in Parallel Logic Programming, in Proceedings of the Logic Programming Conference '87, pp.213-222, ICOT, June 1987

[Shapiro 83]    E. Shapiro; A Subset of Concurrent Prolog and Its Interpreter, ICOT Technical Report, TR-003, 1983

[Shapiro 84]    E. Shapiro; Systems programming in Concurrent Prolog, in Conference Record of the 11th Annual ACM Symposium on Principles of Programming Languages, pp.93-105, ACM, January 1984

[Silverman 86]  W. Silverman, M. Hirsch, A. Houri and E. Shapiro; The Logix System User Manual, Version 1.21, Weizmann Institute, Israel, July 1986

[Smith 84]      B.C. Smith; Reflection and Semantics in Lisp, in Proceedings. of in Conference Record of the 11th Annual ACM Symposium on Principles of Programming Languages, pp.23-35, ACM, January 1984

[Takagi 84]     S. Takagi, T Yokoi, S. Uchida, T. Kurokawa, T. Hattori, T. Chikayama, K. Sakai and J. Tsuji; Overall Design of SIMPOS, in Proceedings. of the Second International Logic Programming Conference, Uppsala, Sweden, pp.1-12, July 1984

[Taki 84]       K. Taki, M. Yokota, A. Yamamoto, H. Nishikawa, S. Uchida, H. Nakashima and A. Mitsuishi; Hardware Design and Implementation of the Personal Sequential Inference Machine (PSI), in Proceedings of the International Conference on Fifth Generation Computer Systems 1984, pp.398-409, ICOT, 1984

[Tanaka 86]   J. Tanaka, K. Ueda, T. Miyazaki, A. Takeuchi, Y. Matsumoto and K. Furukawa; Guarded Horn Clauses and Experiences with Parallel Logic Programming, in Proceedings. of FJCC '86, ACM, Dallas, Texas, pp.948-954, November 1986

[Tanaka 88]   J. Tanaka; Meta-interpreters and Reflective Operations in GHC, in Proceedings of of the International Conference on Fifth Generation Computer Systems 1988, pp.774-783, ICOT, November 1988

[Ueda 85]     K. Ueda; Guarded Horn Clauses, ICOT Technical Report, TR-103, 1985

[Watanabe 88] T. Watanabe and A. Yonezawa; Reflection in an Object-Oriented Concurrent Language, in Proceedings. of ACM Conference on OOPSLA, San Diego, September 1988

[Weyhrauch 80] R. Weyhrauch, Prolegomena to a Theory of Mechanized Formal Reasoning. In Artificial Intelligence 13, pp.133-170, 1980

# Implementation of Full GHC by Communicating Processes

Minoru TERADA

Department of Mathematical Engineering and Information Physics
Faculty of Engineering, University of Tokyo

### Abstract

In this paper an algorithm for interpreting the parallel logic language GHC (Guarded Horn Clauses) is described. The algorithm interprets full GHC programs using several communicating processes, which do not share data objects. To control unification and suspension, an integer (called commit value) is attached to each external references. An implementation of the algorithm on a concurrent lisp is also reported. This algorithm is applicable to conventional languages.

## 1 Introduction

In this paper an algorithm for interpreting the parallel logic language GHC (Guarded Horn Clauses)[1] is described, and an implementation of the algorithm on a concurrent lisp mUtilisp[2, 3] is reported.

In GHC, a clause is separated into the guard part and the body part by a commit operator. Several clauses start execution for a goal-literal, and only one of the clauses which succeeded to solve its guard part gains the right to affect the outer world (the environment belonging to the caller). This is the fundamental mechanism to achieve synchronization in GHC, and called commit mechanism. A clause which has not committed yet (not succeeded to solve its guard part) is not permitted to affect the caller's environment, and if the clause tries to instantiate an unbound variable belonging to the caller, it is suspended until the variable is instantiated by another clause.

There exists a subset of GHC, called Flat GHC (or FGHC), which allows only system-defined predicates (e.g., arithmetic comparison) on the guard part. The execution algorithm for GHC is quite different from that of FGHC, especially in unification. Because the overhead of GHC is certainly heavy compared to FGHC, FGHC is regarded to be enough for practice, and most implementations of GHC were those of FGHC[4, 5].

When we first consider the implementation of a parallel logic language by the interprocess communication, we found that full GHC can be implemented without much effort. So we decided to implement full GHC, and tried to found the basis for the comparison of their overheads.

Our algorithm has the following characteristics:

1. The execution of GHC program is divided into several processes, and their interaction (such as unification) is achieved by interprocess communication with messages;

2. The sharing of data between processes is inhibited as far as possible;

3. To control unification and suspension, an integer (called *commit value*) is attached to every external references;

4. The direction of external reference is constrained from child to parent.

In chapter 2, we describe the restriction for the language. The detail of the algorithm is described in chapter 3. In chapter 4, our implementation on mUtilisp is reported briefly. Various problems of the algorithm are discussed in chapter 5.

# 2 Language specification and restrictions

Our algorithm handles full GHC, and the following three data types are admitted: `integer`, `symbolic atom` and `list` (or `cons`).

We posed the following restrictions on the language:

1. The execution of a clause is separated into three distinct parts (head, guard and body) and they are not overlapped, although these parts could be executed in parallel according to the language specification. (Of course even the body part cannot affect the caller's environment until the clause commits.) This restriction is essential for our algorithm.

2. We support only list (cons) for structured data types. This restriction is not essential, and the addition of general compound-term is not so difficult to do.

# 3 Algorithm

## 3.1 Control

In our algorithm, programs are executed by communicating processes. To execute one goal-literal, several clauses that match the goal start execution in parallel (called *or-parallel*). And each goal-literal included in a clause is executed in parallel (called *and-parallel*). Corresponding to those two parallelisms, there are two types of process: OR and AND. Figure 1 illustrates a simple example of execution.

The followings are the control algorithm for OR and AND:

**OR** (argument: one goal-literal)

1. Collect clauses that match the argument. If no clause is found, go to step 6.

2. Fork AND as a child process for each clause collected in step 1.

3. Wait for reports of commitment from the children.

4a. If any child reports success, grant the child to commit, and tell other children to terminate.

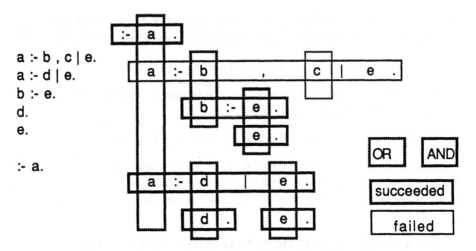

a :- b , c | e.
a :- d | e.
b :- e.
d.
e.

:- a.

Figure 1: Example of execution

4b. If all the children report failure, go to step 6.

5. Wait for the completion of the granted child, and report the result to the parent, and terminate.

6. (Failure) Report failure to the parent and terminate. □

**AND** (arguments: one goal-literal, one clause)

1. Unify the goal and the head of the clause.

2. Fork OR as a child process for each goal-literal in the guard part of the clause.

3. Wait for reports from the children.

4a. If any child reports failure, go to step 9.

4b. If all the children report success, report the success of guard to the parent.

5. Wait for the parent to grant the commitment.

6. If the parent grants the commitment, fork OR as a child process for each goal-literal in the body part of the clause.

7. Wait for reports from the children.

8a. If any child reports failure, go to step 9.

8b. If all the children report success, report success to the parent and terminate.

9. (Failure) Tell other children to terminate, report failure to the parent and terminate. □

Actually processes perform other works than described above. Those works are initiated by messages as follows:

*Instruction of termination* Whenever a process receives a message to terminate, it tells its children to terminate and kill itself.

*Inquiry of value of variables* and *instruction of unification* These messages are sent from a child (or any descendent), and the process should take appropriate action.

## 3.2 Value

### 3.2.1 Type of values

Variables and conses occurred in a clause belong to the AND process which is executing the clause. The process is responsible for the values of variables and the elements of conses. There exist 8 types of value in a cell (figure 2):

(1) Unbound

(2) Unified with another cell (left value)

    (2a) with a variable in the same process

    (2b) with a variable in another process

    (2c) with a car/cdr cell in the same process

    (2d) with a car/cdr cell in another process

(3) Already instantiated (right value)

    (3a) to a constant (integer, symbolic atom)

    (3b) to a cons in the same process

    (3c) to a cons in another process

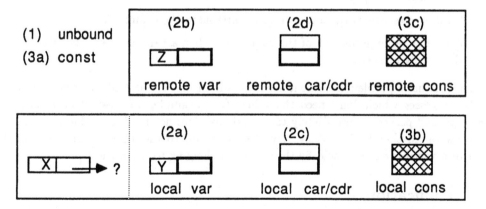

Figure 2: Type of values in a cell

### 3.2.2 Reference to another process

Pointers may refer objects in another process (as shown (2b), (2d) and (3c) in last section).

Such pointer (called *external reference*) is not implemented by direct pointer, in order to prevent object sharing between processes. Rather, it is represented by a record of the following four fields:

**type** The type of referred object, which is one of four types RVAR, RCAR, RCDR and RCONS.

**owner** The name of owner process

**id** The name of the variable or the serial number (within the owner process) of the cons.

**commit value** Explained in 3.3.2.

### 3.2.3 Direction of pointers

In our algorithm, the direction of external reference is constrained to be from-child-to-parent. To achieve this, we need some extra operation on unification (see 3.3.4 Copy-up of cons).

This restriction means that if a process has no child, there exists no external reference to the process. One of the consequences of this is that when a process is about to terminate, because the children of the process are all terminated, no object in the process is necessary any longer. So the entire workspace for the process can be freed, reducing the cost of garbage collection significantly.

### 3.2.4 Propagation of values

Unification of two unbound cells creates a directed link between cells. We call the series of such links *variable chain*. When a variable is instantiated (by getting unified to a constant or a cons), the value should be propagated through the variable chain in which the variable is included. There are several ways to do the propagation:

1. Broadcast to all processes;

2. Sending message to the owner of each variable in the chain;

3. Keep the value in one cell of the chain, and when a variable needs its value, access the cell by message.

The first has a problem because it needs broadcasting. The second may send a message to the processes which don't need the value. (For example, a clause which receives an argument and passes it immediately to the subgoal does not need the value.)

We adopted the third strategy. By the constraint to the direction of pointers, the value of a variable chain is held by the variable belonging to the highest process.

## 3.3 Unification

### 3.3.1 Difference between FGHC and GHC in unification

GHC and FGHC differ most in unification. See the following GHC program:

```
[p1]  a :- true | b(X), ...
[p2]  b(Y) :- c(Y) | ...
[p3]  c(Z) :- true | Z=3.
```

Now p3 is about to instantiate the variable Z, which is linked to the variable X of p1 via variable chain. Because p2 is not committed yet, this unification must be suspended.

This example means that the information necessary to determine the suspension is distributed among the hierarchy of processes. Neither the process trying the unification (p3) nor the owner of the variable (p1) can determine that by itself.

On the other hand, because FGHC does not allow user-defined predicate in the guard part, there is no child for not-committed process. So the suspension is fully determined by the state of the process trying the unification. That is, an attempt to instantiate an unbound external variable in the head or the guard part of a clause causes a suspension.

### 3.3.2  Commit Value

In order to determine whether a unification causes an instantiation or a suspension, any external reference (to cell or structure) maintains an integer, called a *commit value*. A commit value is the number of processes between the referring process and the referred process that have not committed yet. (The status of referred process is not counted while that of referring process is counted.)

In the example in 3.3.1, the variable Z of p3 refers X of p1. The commit value for this external reference is 1, because p2 has not committed yet. Y of p2 also refers X of p1, and its commit value is 1. In general, commit values that reference the same cell (or structure) may differ if referring processes differ.

The commit value makes it very easy to determine the suspension. In a unification, any instantiation of a cell which is designated by an external reference whose commit value is not zero must be suspended.

The cell may be designated by a chain of references, not a single direct reference (figure 3). In such cases, the commit value for the cell is the sum of the commit values of the references.

The commit value for a structure is provided to distribute it to the components. See the following example:

```
[p1]   a :- b(X) | ...
[p2]   b(Y) :- c([Y | nil]) | ...
[p3]   c(Z) :- Z = [A | B] | ...
```

The commit value for A of p3 (to X of p1) is 2 as shown in figure 4.

The calculation of commit value is simple:

1. When a process delivers a term to the child as an argument of the goal literal, unless the term is not atomic (i.e. not a number nor a symbol), the commit value for the term is incremented. If the term is local to the delivering process, it should be transformed into an external reference with commit value 1. (That is, the commit value for a local reference is 0 logically.)

2. When a process commits, it must decrement the commit values of all external references held by the process.

The separate execution of the guard and body (mentioned in chapter 2) plays crucial role for the calculation of the commit value. An intermediate process (a process waiting for its children to terminate) never changes its commit status while the execution of the

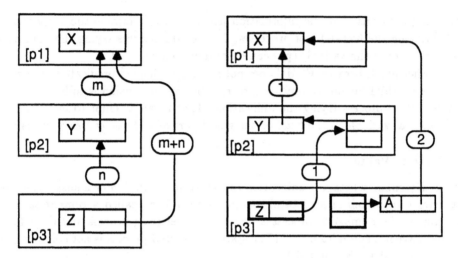

Figure 3: Chain of references          Figure 4: Chain through a cons

leaf children. So once a process has received an external reference, the commit value of the reference is valid until the process terminates.

And the restriction of the direction of external reference (in 3.2.3) is also very important for the algorithm. When a process is about to commit, the process has no children. So the commit values affected by the commitment are only those attached to the external references held by the process.

### 3.3.3  Examples of unification

Unification is divided into two stages:

*FETCHVAR* Acquire the actual value of one term

*UNIFY* Tell the other term to unify with the result of *FETCHVAR*

If any term includes external reference, those stages may need interprocess communication, which is implemented by remote procedure calls. The unifying process sends a message containing the name of the request (*FETCHVAR* or *UNIFY*) to the referred process, and waits for the reply. Receiving the request, the referred process examines the message and takes one of the following actions:

1. Send reply to the unifying process;

2. Forward the request to another process;

3. Queue the request and defer the reply.

In *FETCHVAR* stage, 1 or 2 may occur. If the reference is chained, the request is forwarded. In *UNIFY* stage, any of the three actions may occur. The reply is SUCCEED or FAIL.

Now the algorithm for unification is explained using examples.

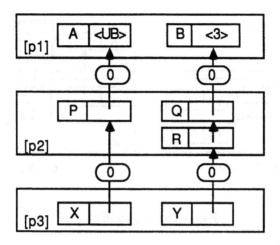

Figure 5: Relationship of variables in [**example 1**]

[**example 1**]  First an example without suspension is presented.

```
[p1]  a :- true | B = 3, b(A, B), ...
[p2]  b(P, Q) :- true | R = Q, c(P, R), ...
[p3]  c(X, Y) :- true | X = Y.
```

**p3** is trying to unify X with Y. (Figure 5 illustrates the relationship of variables.)

**stage 1**  (*FETCHVAR*) In order to acquire the value of X, p3 sends p2 a message. Because the reference is chained to A of p1, the message is forwarded to p1, and the final value ⟨A of p1, commit value is 0⟩ is returned to p3. Notice that the commit value is the sum of the commit values along the forwarding path.

**stage 2**  (*UNIFY*) p3 tries to unify Y with the result of stage 1, sending a message to p2. p2 relays the request to p1, in which the chain of reference ends. p1 is requested to unify the final value of Y ⟨constant 3⟩ with the final value of X ⟨A of p1, commit value is 0⟩. Because the commit value is 0, the variable is instantiated to the constant 3, and the reply of SUCCEED is returned to p3.

[**example 2**]  See how suspension occurs during unification. Suppose the p2 of the last example is not committed yet:

```
[p1]   a :- true | B = 3, b(A, B), ...
[p2']  b(P, Q) :- R = Q, c(P, R) | ...
[p3]   c(X, Y) :- true | X = Y.
```

**stage 1**  (*FETCHVAR*) The result p3 gets is ⟨A of p1, commit value is 1⟩, because the reference from P of p2' to A of p1 has commit value 1.

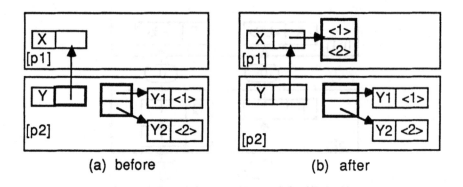

(a) before    (b) after

Figure 6: Copyup of a cons

**stage 2** (*UNIFY*) As in example 1, p1 is requested to unify A to constant 3. But because the commit value for A is not zero, this instantiation must be suspended. p1 stores the request into a queue attached to the variable A, and terminates the service for the message. So p3 cannot get any reply for its request, and keeps waiting for the reply. (This realizes the suspension.)

When the variable A is instantiated later, the queue is scanned and suspended unifications are continued. For example, if A is instantiated to constant 3, SUCCEED message is sent to p3 as a reply, and p3 completes unification. On the other hand, if A is bound to another variable V which belongs to an ancestor of p1, contents of the queue of A are transferred to the variable V, and wait for the instantiation of V.

### 3.3.4 Copy-up of cons

As mentioned in 3.2.3, all the external references must be from-child-to-parent. When a pointer is created as a result of unification, its direction must be considered carefully. In almost all cases this is easy because the direction of a link between two cells is determined by the level of the cells. But the only exception is the case when a cell is instantiated to a cons belonging to the lower process.

```
[p1]  a :- true | b(X).
[p2]  b(Y) :- Y1=1, Y2=2 | Y=[Y1 | Y2].
```

This program unifies the variable X of p1 and a cons of p2. (Those two terms are indicated by boldfaced rectangles in figure 6(a).) It is inhibited to make a pointer from X to the cons, because the pointer is from-parent-to-child. To solve the problem, a new cons whose fields are unbound is allocated in p1 as a value of X, and these two conses are unified in turn (figure 6(b)).

As a result, the cons of p2 was copied to p1, saving the data which will be necessary after the termination of the owner process (p2). That may be seen as a local garbage collection by copying.

```
(defun wait-for ((protocols))
   (cond ((msgq-lookup protocols))
         (t (do ((msg (receive)(receive)) (action))
                ((memq (protocol msg) protocols)
                 (exit msg))
                (setq action (get (protocol msg) 'g:protocol-action))
                (cond ((null action) (msgq-insert msg))
                      (t (funcall action msg)))))))))

(putprop 'TERMINATE (function terminate) 'g:protocol-action)
(putprop 'FETCHVAR (function fvd) 'g:protocol-action)
(putprop 'UNIFY (function ud) 'g:protocol-action)
```

Figure 7: Function wait-for

# 4 Implementation

A prototype for the algorithm is implemented on a concurrent lisp mUtilisp. mUtilisp is an extension of Utilisp[6] to include concurrent processing. It has the following characteristics:

1. Processes are created dynamically (by the function create-process);

2. Processes are not allowed to share lisp objects (such as symbols or lists);

3. Processes communicate by sending and receiving messages.

Any lisp object can be used as a message. But it is copied in order to avoid sharing.

Message is sent by the function send with an argument specifying the receiver process. No broadcast is available.

To receive a message, the function receive is used with an optional argument designating the sender. If there is no messages to receive, the calling process is blocked until a message arrives.

Our algorithm requires to receive only messages of specified types, such as the result of the guard part. And furthermore, the message for termination or unification must be received and processed at any time. Because the language does not support the selection of message by its contents, function wait-for was defined (figure 7). The function receives any message to the process, inspecting the type (called *protocol*) of the message. If a message of specified protocol arrives, the function returns it. If the protocol requires instant action (e.g., termination), the function internally calls the appropriate service routine.

The code contains about 700 lines in the form of lisp source. Although the current implementation lacks arithmetic operations and input-output predicates, it processes fundamental GHC programs. The sample session is shown in figure 8.

```
;------Example "union"--------------------------------
;
; mem(A,[A|R]) :- true | true.
; mem(A,[B|R]) :- A!=B | mem(A,R).
(putprop 'mem '(
   ((A (A . R)) ()         ())
   ((A (B . R)) ((!= A B)) ((mem A R)))) 'two)


; notmem(A,[]) :- true | true.
; notmem(A,[B|R]) :- A!=B | notmem(A,R).
(putprop 'notmem '(
   ((A ())       ()         ())
   ((A (B . R)) ((!= A B)) ((notmem A R)))) 'two)


; union([],X,Y) :- true | X=Y.
; union([H|T],X,Y) :- mem(H,X) | union(T,X,Y).
; union([H|T],X,Y) :- notmem(H,X) | union(T,X,Y2),Y=[H|Y2].
(putprop 'union '(
   ((() X Y)       ()         ((= X Y)))
   (((H . T) X Y) ((mem H X)) ((union T X Y)))
   (((H . T) X Y) ((notmem H X)) ((union T X Y2)(= Y (H . Y2))))
   ) 'three)


> (g:top '((union (1 2) (3 2) Y)))
"or0" (union (rcons "and" 1 1) (rcons "and" 3 1) (rvar "and" Y 1))
"and00" (union (rcons "and" 1 1) (rcons "and" 3 1) (rvar "and" Y 1))
"and01" (union (rcons "and" 1 1) (rcons "and" 3 1) (rvar "and" Y 1))
"and02" (union (rcons "and" 1 1) (rcons "and" 3 1) (rvar "and" Y 1))
"or010" (mem (rcar "and" 1 2) (rcons "and" 3 2))
"or020" (notmem (rcar "and" 1 2) (rcons "and" 3 2))
....(62 lines)....
"or021" SUCCEED
"and02" SUCCEED
"or0" SUCCEED
((union (lcons ? ? 1 nil nil) (lcons ? ? 3 nil nil) (lvar ? Y nil)))
> result-vars
((Y (1 3 2)))
```

Figure 8: Sample session

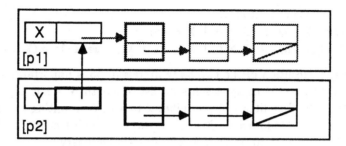

Figure 9: Copyup of multiple conses

# 5 Discussion

## 5.1 Maintenance of Commit Values

As mentioned in 3.3.2, when a clause commits it must decrement all commit values held by the clause. There will be two ways to implement that:

1. Actually decrement all commit values scanning all external references;

2. Only set a flag at the time of commitment, but after that when an external reference is sent to another process its commit value is decremented 'on demand'.

The former seems to be too naive, but it is not so bad because external references at the time of commitment are usually only those given by the parent as the arguments of the goal.

On the other hand, the overhead of the latter will be heavy because there may exist many requests of FETCHVAR or UNIFY from child processes.

(Certainly pathological cases exist; the following program is one of such cases.

```
[p1]   a :- b([1, 2, 3, ...]).
[p2]   b(X) :- c(X, Y) | ...
[p3]   c(L, A) :- L = [] | A = [].
[p4]   c(L, A) :- L = [H | T] | A = [L | A1], c(T, A1).
```

When p2 commits, its variable Y holds a list which is composed from the list of p1. Each cons in the list contains an external reference to the cons cell of p1. Notice that although X of p2 points the list of p1, it causes only a single external reference.)

## 5.2 Overhead of Copy-up conses

Although the explanation of copy-up in 3.3.4 is focused to single cons, several conses may have to get copied up if the first cons includes a reference to another cons belonging to a lower process (figure 9). Those conses are necessary for the upper process into which they are copied, so the copy-up is inevitable anyway.

But in some situation, unnecessary intermediate copy-up may occur. See the following example:

```
[p1]   a :- make_list(X, 100).
[p2]   make_list(X, N) :- N = 0 | X = nil.
[p3]   make_list(X, N) :- N > 0 | X = [N | X1], make_list(X1, N-1).
```

The order of the execution of the two body literals in p3 is important. If the second literal (make_list(X1, N-1)) completes first, a list of length $N - 1$ is copied up to the process. After that the first literal of p3 unifies X to a cons, resulting a copy-up of the cons. But the copy-up is followed by $N - 1$ copy-ups of the list cells already copied to the process. Thus, in this situation $O(N^2)$ copy-ups are necessary.

On the other hand, if the first literal (X = [N | X1]) completes first, the result of the second literal (a list of length $N - 1$) is copied up directly to p1, the target process. In this situation, only $O(N)$ copy-ups are necessary.

Probably this problem should be solved as a matter of programming style. One of the remedy for that is to execute unifications (e.g., the first literal) prior to other literals.

## 5.3 Optimization

The current version of the algorithm lacks optimizations. One of the most necessary optimizations is the tail recursion optimization, or more generally the tail call optimization.

It saves the number of processes by not forking a subprocess for the last goal-literal of a clause. The parent process itself executes the literal. But in our algorithm it is not easy to implement this because even for the last literal there may be several clauses to be executed in parallel (OR parallelism).

One of the solutions is to merge the child process for the last literal when it is about to commit, because at the commitment only one child process can survive. The rest of its clause (i.e. body part) is sent to the parent along with its local variables and conses. Several problems are left such as the conflict of variable names, the overhead of process merging.

## 5.4 Deadlock

Various program errors are often detected as a deadlock in GHC, so its detection is necessary for a practical implementation. Although current implementation lacks the detection, it will be not so hard to implement it.

Because the suspension of the process is implemented using the blocking by receiving messages, the process never becomes runnable again until the suspension is released. So if there exists no runnable process, it is considered that a deadlock has occurred.

If the suspension were implemented by busy wait (the suspended process itself examines the variable periodically), more complex method would be necessary.

## 5.5 Possibility of implementation

Although the prototype implementation was on a lisp, it is possible to use other languages. Because the algorithm does not need garbage collection, it may be implemented on a conventional language if it supports multiprocessing and basic communication. For example, the multiprocess package on the unix C language[7] can be used for that.

It will be a good property for multiprocessors that no data is shared between processes. But the implementation on multiprocessors is not investigated yet.

# 6 Conclusions

An algorithm for interpreting full GHC program is presented, and a prototype implementation of the algorithm on a concurrent lisp is reported.

The algorithm can be implemented on conventional languages, and has features suitable for multiprocessors.

# Acknowledgements

The author would like to thank Professor Eiiti Wada for giving us the opportunity to do this work and Dr. Hideya Iwasaki, Mr. Tetsuro Tanaka and Mr. Koichi Konishi for their helpful discussions and useful advices.

# References

[1] K. Ueda: Guarded Horn Clauses, Logic Programming '85, E. Wada (ed.), Lecture Notes in Computer Science 221, Springer-verlag (1986).

[2] H. Iwasaki: Programming and Implementation of a Multi-processing Lisp (in Japanese), Trans. IPS Japan, Vol. 28 No. 5 (1987).

[3] H. Iwasaki: mUtilisp Manual, METR 88-11, Department of Mathematical Engeneering and Information Physics, Faculty of Engeneering, University of Tokyo (1988).

[4] T. Miyazaki and K. Taki: Flat GHC Implementation on Multi-PSI (in Japanese), The Login Programming Conference '86 (1986).

[5] K. Fujimura, M. Kurihara and I. Kaji: An Implementation of GHC compiler on the LISP Systems (in Japanese), Trans. IPS Japan, Vol. 28 No. 7 (1987).

[6] T. Chikayama: Implementation of the Utilisp System (in Japanese), Trans. IPS Japan, Vol. 24 No. 5 (1983).

[7] Y. Tada and M. Terada: Primitives for Testing Environment of Concurrent Processes (in Japanese), IPS Japan WGOS, No. 33-2 (1986).

[8] M. Terada, H. Iwasaki, T. Tanaka, K. Konishi, K. Shirakawa and E. Wada: Implementation of GHC on the concurrent lisp (in Japanese), IPS Japan WGSYM, No. 44-3 (1988).

# Inference Methods and Semantics
# on Or-type Knowledge Bases

Hiroshi SAKAI

Information Science Center, Kyushu Institute of Technology

680, Kawazu, Iizuka, Fukuoka 820, Japan

## ABSTRACT

Or-type knowledge is information which has some disjunctive conclusions, for example, $(A \lor B) \leftarrow C$. We often face with this type of knowledge in our everyday lives. There are several problems to deal with such type of knowledge in computer systems. In general, it is difficult to represent the or-type knowledge in Horn logic. In this paper, we extend first order formulas and define the interpretations for them in a three valued logic. According to the discussion, a Horn clause is also extended so as to deal with the or-type knowledge. We show a fixpoint theorem, the soundness and completeness of a resolution.

## 1. Introduction

Let us consider the following example in order to clarify the problem of or-type knowledge. In reality, the following rule1 is not a Horn clause, and this kind of knowledge are rarely dealt with in the usual logic programming.

( rule1 )  place(X, kitakyushu_city)$\lor$place(X, iizuka_city) :- staff(X, kit)

( rule2 )  address(X, fukuoka) :- place(X, fukuoka_city)$\lor$

place(X, kitakyushu_city)$\lor$place(X, iizuka_city)

( fact1 )  staff(taro, kit)

First rule means that if a person is on the staff of KIT ( Kyushu Institute of Technology ), the place of his employment is in either Kitakyushu City or Iizuka City. We call this kinds of knowledge or-type knowledge. The second rule means that if the place of his employment is in Fukuoka City or Kitakyushu City or Iizuka City, his address is in Fukuoka Prefecture. The fact1 means Taro is on the staff of KIT.

First we consider an aspect of logical semantics of our problem. In the above example,

( fact2 )　place(taro, kitakyushu_city)$\lor$place(taro, iizuka_city)

is logically true by the rule1 and the fact1, and

( fact3 )　address(taro, fukuoka)

is also logically true by the rule2 and the fact2.

Now consider the aspect of the formal inference on the same example. We can formally infer fact2 by the rule1 and the fact1. However, neither

place(taro, kitakyushu_city)

nor

place(taro, iizuka_city)

can formally be inferred. In this case, using the *closed world assumption (CWA)* [1] would lead to a contradiction. Furthermore, in most logic programming languages, the rule2 means that one of the following clauses holds:

address(X, fukuoka) :- place(X, fukuoka_city)

address(X, fukuoka) :- place(X, kitakyushu_city)

address(X, fukuoka) :- place(X, iizuka_city)

Hence, formally fact3 can not be inferred. Some logically true facts can not be formally inferred in this example. The logically true fact3 can not be proved by using the *SLD-resolution* [2] , either.

The importance of the or-type knowledge and the hardness of handling it have been pointed out in [3]. Loveland [4] has also studied the related problems, but has not discussed the semantics of his system. Lloyd [5] has studied a system which allows any first order formula in the body of program clauses. However, he has not discussed the head of the program clause. Incomplete information has also been studied in [6,7,8], but these discussions are based on relational database theory, and the incompleteness of facts is only dealt with. We deal with not only the incompleteness of facts but also the incompleteness of rules. In this paper, we study and develop a system in which or-type knowledge can easily be represented, and discuss semantics of the system.

## 2. Declarative Semantics of Or-type Knowledge Bases

In this section, we extend first order formulas, and give the interpretations for the formulas. According to the extended formulas, an or-type knowledge base is formally defined in Section 2.3.

### 2.1. Extended Formulas and Their Interpretations

**DEFINITION 1.** An *alphabet* consists of the following classes of symbols:

(1) *variables*

(2) *constants*

(3) *predicates*

(4) *connectives* : "$\vee$", "$\wedge$", "$\neg$", "$\leftarrow$" and "$\leftrightarrow$"

(5) *quantifiers* : $\forall$ ( the universal quantifier ) and $\exists$ ( the existential quantifier )

(6) *punctuation symbols* : "(", ")", ". " and ","

In this paper, we do not consider function symbols for simplicity, so a term is a variable or a constant.

**DEFINITION 2.** If $p$ is an $n$-ary predicate symbol and $t_1,...,t_n$ are terms, then $p(t_1,\cdots,t_n)$ is called an *atomic formula* ( or an *atom* ). An atom that contains no variables is called a *ground atom*.

Now, we introduce a set of formulas called elementary formulas.

**DEFINITION 3.** An *elementary formula* is defined inductively as follows:

(1) An atom is an elementary formula.

(2) If $P_1,\cdots,P_m$ are distinct finite atoms, then $P_1;P_2;\cdots;P_m$ is an elementary formula.

We denote the set of all elementary formulas by *EF*, and call an elementary formula which does not contain variables a *ground elementary formula*. The set of all atoms which are used to construct an elementary formula $P$ is denoted by $Atom(P)$. For example,

$$Atom(P_1;P_2;\cdots;P_m)=\{P_1,P_2,\cdots,P_m\}.$$

Intuitively a ground elementary formula $P$ is *True* if at least one element of $Atom(P)$ is *True*; however it is sometimes impossible to decide which specific elements of $Atom(P)$ are *True*.

We extend formulas by the elementary formulas.

**DEFINITION 4.** An *extended formula* is defined inductively as follows:

(1) An elementary formula is an extended formula.

(2) If $P$ and $Q$ are extended formulas, then so are $(\neg P)$, $(P \wedge Q)$, $(P \vee Q)$, $(P \rightarrow Q)$, $(P \leftrightarrow Q)$.

(3) If $P$ is an extended formula and $x$ is a variable of $P$, then $(\forall xP)$ and $(\exists xP)$ are extended formulas.

First order formula is a special extended formula, and in the rest of this paper we use a "formula" instead of "extended formula". A formula which does not contain free variables is called a *closed formula*. A formula with free variables is assumed to be universally quantified, and thus we always consider only closed formulas.

We define an interpretation for ground elementary formulas, and give the interpretations for formulas.

**DEFINITION 5.** For any domain $D$ and a set of elementary formulas $EF$,

$Base(D)=\{Q \mid Q$ is a ground elementary formula constructed by
substituting an element of $D$ for any argument of an
elementary formula $P(\in EF)\}$.

**DEFINITION 6.** For any domain $D$, a mapping from $Base(D)$ to $\{T(\text{true}), F(\text{false}), \perp(\text{undefined})\}$ is called a *relation* on the $Base(D)$.

**PROPOSITION 1.** An assignment $\zeta_I$, which depends on $I$ ( $\in 2^{Base(D)}$ ) and satisfies the following conditions, is a relation on the $Base(D)$.

(1) $\zeta_I(P) = T$ ( $P \in I$ )

(2) $\zeta_I(P) = T$ ( $Atom(Q) \subseteq Atom(P)$ for some $Q( \in I )$ )

(3) $\zeta_I(P) = F$ ( $P$ is a ground atom, and $P \notin Atom(Q)$ for any $Q( \in I )$ )

(4) $\zeta_I(P) = F$ ( $\zeta_I(R) = F$ for any ground atom $R( \in Atom(P) )$ )

(5) $\zeta_I(P) = \perp$ ( $Atom(P) \subseteq Atom(Q)$ for some $Q( \in I )$ and $Atom(R) \not\subseteq Atom(P)$ for any
$R( \in I )$ )

(6) $\zeta_I(P) = \perp$ ( otherwise )

[Sketch of Proof] For any $P( \in Base(D) )$, there are two cases to be considered.

(1) There exists $Q( \in I )$ such that $Atom(P) \cap Atom(Q) \neq \varnothing$.

(2) There exists no $Q( \in I )$ such that $Atom(P) \cap Atom(Q) \neq \varnothing$. ∎

According to this proposition, we define interpretations for ground elementary formulas.

**DEFINITION 7.** An *interpretation for ground elementary formulas M* is a quadruple

$$M = \, <D, F, I, \zeta_I>,$$

where

$D$ is a domain,

$F$ is an assignment from a constant to an element of $D$,

$I$ is a subset of $Base(D)$,

$\zeta_I$ is a relation defined in Proposition 1.

Since a relation $\zeta_I$ is uniquely defined by $I$, from now on we identify $I$ with $\zeta_I$.

**DEFINITION 8.** Let $M$ be an interpretation for ground elementary formulas. For the relation $I$ in $M$, $Ker(I)$ is as follows:

$$Ker(I) = \{ A \in I \,|\, \text{there is no } B( \in I ) \text{ s.t. } Atom(B) \subset Atom(A) \}$$

$Ker(M)$ is also defined as follows:

$$Ker(M) = \, < D, F, Ker(I), \zeta_{Ker(I)} >$$

By Proposition 1 and $Ker$ operation,

$$\{ A \in Base(D) \,|\, A \text{ is assigned } T \text{ by the relation } Ker(I) \}$$

$$=\{A \in Base(D) \mid A \text{ is assigned } T \text{ by the relation } I\}$$

holds. Therefore, we call $Ker(I)$ non-redundant relation with respect to the assignment value true, and call $Ker(M)$ non-redundant interpretation.

**EXAMPLE 1.** For simplicity, take propositional variables $g_1$, $g_2$ and $g_3$, and any domain $D$. In this case,

$$Base(D) = \{g_1, g_2, g_3, g_1;g_2, g_2;g_3, g_3;g_1, g_1;g_2;g_3\}.$$

Let a relation $I$ be $\{g_1, g_1;g_2\}$, then

$$Ker(I) = \{g_1\}, \quad \zeta_I(g_1) = \zeta_I(g_1;g_2) = \zeta_I(g_1;g_3) = \zeta_I(g_1;g_2;g_3) = T,$$

$$\zeta_I(g_3) = F, \quad \zeta_I(g_2) = \zeta_I(g_2;g_3) = \perp.$$

**DEFINITION 9.** A mapping $\rho$ is defined by the following tables and equations:

| $\neg P$ | |
|---|---|
| $T$ | $F$ |
| $F$ | $T$ |
| $\perp$ | $\perp$ |

| $P \wedge Q$ | $T$ | $F$ | $\perp$ |
|---|---|---|---|
| $T$ | $T$ | $F$ | $\perp$ |
| $F$ | $F$ | $F$ | $F$ |
| $\perp$ | $\perp$ | $F$ | $\perp$ |

| $P \vee Q$ | $T$ | $F$ | $\perp$ |
|---|---|---|---|
| $T$ | $T$ | $T$ | $T$ |
| $F$ | $T$ | $F$ | $\perp$ |
| $\perp$ | $T$ | $\perp$ | $\perp$ |

| $P \rightarrow Q$ | $T$ | $F$ | $\perp$ |
|---|---|---|---|
| $T$ | $T$ | $F$ | $\perp$ |
| $F$ | $T$ | $T$ | $T$ |
| $\perp$ | $T$ | $\perp$ | $\perp$ |

| $P \leftrightarrow Q$ | $T$ | $F$ | $\perp$ |
|---|---|---|---|
| $T$ | $T$ | $F$ | $\perp$ |
| $F$ | $F$ | $T$ | $\perp$ |
| $\perp$ | $\perp$ | $\perp$ | $\perp$ |

$$\forall x P(x) = \bigwedge_{d \in D} P(d), \quad \exists x P(x) = \bigvee_{d \in D} P(d).$$

In the above tables, the first lines mean the truth values of $Q$ and, the first columns mean the truth values of $P$.

The logic defined by the above truth table is generally called *Kleene's three valued logic* [9].

**DEFINITION 10.** An *interpretation for formulas $N$* is a quintuple

$$N = <D, F, I, \zeta_I, \rho>,$$

where $D, F, I$ and $\zeta_I$ are the same definitions as in the interpretation $M$, and $\rho$ is the mapping in Definition 9.

From now on, we also use "interpretation" for "interpretation for formulas". *Ker* operation for an interpretation $N$ is the same as in Definition 8. We show a proposition for the subsequent discussion.

**PROPOSITION 2.** By $A = B$ we denote that $A$ and $B$ have the same truth table. The following relations hold:

(1) $(P \leftarrow Q) = (\neg P \vee Q)$

(2) $(\neg(P \vee Q)) = (\neg P \wedge \neg Q)$

(3) $(\neg(P \wedge Q)) = (\neg P \vee \neg Q)$

(4) $((P \vee Q) \wedge R) = ((P \wedge R) \vee (Q \wedge R))$

(5) $((P \wedge Q) \vee R) = ((P \vee R) \wedge (Q \vee R))$

## 2.2. Model Theory of Extended Formulas

In this section, we discuss the model theory of formulas.

**DEFINITION 11.** Let $P$ be a closed formula.

(1) An interpretation which assigns $T$ to the formula $P$ is called a *positive model* of $P$.

(2) An interpretation which assigns $F$ to the formula $P$ is called a *negative model* of $P$.

(3) An interpretation which assigns $\perp$ to the formula $P$ is called an *incomplete model* of $P$.

For any formula $P$ and any interpretation $N$, if the relation $I$ in $N$ does not have enough information to interpret $P$, then the interpretation $N$ becomes an incomplete model for formula $P$.

**EXAMPLE 2.** Under the same conditions as in Example 1, put a formula $P = g_1 ; g_2$. Then, $P$ is a closed formula. An interpretation with a relation $\{ g_1 ; g_2 ; g_3 \}$ is an incomplete model of $P$. An interpretation with a relation $\{ g_1 \}$ or $\{ g_1, g_3 \}$ is a positive model of $P$.

**DEFINITION 12.** Let $S$ be a finite set of closed formulas.

(1) An interpretation which assigns $T$ for any formula in $S$ is called a *positive*

*model* of *S*.

(2) An interpretation which assigns *F* for some formulas in *S* is called a *negative model* of *S*.

(3) Another interpretation, except (1) and (2), is called an *incomplete model* of *S*.

**PROPOSITION 3.** Let *S* be a finite set of closed formulas.

(1) An interpretation *N* is a positive model if and only if *N* is a positive model of $\wedge_{P \in S} P$.

(2) An interpretation *N* is a negative model if and only if *N* is a negative model of $\wedge_{P \in S} P$.

(3) An interpretation *N* is an incomplete model if and only if *N* is an incomplete model of $\wedge_{P \in S} P$.

**DEFINITION 13.** Let *S* be a finite set of closed formulas.

(1) We say *S* is *satisfiable* if there exists a positive model of *S*, especially we say *S* is *valid* if there is no negative model of *S*.

(2) We say *S* is *unsatisfiable,* if there is no positive model of *S*.

**EXAMPLE 3.** Under the same conditions as in Example 1, let a formula *P* be $(g_1 \vee \neg g_1)$. *P* is a closed formula. Any interpretation which assigns *T* or *F* to the propositional variable $g_1$ is a positive model of *P*. An interpretation which assigns $\perp$ to $g_1$ is an incomplete model of *P*, but there exists no negative model of *P*. Namely, *P* is valid.

Now we define two types of logical consequences.

**DEFINITION 14.** Let *S* be a finite set of closed formula and *P* be any closed formula.

(1) We say *P* is a $\square$-*logical consequence* of *S* if, any positive model for *S* is also a positive model for *P*.

(2) We say *P* is a $\diamond$-*logical consequence* of *S* if, there exists a positive model for *S* and *P*.

The definition of a $\square$-logical consequence is the same as that normal logical consequence. The $\square$-logical consequence defines some formulas which strictly hold under the or-type knowledge. The $\Diamond$-logical consequence defines some formulas, which may be true in some cases.

$\{P\,|\,P$ is a $\Box$-logical consequence of $S\,\}\subseteq\{P\,|\,P$ is a $\Diamond$-logical consequence of $S\,\}$

is obvious from the definition.

**EXAMPLE 4.** Under the same conditions as in Example 1, let $S$ be $\{g_1;g_2\}$. Then,

$\{P\,|\,P$ is a $\Box$-logical consequence of $S\,\}=\{g_1;g_2,\ g_1;g_2;g_3\}$,

$\{P\,|\,P$ is a $\Diamond$-logical consequence of $S\,\}=\{g_1,\ g_2,\ g_1;g_2,\ g_1;g_3,\ g_2;g_3,\ g_1;g_2;g_3\}$.

Now we discuss interpretations with a fixed domain and a fixed assignment for constants.

**DEFINITION 15.** Let $N$ and $N'$ be interpretations which have the same domain and the same assignment for constants. Let $I$ and $I'$ be relations in $N$ and $N'$, respectively. $N'$ is called an *extended interpretation* of $N$ and denoted by $N'\leqq N$ if the following two conditions are satisfied.

(1) For any $P'(\in I')$, there exists $P(\in I)$ s.t. $(\varnothing\neq)Atom(P')\subseteq Atom(P)$.

(2) For any $P(\in I)$, there exists $P'(\in I')$ s.t. $(\varnothing\neq)Atom(P')\subseteq Atom(P)$.

Intuitively the knowledge in $N'$ is more detailed than that in $N$.

**DEFINITION 16.** Suppose $N$ and $N'$ are two interpretations with the same domain and the same assignment for constants. Let $I$ and $I'$ be a relation in $N$ and $N'$, respectively. We say $N'$ is *included* by $N$ if $I'\subseteq I$ holds, and denote it by $N'\subseteq N$.

**EXAMPLE 5.** Under the same conditions as in Example 1, take four interpretations $N_1, N_2, N_3, N_4$ with the following relations, respectively,

$$I_1=\{g_1\},\ I_2=\{g_1,g_3\},\ I_3=\{g_1;g_2,g_2;g_3\},\ I_4=\{g_1;g_2;g_3\}.$$

Then,

$$N_1\leqq N_4,\ N_2\leqq N_3\leqq N_4 \text{ and } N_1\subseteq N_2$$

hold, but

$$N_1\leqq N_2,\ N_2\subseteq N_1 \text{ and } N_2\subseteq N_3$$

do not hold.

**PROPOSITION 4.** Let $S$ be a finite set of closed formulas.

(1) If $N$ is a positive model of $S$, then any extended interpretation of $N$ is a positive model of $S$.

(2) If $N$ is a negative model of $S$, then any extended interpretation of $N$ is a negative model of $S$.

[Sketch of Proof] By Proposition 2, any closed formulas can equivalently be transformed to a disjunctive normal form.  ∎

According to Proposition 4, it is convenient to deal with a set of positive models which have more incomplete relations.

**DEFINITION 17.** Let $S$ be a set of closed formulas, $D$ be a domain and $F$ be an assignment for constants. We define a *Maximum model Maxm(S,D,F)* and a *Maximum relation Maxr(S,D,F)* as follows:

$Maxm(S,D,F) = \{ Ker(N) \mid Ker(N)$ is a positive model of $S$ on $D$ with

the assignment $F$, and there is no positive model $Ker(N')$

$(\neq Ker(N))$ for $S$ such that $Ker(N) \leq Ker(N') \}$.

$Maxr(S,D,F) = \{ I \in 2^{Base(D)} \mid I$ is a relation of a positive model in $Maxm(S,D,F) \}$.

**PROPOSITION 5.** Let $P$ be a closed formula, $D$ be a domain and $F$ be an assignment for constants. Then the following two propositions are equivalent.

(1) Any element in $Maxm(S,D,F)$ assigns $T$ to a closed formula $P$.

(2) Any positive model $N(= <D, F, I, \zeta_I, \rho>)$ for $S$ assigns $T$ to a closed formula $P$.

[Proof] Trivial by Proposition 4 and Definition 17.  ∎

We have only to consider the set $Maxm(S,D,F)$ for the decision of a $\square$-logical consequence by Proposition 5 and Definition 14.


## 2.3. Semantics of Or-type Knowledge Bases

Now we discuss a class of closed formulas.

**DEFINITION 18.** *Or-type knowledge base* is a finite set of closed formulas made by substituting an elementary formula for an atom in Horn clauses.

Clearly, a set of Horn clauses is an or-type knowledge base. The following incomplete knowledge can be represented in the or-type knowledge base as $C \leftarrow A_1; A_2; A_3, B_1; B_2; B_3$.

If at least one element of $A_1$, $A_2$ and $A_3$ hold, and

if at least one element of $B_1$, $B_2$ and $B_3$ hold, then $C$ holds.

**PROPOSITION 6.** Let $S$ be an or-type knowledge base and suppose $S$ has a positive model. Then $S$ has a positive model with the Herbrand universe $U_S$ as its domain and an assignment $F$ for constants which assigns any constant to itself.

[Proof] Let $N$ be a positive model of $S$ and $I$ be its relation, and let

$$\Gamma = \{ A \in Base(U_S) \mid A \text{ is assigned } T \text{ with respect to } I \}.$$

An interpretation $N(= < U_S, F, \Gamma, \zeta_I, \rho >)$ is clearly a positive model. ∎

According to this proposition, we define an interpretations for an or-type knowledge base.

**DEFINITION 19.** An *interpretation $N$ for an or-type knowledge base $S$* is a quintuple

$$N = < U_S, F, I, \zeta_I, \rho >,$$

where

$U_S$ is the Herbrand universe of $S$,

$F$ is a constant assignment which assigns any constant to itself,

$I$, $\zeta_I$, $\rho$ are the same as in Definition 10.

**PROPOSITION 7.** Let $S$ be an or-type knowledge base, and

$$N = < U_S, F, I, \zeta_I, \rho >$$

be an interpretation for $S$. Then, an interpretation with a relation

$$\bigcap_{I \in Maxr(S, U_s, F)} I$$

is a non-redundant positive model of $S$.

We denote the relation($= \bigcap_{I \in Maxr(S, U_s, F)} I$) by $R_S$, and say the interpretation $N_S(= < U_S, F, R_S, \zeta_{R_S}, \rho >)$ *a least positive model* of $S$.

Now we show the relation between $R_S$ and the $\square$-logical consequence.

**THEOREM 8.** Let $S$ be an or-type knowledge base. Then

$$R_S = Ker(\{ A \in Base(U_S) \mid A \text{ is a } \square\text{-logical consequence of } S \}).$$

[Proof]

$A \in Ker(\{A \in Base(U_S) \mid A$ is a $\Box$-logical consequence of $S\})$

$\Leftrightarrow$ $A$ is assigned $T$ by any relation $I \in Maxr(S, U_S, F)$. ( by Proposition 5 )

$\Leftrightarrow$ there exists $Q(\in I)$ s.t. $Atom(Q) \subseteq Atom(A)$ for any $I \in Maxr(S, U_S, F)$.

$\Leftrightarrow$ there exists $Q(\in I)$ s.t. $Atom(Q) = Atom(A)$ for any $I \in Maxr(S, U_S, F)$.

( by $Ker$ operation )

Therefore, $A = Q \in I$ for any $Maxr(S, U_S, F)$. ∎

We define two mappings.

**DEFINITION 20.** Let $S$ be an or-type knowledge base, and $U_S$ be a Herbrand universe of $S$. We define two mappings $\Box T_S$ and $\Diamond T_S$ from $2^{Base(U_S)}$ to $2^{Base(U_S)}$ as follows:

(1) $\Box T_S(I) = \{A \in Base(U_S) \mid$

    (a) $A \leftarrow P_1, P_2, \cdots, P_n$ is a ground instance [2] of a formula in $S$,

    (b) For any $P_i (1 \leq i \leq n)$, there exists $Q(\in I)$ s.t. $Atom(Q) \subseteq Atom(P_i)$,

    (c) For any $R(\in I)$, $Atom(R) \not\subseteq Atom(A)\}$.

(2) $\Diamond T_S(I) = \{A \in Base(U_S) \mid$

    (a) $A \leftarrow P_1, P_2, \cdots, P_n$ is a ground instance of a formula in $S$,

    (b) For any $P_i (1 \leq i \leq n)$, there exists $Q(\in I)$ s.t. $Atom(Q) \cap Atom(P_i) \neq \emptyset$,

    (c) For any $R(\in I)$, $Atom(R) \not\subseteq Atom(A)\}$.

**PROPOSITION 9.** Two mappings $\Box T_S$ and $\Diamond T_S$ are continuous, and there exist least fixpoints of them. Furthermore,

$$lfp(\Box T_S) = \Box T_S \uparrow \omega,$$

$$lfp(\Diamond T_S) = \Diamond T_S \uparrow \omega,$$

$$lfp(\Box T_S) \subseteq lfp(\Diamond T_S)$$

hold.

[ Proof ] Similar to Proposition 5.1 in [2]. ∎

**PROPOSITION 10.** Let $S$ be an or-type knowledge base. An interpretation $N(= <U_S, F, I, \zeta_I, \rho>)$ for $S$ satisfies $I \in Maxr(S, U_S, F)$ if and only if $\Box T_S(I) \subseteq I$.

[Proof] Similar to Proposition 6.4 in [2]. ∎

We show that $N_S$ is characterized by the least fixpoint of $\Box T_S$.

**THEOREM 11.** Let $S$ be an or-type knowledge base, and $U_S$ be a Herbrand universe of $S$.

(1) $R_S$

$= Ker(\{A \in Base(U_S) \mid A$ is a $\Box$-logical consequence of $S\})$

$= lfp(\Box T_S)$

$= \Box T_S \uparrow \omega.$

(2) $\{A \in Base(U_S) \mid A$ is assigned $T$ by the relation $lfp(\Diamond T_S)\}$

$= \{A \in Base(U_S) \mid A$ is assigned $T$ by the relation $\Diamond T_S \uparrow \omega\}$

$\subseteq \{A \in Base(U_S) \mid A$ is a $\Diamond$-logical consequence of $S\}$

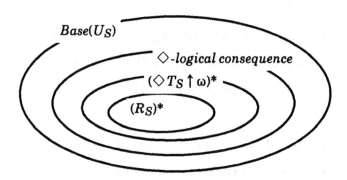

**Fig.1** Relationship between rules.

In Fig. 1, $(R_S)^*$ and $(\Diamond T_S \uparrow \omega)^*$ imply the ground elementary formula assigned $T$ by the relation $R_S$, and $\Diamond T_S \uparrow \omega$, respectively.

[Proof]

(1) By Theorem 8,

$$R_S = Ker(\{A \in Base(U_S) \mid A \text{ is a } \Box\text{-logical consequence of } S\}).$$

Then, by Proposition 9,

$$lfp(\Box T_S) = \Box T_S \uparrow \omega, \quad lfp(\Diamond T_S) = \Diamond T_S \uparrow \omega, \quad lfp(\Box T_S) \subseteq lfp(\Diamond T_S)$$

$$R_S = \cap_{I \in Maxr(S,U_s,F)} I$$

$$= glb\{I \in 2^{Base(U_S)} \mid \Box T_S(I) \subseteq I\} \text{ (by Proposition 11)}$$

$= lfp(\Box T_S)$ ( by Proposition 5.1 in [2] ).

(2) is trivial. ∎

## 3. Procedural Semantics of Or-type Knowledge Bases

This section studies the procedural semantics of or-type knowledge bases. We omit some definitions, which depend on [2].

### 3.1. Two Resolutions

We discuss an aspect of proof theory of the or-type knowledge bases. First, we extend the *SLD*-resolution.

**DEFINITION 21.** Take a goal $G$ and a rule $C$,

$$G: \leftarrow P_1, P_2, \cdots, P_n,$$

$$C: Q \leftarrow R_1, R_2, \cdots, R_m,$$

and let $CR$ be a computation rule [2]. We define a $\Box$-*resolution* and a $\Diamond$-*resolution* as follows:

(1) If there exists a substitution $\theta$ which satisfies (a) and (b):

(a) $P_l$ is the selected atom given by the computation rule $CR$,

(b) $Atom(Q\theta) \subseteq Atom(P_l\theta)$,

then we derive a new goal $G'$

$$G': \leftarrow (P_1, \cdots, P_{l-1}, R_1, R_2, \cdots, R_m, P_{l+1}, \cdots, P_n)\theta.$$

$G'$ is a $\Box$-*resolvent* of $G$ and $C$. We say $\theta$ a $\Box$-*unifier*, and the condition (b) specifies a $\Box$-*unification*.

(2) If there exists a substitution $\theta$ which satisfies (a) and (b):

(a) $P_l$ is the selected atom given by the computation rule $CR$,

(b) $Atom(Q\theta) \cap Atom(P_l\theta) \neq \emptyset$,

then we derive a new goal $G'$

$$G': \leftarrow (P_1, \cdots, P_{l-1}, R_1, R_2, \cdots, R_m, P_{l+1}, \cdots, P_n)\theta.$$

$G'$ is a $\Diamond$-*resolvent* of $G$ and $C$. We say $\theta$ a $\Diamond$-*unifier*, and the condition (b) specifies a $\Diamond$-*unification*.

**DEFINITION 22.** Let $S$ be an or-type knowledge base, $G$ be a goal and $CR$ be a computation rule.

(1) A $\Box$-*refutation* of $S \cup \{G\}$ via $CR$ is a finite sequence of $\Box$-resolutions which has the empty clause as the last goal in the sequence.

(2) A $\Diamond$-*refutation* of $S \cup \{G\}$ via $CR$ is a finite sequence of $\Box$-resolutions or $\Diamond$-resolutions which has the empty clause as the last goal in the sequence and at least one $\Diamond$-resolution is in the sequence.

**DEFINITION 23.** Let $S$ be an or-type knowledge base, $U_S$ be the Herbrand universe.

(1) A $\Box$-*success set* is the set of all ground elementary formula $A$ in $Base(U_S)$ such that $S \cup \{\leftarrow A\}$ has a $\Box$-refutation.

(2) A $\Diamond$-*success set* is the set of all ground elementary formula $A$ in $Base(U_S)$ such that $S \cup \{\leftarrow A\}$ has a $\Diamond$-refutation.

## 3.2. Soundness of the $\Box$-resolution

We show the soundness of the $\Box$-resolution in this section.

**THEOREM 12.** Let $S$ be an or-type knowledge base, and a goal $G$ be

$$G: \leftarrow P_1, P_2, \cdots, P_m.$$

If there exists a $\Box$-refutation for $S \cup \{G\}$ via a computation rule $CR$, and $\theta$ is the composition of all $\Box$-unifiers, then $\forall ((P_1, P_2, \cdots, P_m)\theta)$ is a $\Box$-logical consequence of $S$.

[Proof] The result is proved by induction on the length of the $\Box$-refutation.

[Base step]

In this case, $G$ is a goal of the form $\leftarrow P_1$, and there exists $Q(\in S)$ and substitution $\theta$ such that $Atom(Q\theta) \subseteq Atom(P_1\theta)$. Since $Q\theta$ is an instance of a unit clause of $S$, $\forall (P_1\theta)$ is a $\Box$-logical consequence of $S$.

[Induction step]

Suppose that $G: \leftarrow P_1, P_2, \cdots, P_m$ has a $\Box$-refutation of length $k$, and $\theta_1, \cdots, \theta_k$ are substitutions. Since $G$ has a $\Box$-refutation, there exists a rule $C$,

$$C: Q \leftarrow R_1, R_2, \cdots, R_l,$$

and a selected atom $P_i$ which satisfies $Atom(Q\theta_k) \subseteq Atom(P_i\theta_k)$. By the induction hypothesis,

$$\forall((P_1,\cdots,P_{i-1},R_1,\cdots,R_l,P_{i+1},\cdots,P_m)\theta_1,\cdots,\theta_k)$$

is a $\square$-logical consequence of $S$. Therefore,

$$\forall((R_1,\cdots,R_l)\theta_1,\cdots,\theta_k)$$

is a $\square$-logical consequence of $S$. Consequently, $\forall(Q\theta_1,\cdots,\theta_k)$ and $\forall(P_i\theta_1,\cdots,\theta_k)$ are $\square$-logical consequence of $S$. Hence, $\forall((P_1,P_2,\cdots,P_m)\theta_1,\cdots,\theta_k)$ is a $\square$-logical consequence of $S$. ∎

**COROLLARY 13.** Let $S$ be an or-type knowledge base. Then

$\square$-success set of $S \subseteq \{A \in Base(U_S) \mid A$ is a $\square$-logical consequence of $S\}$.

[Proof] Take any $A \in (\square$-success set of $S$ ). By the definition of success set, $S \cup \{\leftarrow A\}$ has a $\square$-refutation with respect to some computation rule. Since $A$ is an element of $Base(U_S)$, $A(=\forall A)$ is a $\square$-logical consequence of $S$. ∎

## 3.3. Completeness of the $\square$-resolution

We show the completeness of the $\square$-resolution.

**THEOREM 14.** $Ker(\square$-success set of $S$ ) $= R_S$.

[Proof] By Theorem 11, $R_S = \square T_S \uparrow \omega$. By induction on the length, we show that if $A \in \square T_S \uparrow n$, then $S \cup \{\leftarrow A\}$ has a $\square$-refutation. If it is proved, the following relation holds,

$Ker(\{A \in Base(U_S) \mid A$ is a $\square$-logical consequence of $S\})$

$= R_S$　( by Theorem 8 )

$= \square T_S \uparrow \omega$　( by Theorem 11 )

$\subseteq \square$-success set of $S$.

By the definition of the $\square$-refutation, for any element $B$ in $\{A \in Base(U_S) \mid A$ is a $\square$-logical consequence $\}$, there exists an element $A$ in $Ker(\{A \in Base(U_S) \mid A$ is a $\square$-logical consequence $\})$, which satisfies

$$Atom(A) \subseteq Atom(B).$$

If the ground elementary formulas $A$ has a $\square$-refutation, then the ground elementary formula $B$ also has a $\square$-refutation. Namely,

$\{A \in Base(U_S) \mid A$ is a $\square$-logical consequence of $S\} \subseteq \square$-success set of $S$

holds. Hence by Corollary 13,

$\square$-success set of $S = \{A \in Base(U_S) \mid A$ is a $\square$-logical consequence of $S\}$.

By $Ker$ operation,

$Ker(\square$-success set of $S)$

$= Ker(\{A \in Base(U_S) \mid A$ is a $\square$-logical consequence of $S\})$

$= R_S$.

Now, we show the proof of "$A \in \square T_S \uparrow n$, then $S \cup \{\leftarrow A\}$ has a $\square$-refutation".

[Base step]

If $A \in \square T_S \uparrow 1$, then $A$ is a unit clause and $S \cup \{\leftarrow A\}$ has a $\square$-refutation.

[Induction step]

If $A \in \square T_S \uparrow k$, then there exist a rule $C : Q \leftarrow P_1, \cdots P_m$ which satisfies (a) and (b).

(a)  There exist a substitution $\theta$ such that $A = Q\theta$,

(b)  For each $i$ ( $1 \leq i \leq m$ ), there exists a ground elementary formula
$R_i\theta \in \square T_S \uparrow (k\text{-}1)$ such that $Atom(R_i\theta) \subseteq Atom(P_i\theta)$.

By the induction hypothesis, $S \cup \{\leftarrow P_i\theta\}$ has a $\square$-refutation for each $i$ ( $1 \leq i \leq m$ ). Therefore, $S \cup \{\leftarrow R_i\theta \mid Atom(R\theta) \subseteq Atom(P_i\theta)\}$ also has a $\square$-refutation, and $S \cup \{\leftarrow A\}$ has a $\square$-refutation.  ∎

**LEMMA 15.** Let $S$ be the or-type knowledge base, $A$ be an elementary formula. If $\forall(A)$ is a $\square$-logical consequence of $S$, then there exist a $\square$-refutation of $S \cup \{\leftarrow A\}$ with the identity substitution as the computed answer substitution.

[Proof] By Theorem 14 and Lemma 8.5 in [2].  ∎

**LEMMA 16.** Let $S$ be an or-type knowledge base, $G$ be a goal and $\theta$ be a substitution. If there exists a $\square$-refutation with respect to $S \cup \{G\theta\}$, then there exists a $\square$-refutation with respect to $S \cup \{G\}$.

[Proof] By Lemma 8.2 in [2].  ∎

**THEOREM 17.** Let $S$ be an or-type knowledge base, $G$ a goal and $\theta$ be a substitution. If $G\theta$ is a $\square$-logical consequence of $S$, then there exists a $\square$-refutation of $S\cup\{G\}$ via a computation rule $CR$.

[Proof] Let goal $G$ be $\leftarrow P_1,\cdots P_m$. Since $G\theta$ is a $\square$-logical consequence of $S$, $\forall((P_1,\cdots P_m)\theta)$ is a $\square$-logical consequence of $S$. Namely, $\forall((P_i)\theta)$ is a $\square$-logical consequence of $S$ for any $i(1\leq i\leq m)$. By Lemma 15, there exists a $\square$-refutation of $S\cup\{\leftarrow(P_i)\theta\}$ with the identity substitution as the computed answer substitution for any $i(1\leq i\leq m)$. By combining these $\square$-refutations of $S\cup\{\leftarrow(P_i)\theta\}(1\leq i\leq m)$, we can make a $\square$-refutation of $S\cup\{G\theta\}$ with the identity substitution. Lemma 16 shows there exists a $\square$-refutation of $S\cup\{G\}$. ∎

## 4. Discussion

In this paper, we gave a definition of a system, where or-type knowledge can easily be represented. We have introduced an interpretation of formulas in the three valued logic, and discussed the declarative semantics, fixpoint semantics and procedural semantics. Furthermore, we have shown the $\square$-logical consequence, $\square T_S \uparrow \omega$ and the $\square$-refutation characterize the same class of formula. We have also shown that the $\square$-resolution can be used as a $\square$-theorem prover in the or-type knowledge bases. However, there are some problems to be solved.

(1) unification algorithm

(2) properties of the $\diamondsuit$-resolution

(3) computation rule

(4) selection of input clause

## ACKNOWLEDGMENT

I am deeply grateful to Prof. Setsuo Arikawa of Kyushu University for his constant support and encouragement.

# REFERENCES

[1] R. Reiter : On Closed World Databases, In *Logic and Databases*, H. Gallaire
    Eds., 1979.

[2] J.W. Lloyd : *Foundation of Logic Programming*, Springer-Verlag, 1984.

[3] Tanaka and Katsuno : Ko-sui-jun Database (unpublished manuscript in
    Japanese ).

[4] D.W. Loveland : Near-Horn Prolog, Proc. 4th Int. Conf. on Logic Programming,
    1987.

[5] J.W. Lloyd and R.W. Toper : Making Prolog More Expressive, Journal of the
    Logic Programming vol.3, 1984.

[6] E.F. Codd : Extending the Database Relational Model to Capture More Meaning,
    ACM Transaction on Database Systems, vol.4, no.4, 1979.

[7] W. Lipski : On Semantic Issues Connected with Incomplete Information
    Databases, ACM Transaction on Database Systems, vol.4, no.3, 1979.

[8] W. Lipski : On Databases with Incomplete Information, Journal of the ACM,
    vol.28, no.1, 1981.

[9] R.Turner : *Logics for Artificial Intelligence*, Ellis Horwood, 1984.

## APPENDIX : Simple Realization of a □-prover in Prolog

The following program is the or-type knowledge base in introduction. We simply realized the following interpreter for the or-type knowledge base. We have used the unification algorithm in Prolog.

<u>Program</u>

```
or2(stay(X, kitakyu), stay(X, iizuka)) :- staff(X, kit).
address(X, fukuoka) :- or3(stay(X, fukuoka), stay(X, kitakyu), stay(X, iizuka)).
staff(taro, kit).
```

<u>Interpreter</u>

```
box(X) :- write('START BOX RESOLUTION!!'), nl, X, unique(b(X)),
write('FIND BOX REFUTATION!!').
```

box(X) :- write('END OF BOX RESOLUTION!!').

set :- retract(b(X)), fail.

set :- write('READY, PLEASE ENTER BOX QUERY!!').

unique(X) :- not(X), assert(X).

or2(X,Y) :- X;Y.

or3(X,Y,Z) :- or2(X,Y);or2(Y,X);or2(X,Z);or2(Z,X);or2(Y,Z);or2(Z,Y).

## xecution of Program by the Interpreter

| ?-set.

READY, PLEASE ENTER BOX QUERY!!

yes

| ?-box(live(X, fukuoka)).

START BOX RESOLUTION!!

FIND BOX REFUTATION!!

X = taro;

END OF BOX RESOLUTION!!

X = X;

no

| ?-set.

READY, PLEASE ENTER BOX QUERY!!

yes

| ?-box(or2(staff(X, kyushu), staff(X, kit))).

START BOX RESOLUTION!!

FIND BOX REFUTATION!!

X = taro;

END OF BOX RESOLUTION!!

X = X;

no

| ?-

# ACCESS PROGRAM TO MINIMIZE REDUNDANT REFUTATIONS ON THE NETWORK DATABASE SYSTEM

Makoto TAKIZAWA, Motoshi KATSUMATA, and Shinichi NAGAHORA

Dept.of Information and Systems Engineering

Tokyo Denki University

Ishizaka, Hatoyama-cho, Hiki-gun, Saitama 350-03, JAPAN

This paper presents how to generate access programs which get all answer substitutions from the network database without duplicate refutations from Prolog goal clauses and a Prolog view of the conventional network database system. We show an improvement of the Prolog refutation procedure by taking advantage of the network model. In our system, redundant refutations, which occur while finding all answer substitutions for given goals, are prevented in addition to preventing meaningless backtracking to find one refutation by intelligent backtracking. We show that our system is superior to the conventional Prolog system in performance.

## 1. INTRODUCTION

Information systems are composed of heterogeneous database systems interconnected by communication networks. Users want to manipulate these database systems independently of their heterogeneity and distribution[20]. Data structures and procedures can be defined recursively and uniformly in Prolog[6,16] while conventional database languages like SQL[9] cannot. Our distributed database system[20,21,22,23] provides users with common Prolog views on heterogeneous database systems. This view is named a fact base system (FBS) which provides a set of Prolog ground unit clauses, and operations for manipulating them. That is, users can manipulate heterogeneous database systems in Prolog as if they were fact base systems. How to provide Prolog views on the relational database systems[8] has been discussed in [4,13,25,etc.]. Also, the logical relation between Prolog systems and the network database systems have been discussed in [21,22]. [24] discusses how to find efficient access path to the relational database system and shows the way of translating Prolog goal clauses into relational set-at-a-time operations. In this paper, we discuss how to find efficient navigational, i.e. record-at-a-time, operations on the network database for Prolog goal clauses and discuss how to reduce the number of redundant answers and navigational accesses to N. Intelligent backtracking[3] aims at avoiding meaningless backtrackings to find a refutation. In this paper, we present a refutation procedure which reduces redundant refutations in addition to conventional intelligent back-tracking. Also, we show the evaluation by comparing our system and conventional Prolog system.

In Section 2, we present a Prolog view on the conventional network database system. In Section 3, we show problems in conventional Prolog refutation procedure. In section 4, we show how to compile a goal clause to an access procedure to the network database system. In section 5, we show the evaluation of our system.

## 2. PROLOG VIEWS ON NETWORK DATABASE SYSTEM

An abstract model of the conventional network model[7,19] is presented.

### 2.1 Network Data Structure

The network data structure is composed of entity (E) types and function (F) types. An E type is a totally ordered set of E tuples, each of which is identified by its identifier. Each E tuple is composed of attribute values. The E type corresponds to a record type, E tuple to a record occurrence, and identifier to a database (db) key in the conventional network model[7]. An F type S represents a partial function from an E type $E_1$ to $E_2$. Each element $<a,b>$ of S is an F tuple. For every b in $E_2$, a subset $R[b]$ of F tuples $<a,b>$ in R is totally ordered. The F type corresponds to a set type and $R[b]$ a set occurrence in [7]. Fig.1 shows an example of a network data structure on suppliers (s), parts (p), and parts-subparts relations (b).

Tuples in N are navigationally accessed according to the ordering by the data operations, which correspond to the conventional DML operations[19].

### 2.2 Prolog View of Network Database

A Prolog view D for the network database N is composed of a fact base (FB) and a rule base (RB). The FB is a collection of ground unit clauses, and the RB is a collection of rule clauses. There exists an (m+1)-ary predicate symbol A for each E type A which has m attributes $A_1,...,A_m$, a binary predicate symbol C for each F type C, and a constant symbol c for each value c in N. Each clause $A(@a,a_1,...,a_m)$ in the FB denotes an E tuple $<@a,a_1,...,a_m>$ with identifier @a and m attribute values $a_1,...,a_m$ in an E set A, and $C(@a,@b)$ denotes an F tuple $<<@a,...>,<@b,...>>$ in an F type C from an E type A to B. Fig.2 shows the FB for Fig.1. Here, constant symbols prefixed by @ denote the identifiers of E tuples. For example, a clause sp(@p1,@s1) denotes an F tuple $<<@p1,c>,<@s1,a>>$ in Fig.1.

(1) network schema <u>N</u>

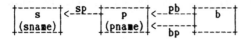

(2) network database N

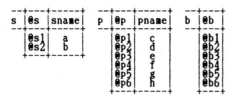

**Fig.1** Network Database

```
D ={s1) s(@s1,a).   s2) s(@s2,b).   p1) p(@p1,c).   p2) p(@p2,d).   p3) p(@p3,e).
    p4) p(@p4,f).   p5) p(@p5,g).   p6) p(@p6,h).   b1) b(@b1).   b2) b(@b2).
    b3) b(@b3).   b4) b(@b4).   b5) b(@b5).   b6) b(@b6).   sp1) sp(@p1,@s1).
    sp2) sp(@p2,@s1).   sp3) sp(@p3,@s1).   sp4) sp(@p4,@s1).   sp5) sp(@p5,@s2).
    sp6) sp(@p6,@s2).   pb1) pb(@b1,@p1).   bp1) bp(@b1,@p2).   pb2) pb(@b2,@p1).
    bp2) bp(@b2,@p3).   pb3) pb(@b3,@p2).   bp3) bp(@b3,@p5).   pb4) pb(@b4,@p3).
    bp4) bp(@b4,@p5).   pb5) pb(@b5,@p3).   bp5) bp(@b5,@p6).   pb6) pb(@b6,@p6).
    bp6) bp(@b6,@p5). }
```

**Fig.2.    Fact Base(FB) of Fig.1**

## 3.  PROBLEMS IN PROLOG REFUTATION PROCEDURE

Let $?-(B_1,...,B_m)\theta$ be a goal clause H where $\theta$ is a substitution. For an atom $B_j$ selected by a computation rule and an input clause $B:- A_1,...,A_k$ where there exists a unifier $\sigma$ such that $B_j\theta\sigma = B\sigma$, $?-(B_1,...,B_{j-1},A_1,...,A_k,B_{j+1},...,B_m)\theta\sigma$ is a resolvent [Fig.3]. This is an SLD resolution[2,16,17]. Variables which denote identifiers in the network database N are primary. Underlined atoms denote selected ones.

Let us consider a goal $G = ?-s(S,?X),p(P,Y),sp(P,S)$ for N, where X is a target variable, i.e. users want to get substitutions of X. Variables S and P are said to be primary since both denotes identifiers. Fig.4 shows an SLD tree[17] by the Prolog refutation procedure where atoms are selected from left to right in G. From Fig.2, there are two clauses of s in D, and six ones of p. Also, since sp denotes a function from p to s, there is at most one clause for a pair of s and p clauses. Atoms s(S,?X) and p(P,Y) share no variable. Hence, 2*6=12 deductions are done and 2+2*(6+6)=26 tuples are derived from N to obtain all refutations. Next, an SLD tree by another computation rule which selects atoms in an order, s, sp, p, is shown in Fig.5. Since for each s(@k,...), only clauses of sp(...,@k) can be accessed, totally six deductions are done, and 14 tuples are derived. Therefore, if atoms are selected based on the data structure, a search space to find refutations is reduced.

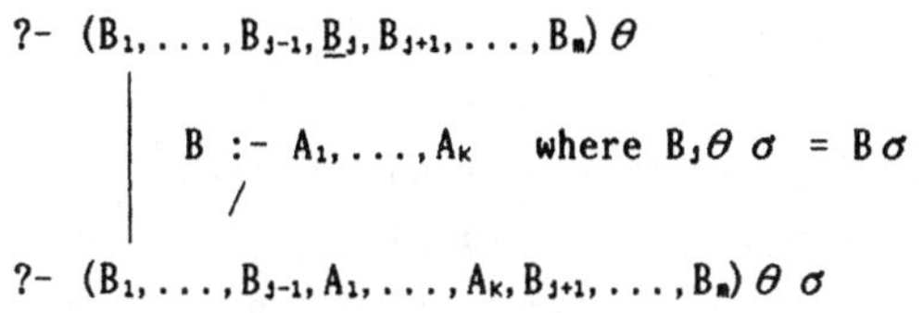

$$?- (B_1,\ldots,B_{J-1},\underline{B_J},B_{J+1},\ldots,B_n)\,\theta$$

$$B :- A_1,\ldots,A_k \quad \text{where } B_J\theta\,\sigma = B\sigma$$

$$?- (B_1,\ldots,B_{J-1},A_1,\ldots,A_k,B_{J+1},\ldots,B_n)\,\theta\,\sigma$$

**Fig.3.** SLD Resolution.

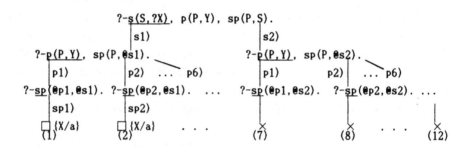

**Fig.4** SLD Tree by Prolog Procedure.

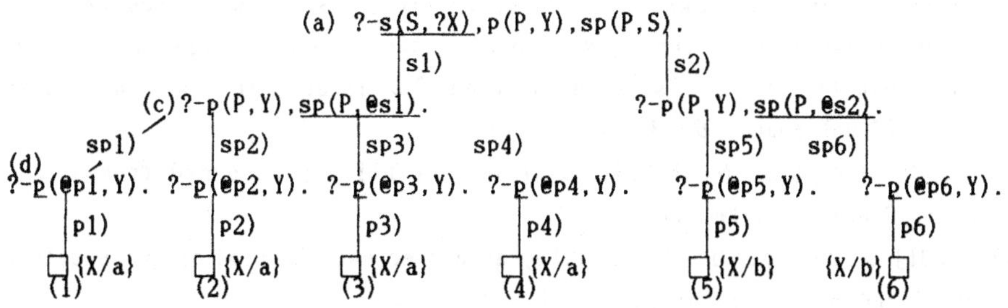

**Fig.5** SLD Tree by Another Procedure.

Refutations (1)~(4) in Fig.5 have the same answer substitutions {X/a}. Thus, if multiple refutations have the same answer substitutions, they are said to be redundant. (1)~(4) are redundant. In order to get a set of answer substitutions for target variables, it is meaningless to obtain the refutations (2)~(4) after (1) is obtained. Another substitution {X/b} can be obtained by backtracking from (d) to (a). In this paper, we try to prevent these redundant refutations.

## 4. ACCESS PROGRAM

We consider a program which derives all the answer substitutions for a goal clause G by navigationally accessing tuples in N.

### 4.1 Basic Behaviors of Cells

In this paper, we assume that every goal clause G contains no rule atoms. In our system, if G includes a rule R, R is replaced with the body of the rule clause unifiable with R. In this paper, recursive rules are not considered.

An access program for a goal clause G is composed of cells interconnected by one-way channels. Each cell C denotes an atom C in G. C is composed of an ordered set $D(C)$, i.e. E type or F type, in N, state variable $P(C)$, and two input ports, i.e. C:FS(FirSt) and C:NX(NeXt), and two output ports, i.e. C:SC(SuCcess) and C:FL (FaiLure). There are special cells named ST and OUT. Cells A and B are connected by a one-way channel A:O→B:I from an A's output port A:O to a B's input port B:I. Data unit named a token is transmitted through the channel. Cells behave as follows.

[Cell ST] (1) First, ST sends an identity substitution $\varepsilon$ as a token at ST:SC.
    (2) On receipt of a token at ST:NX, ST makes all cells terminate.
[Cell C] (1) On receipt of a token $\theta$ at C:FS, $D(C)$ is sequentially accessed based on its ordering relation. That is, record types and set types [7] are navigationally accessed in the conventional network database system. If a tuple t, such that $t\sigma = C\theta\sigma$, is found, a token $\theta\sigma$ is sent at C:SC and t is stored in $P(C)$. If not found, $\theta$ is sent at C:FL.
    (2) On receipt of $\theta$ at C:NX, $D(C)$ is sequentially accessed from a tuple t in $P(C)$. C behaves like (1).
[Cell OUT] On receipt of $\theta$ at OUT:FS, an answer substitution of $\theta$ is output to the user, and $\theta$ is sent at OUT:FL.□

In Fig.6, an access program for a goal   ?- p(P,?Y),pb(B,P),p(?PP,X),b(B),bp(B,?PP) is shown, which represents the Prolog refutation procedure. For example, if a tuple t unifiable with p(P,?Y) is derived from the E type p in N in the cell (1), the substitution $\theta$ such that $p(P,?Y)\theta = t$ is sent to (2) via (1):SC→(2):FS. If (4) fails, (4) sends a token to (3) via (3):FL→(2):NX. However, since substitutions obtained by (3) include no binding of the variable B in (4), backtracking from (4) to (3) is meaningless. Further, this program does not accesses N by making use of the data structure of N.

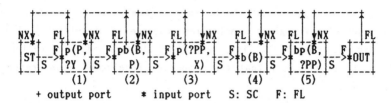

**Fig.6** Prolog Access Program.

Here, if C:FL→A:NX and C:SC→B:FS, let parent(C) and next(C) denote cells A and B, respectively. Also, let prior(A) denote C. parent(C) shows a cell to be backtracked from C and next(C) shows a next selected atom. In Fig.6, (3)= parent(4) and (3)= next(2). If a cell A has no cell B such that A = parent(B), A is said to be a leaf. (5) is a leaf in Fig.6.

## 4.2 Computation Rule Based on the Network Data Structure

First, we consider a computation rule which selects atoms according to the underlying data structure in N. Relationships among types in N are denoted by shared primary variables among the atoms which denote the types. For atoms A and B, and a substitution $\theta$, if $A\theta$ and $B\theta$ include the same variable X, A and B are said to share X on $\theta$.

Now, a computation rule SP for a goal clause G is given as follows. Here, cost($A\theta$) gives an expected number of tuples to be accessed to find an input clause whose head is unifiable with $A\theta$. It is defined later. A function vinst(A,$\theta$) returns $\theta\{X/c_X\}$ where X is an uninstantiated variable X in $A\theta$ and $c_X$ is an unused constant symbol.

**[Simple computation rule SP]** (0) Initially, A = C = NULL, $\theta_0 = \theta_X = \varepsilon$, and j = 0.
(1) Select an atom B whose cost($B\theta_0$) is the minimum in G. Go to (3).
(2) For a cell P = parent(A), select an atom B in G whose cost($B\theta_P$) is the minimum among ones which share variables with P on $\theta_P$.
(3) [B is found] Construct a cell B. If A = NULL, then make a channel B:FL→ST:NX, else B:FL→P:NX and C:SC→B:FS. C = B, $\theta_B$ = vinst(B,$\theta_A$), remove B from G, A = B, j = j+1, $\theta_j = \theta_{j-1}\theta_B$. Go to (2).
(4) [B is not found]
    4-1) If G is empty, make C:SC→OUT:FS and OUT:FL→ST:NX, and terminate.
    4-2) If parent(A) is not ST, A = parent(A) and go to (2).

4-3) If parent(A) = ST, then select an atom B whose cost($B\theta_j$) is the minimum. Make C:SC→B:FS and B:FL→A:NX. C = B, $\theta_B$ = vinst(B,$\theta_j$), A = B, and remove B from G. j = j+1, $\theta_j = \theta_{j-1}\theta_B$. Go to (2).□

A sequence of atoms obtained by the SP is represented by an ordered tree where depth-first order of cells gives a selection sequence of atoms[21,22]. Fig.7 shows the tree obtained by the SP for Fig.6, and Fig.8 shows a deduction by the SP. From Fig.7 and Fig.1, it is clear that the sequence of selected atoms represents an access path in N.

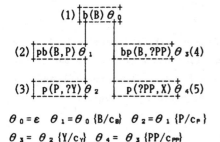

(1) $\boxed{b(B)\,\theta_0}$

(2) $\boxed{pb(B,P)\,\theta_1}$   $\boxed{bp(B,?PP)\,\theta_3}$(4)

(3) $\boxed{p(P,?Y)\,\theta_2}$   $\boxed{p(?PP,X)\,\theta_4}$(5)

$\theta_0 = \varepsilon$   $\theta_1 = \theta_0\,\{B/c_B\}$   $\theta_2 = \theta_1\,\{P/c_P\}$
$\theta_3 = \theta_2\,\{Y/c_Y\}$   $\theta_4 = \theta_3\,\{PP/c_{PP}\}$

**Fig.7** Navigational Tree.

?-(p(P,?Y),pb(B,P),b(B),bp(B,?PP),
   p(?PP,X))$\theta_0$
        $\mid$  b(...).
?-(p(P,?Y),pb(B,P),bp(B,?PP),p(?PP,X))$\theta_1$
        $\mid$  pb(...).
?-(p(P,?Y),bp(B,?PP),p(?PP,X))$\theta_2$
        $\mid$  p(...).
?-(bp(B,?PP),p(?PP,X))$\theta_3$
        $\mid$  bp(...).
?-p(?PP,X)$\theta_4$
        $\mid$  p(...).
   $\Box$   $\theta_5$     $\theta_5 = \theta_4\,\{X/c_X\}$

**Fig.8** Deduction by SP.

Fig.9 shows an access program obtained by the SP, which accesses navigationally tuples in N. Since a cell (1) is a parent of (4) in Fig.7, there exists a channel (4):FL→(1):NX. If (4) fails, (1) is resolved by our refutation procedure as shown in Fig.9 although (3) is resolved in the Prolog. Thus, our program not only accesses N by taking advantage of the access path supported by N but also prevents meaning-less backtrackings.

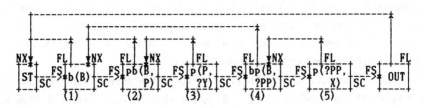

**Fig.9** Access Program.

A rightmost cell which includes target variables in the access program is said to be a target cell. In Fig.9, (4) is a target cell of a variable PP. There exists a function from (1) to (2). Hence, even if we backtrack from (3) to (2), (2) fails since for every clause unifiable with (1) there exists at most one clause unifiable with (2).

[Improvement] For a cell C, let B be parent(C) and A be parent(B). If there exists a function from a type denoted by A to a type denoted by B in the network database N, then remove C:FL→B:NX and add C:FL→A:NX.□

By the above improvement, an access program S as shown in Fig.10 is obtained.

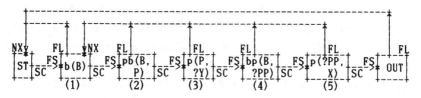

Fig.10 Improved Access Program S.

## 4.3 Reduction of Redundant Refutations

Next, we try to get all answer substitutions without redundant refutations. Although the access program S in Fig.10 can find a refutation without meaningless backtrackings by taking advantage of the underlying data structure, all the answer substitutions cannot be obtained. After one refutation is found, the same backtrackings as the Prolog program are required, which are denoted by edges +++> as shown in Fig.11.

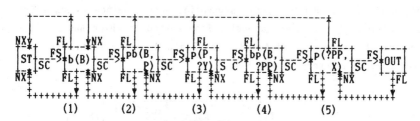

Fig.11 Access Program with Prolog backtrackings.

An access program T is considered to be a sequence of cells $\langle ST, C_1, \ldots, C_m, OUT \rangle$ where $C_{j+1} = next(C_j)$ for $j=1,\ldots,m-1$. For example, S in Fig.10 is $\langle ST,b,pb,p,bp,p,OUT \rangle$. Let root(T) be $C_1$ and last(T) be $C_m$. $C_j$ is said to be greater than $C_h$, written as $C_h <_T C_j$, iff j>h. A cell B is a descendent of a cell A in T if A= parent(B) or parent(B) is a descendent of A. tail(A) is an A's descendent B if there exists no A's descendent C such that B $<_T$ C. Let a subtree of A, Sub(A), be a substring $\langle A,A_1,\ldots,A_n \rangle$ of T where $A_n=$ tail(A). According to the definition of the SP, it is clear that Sub(A) includes only and all descendants of A. The following notations are introduced.

ltarg(A)= a greatest target cell B where B $<_T$ A.

rtarg(A)= a least target cell B where A $<_T$ B.

join(A,B)= a least common ancestor of A and B.

njoin(A,B)= an ancestor D of A such that join(A,B) = parent(D).

rjoin(A)= njoin(rtarg(A),A).

ljoin(A)= njoin(A,ltarg(A)).

In Fig.11, join(3,4) = 1, njoin(3,4) = 3, rjoin(2) = 3, ljoin(5)= 5, rtarg(3) = 4, and tlast(T) = 4.

For a cell A in T, suppose that there are n cells $B_1,...,B_n$ where A = parent($B_j$) for j=1,...,n. Let $T_j$ be Sub($B_j$). Suppose that a substitution $\theta_A$ is obtained by the resolution of A. Let Ans($B_j$) be a set of refutations obtained from $T_j\theta_A$. According to the property of T, any two $T_j\theta_A$ and $T_k\theta_A$ have no common uninstantiated variable. This means that Ans($B_j$) can be obtained independently of other $T_k(k\neq j)$. In the Prolog program, for each $A\theta_A$, a cartesian product $CA_A$ = Ans($B_1$) x...x Ans($B_n$) is obtained. Here, let $T_{MK}$ be a subtree which includes targets in $T_1,...,T_n$ (k=1,...,P, p$\leq$n). In our method, only a projection of $CA_A$ on $T_{m1},...,T_{mp}$, i.e. $AA_A$= Ans($B_{m1}$) x...x Ans($B_{mp}$) is accessed. Since it is clear that $|CA_A| \geq |AA_A|$, we can get all the answer substitutions in less accesses to N than the Prolog program.

In one method to get $CA_A$, each Ans($B_j$) is stored in the intermediate storage and then the cartesian product is taken by accessing them. If Ans($B_j$) is so small to be stored in a main memory, the cartesian product can be efficiently taken. In a case of database, since Ans($B_j$) is too large to be stored in the main memory, it has to be stored in the files. However, only sequential access method is supported on the intermediate files. So, we adopt a nested-loop method in which Ans($B_1$) is obtained in the outermost loop,..., and Ans($B_n$) is obtained in the innermost loop, where tuples are accessed in every loop.

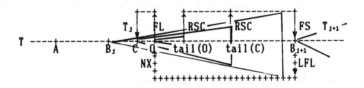

Fig.12  Access Program

Suppose that the resolution of $B_{j+1}$ fails in the deduction, i.e. all answer substitutions in Ans($B_{j+1}$) are already obtained, and that $T_j$ includes a target cell O [Fig.12]. By backtracking from $B_{j+1}$ to O, resolutions for Sub(O) are executed. When the resolution of tail(O) succeeds, a new answer substitution for Sub($B_j$) is obtained. Now, resolutions are forwarded to $B_{j+1}$ from tail(O). Here, Ans($B_j$) is obtained again by resolutions for $T_{j+1}$. If O fails, we backtrack to C = parent(O) and resolutions of Sub(C) are done. On success of the resolution of tail(C), $T_{j+1}$ is resolved by forwarding to $B_{j+1}$. By this program, $AA_R$ can be obtained instead of $CA_R$. Here, for every cell C in $T_j$, rjoin(C) is $B_{j+1}$ and ltarg($B_{j+1}$) is O. To represent the backtracking from $B_{j+1}$ to O and the forwarding from cells in $T_j$ to $B_{j+1}$, new output ports LFL and RSC are introduced. The backtracking and forwarding are denoted by channels $B_{j+1}$:LFL→O:NX and tail(O):RSC→$B_{j+1}$:FS, respectively.

We show a general computation rule GP for reducing redundant refutations by adding these new channels.

[General Computation Rule GP] GP is obtained by modifying SP as follows.
(1) Remove OUT:FL→ST:NX, and add  OUT:FL→tlast(T):NX.
(2) For each cell A, if for some C, A = rjoin(C), then add A:LFL and A:LFL→ltarg(A):NX.
(3) For each leaf A, if Sub(ljoin(A)) includes a target cell, then add A:RSC, and A:RSC→rjoin(A):FS if rjoin(A) exists, A:RSC→OUT:FS otherwise.□

A general access program is one generated by the GP. Fig.13 shows a general access program T for Fig.10. Since tlast(T) is (4), OUT:SC→(4):NX. Since (4) = nrjoin(3,4), (4):LFL→(3):NX and (3):RSC→(4):FS.

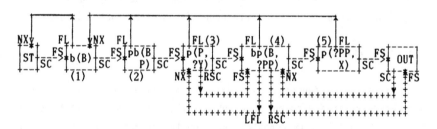

**Fig.13  General Access Program.**

Two kinds of tokens have to be distinguished, one for finding the first refutation and one for finding all answer substitutions. A token is a 4-tuple <Type, Begin, End, Substitution>, where Type indicates a kind of token, i.e. F shows the first type and N the second type, Begin and End indicate a subtree <Begin,...,End> in T. First, Begin = root(T) and End = last(T). When a token t is sent via A:LFL→B:NX, t's Begin is B and End is C = tail(B). After resolutions of Sub(B), a token has to be sent from C via C:RSC→A:FS. On success of resolution of C, C decides at which port SC or RSC a token is sent. If End is C, it is sent at RSC, otherwise at SC. Each cell behaves as follows.

[Cell ST] (1) First, ST sends a token $<F, root(T), last(T), \varepsilon>$ at ST:SC.

(2) On receipt of a token at ST:NX, ST makes all cells terminate.

[Cell A] (1) On receipt of $<N, B, E, \theta>$ at A:FS or A:NX, if B = E = _, let B be A and E be tail(A). If $A <_T B$, let B be A and E be tail(A).

(2) D(A) is accessed as the same as SP. If an unifiable tuple t in D(A) with $A\theta$ is obtained, where $A\theta\sigma = t\sigma$,

(2-1) If E = A, then $<N, \_, \_, \theta\sigma>$ is sent at A:RSC.

(2-2) If $B \leq_T A <_T E$, $<N, B, E, \theta\sigma>$ is sent at A:SC.

(3) If no unifiable tuple is obtained,

(3-1) If $B <_T A \leq_T E$, then $<N, B, E, \theta>$ is sent at A:FL.

(3-2) If A=B and rjoin(C)=A, then $<N, \_, \_, \theta>$ is sent at A:FL.

(3-3) Otherwise, $<N, \_, \_, \theta>$ is sent at A:FL.

[Cell OUT] On receipt of $<\ldots, \theta>$ at OUT:FS, an answer substitution from $\theta$ is output and $<N, \_, \_, \theta>$ is sent at OUT:FL. □

[Proposition] By the GP, all answer substitutions for a goal G are obtained by less redundant refutations than the Prolog refutation procedure.

[Proof] Let T be a general access program for G. Suppose that for a cell A in T, there are n cells $B_j$ such that A = parent($B_j$) in T (j=1,...,n). Let $T_j$ be a subtree sub($B_j$). Let O be a subset $\{O_1, \ldots, O_m\} \subseteq \{B_1, \ldots, B_n\}$ where Sub($O_k$) includes target cells(k=1,...,m). Suppose that $T_j\theta_A$ includes $N_{Bj}$ refutations. In the Prolog system, N = $N_{B1} * \ldots * N_{Bn}$ refutations are required to get all answer substitutions of Sub(A)$\theta_A$. On the other hand, in T, since only one refutation is obtained for $T_j\theta_A$ where $B_j$ is not in O, M = $N_{O1} * \ldots * N_{Om}$ refutations are done. It is clear that M is less than N. ∎

### 4.4 Access Cost

Let us consider the cost functions cost($A\theta$) for a cell A and a substitution $\theta$. Let $O_A$ be an ordered set in N denoted by A and $\sigma_A$ be the probability that each tuple in $O_A$ is unifiable with A. $\sigma_A$ is computed based on the selectivities[14] of attributes in the set. Let $FS_A$ be the expected number of tuples which are accessed in $O_A$ to get all unifiable tuples with A. $FS_A$ depends on the access path supported by $O_A$. If $O_A$ has no access path, $FS_A$ is $|O_A|$. If the j-th attribute of $O_A$ has an access path and it is instantiated in A, $FS_A$ is $\sigma_{Aj} * |O_A|$ where $\sigma_{Aj}$ is the selectivity of the j-th attribute.

For two cells A and B, the connectivity $CN_{AB}$ from A to B is the average number of tuples accessed in $O_B$ to find tuples by which common uninstantiated variables of A and B are instantiated. If B denotes an F type and A is its range, $CN_{AB}$ is an average number of tuples $<r, p>$ for each tuple p. In the conventional network model, the connectivity[20] represents an average number of member record occurrences for each owner record occurrence and a probability that each member has an owner in a set type [7]. Now, we consider the cost of a general access program T.

First, let S be a subtree of a cell A where A = parent($B_j$) (j=1,...,n) in T. Let $S_j$ be Sub($B_j$). Let $C_s$ be an expected number of tuples accessed in order to obtain all the answers for each tuple in A, and $S_s$ be an expected number of answers for S. $C_s$ is given by $(N_s + F_s) \sigma_A + 1$. $N_s$ and $F_s$ are the expected numbers of tuples accessed for subtrees $T_j$ which contain target cells and none, respectively.

$F_s = \sum_{j=1,...,n} FCC_{ABj} * C_{sj}$.

$FCC_{ABj} = CN_{ABj} / (1 + CN_{ABj} * \sigma_{Bj})$ if $T_j$ includes no target cells, 0 otherwise.

$FCC_{ABj}$ is an expected number of tuples in $B_j$ to find one tuple which satisfies the condition of $B_j$.

$N_s = NCC_{AB1} * C_{s1} + SS_{s1} * ( NCC_{AB2} * C_{s2} + SS_{s2} * ( NCC_{AB3} * C_{s3} + ... + SS_{sn-1} * ( NCC_{ABn} * C_{sn}) ...))$

$NCC_{ABj} = CN_{ABj}$ if $S_j$ includes target cells, 0 otherwise.

$SS_{sj} = S_{sj}$ if $S_j$ includes target cells, 1 otherwise.

The expected number $S_s$ of answers is given as follows.

$S_s = \sigma_A * \prod_{j=1,...,n} ACC_{ABj} * SS_{sj}$

$ACC_{ABj} = CN_{ABj}$ if $S_j$ includes target cells, 1 otherwise.

As a result, an expected number $CT_T$ of tuples accessed for T in order to obtain all the answers is as follows.

$CT_T = FS_{root(T)} * CT_T$.

The total cost $COST_T$ is a weighted summation of $CT_T$ and $S_T$.

$COST_T = WC * COST_T + WS * S_T$.

For a goal G, it is difficult to compute $C_T$ and $S_T$ for every possible access program T. So, we use the heuristics based on following access functions. Here, suppose that for an atom A there are n atoms $B_j$ which share common variable with A (j=1,...,n) on $\theta$. Two cost functions are considered.

$cost_1(B_j, \theta) = CN_{ABj}$

$cost_2(B_j, \theta) = CN_{ABj} * (1 + \sigma_{Bj} * \Gamma(a,b))$

Here, $\Gamma(a,b) = a * (1 - b^{n-1}) / (1 - b)$, $a = \sum_{k=1,...,j-1,j+1,...,n} CN_{ABk} / (n-1)$, and $b = \sum_{k=1,...,j-1,j+1,...,n} \sigma_{Bk} / (n-1)$. In $cost_1$, cells are selected among the nearest neighbor cells. In $cost_2$, the effect of resolution of $T_j$ to other $T_k$ is taken account to.

## 5. EVALUATION

Our system named LIP (Logic Interface Processor on database system) has been already implemented in UTI-Lisp[5] on M-380Q, whose fact base and rule base are implemented by the relational database management system AIM/RDB[1][Fig.14]. Since a network database system AIM/DB cannot be used in our university, a network database simulator is implemented as a Fortran application program of AIM/RDB. Fig.15 shows a network database used by the evaluation.

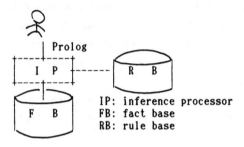

IP: inference processor
FB: fact base
RB: rule base

**Fig.14    LIP**

+----------+ T1 +-------------+ Ls +---------+ Ss +----------+ Sp +-------------+
|T(eacher) +--->|L(aboratory) |<---+St(udent) |<---+Sb(place) +--->|P(refecture) |
+----------+    +-------------+    +---------+    +----------+    +-------------+

**Fig.15   Network Database**

For goal clauses, the following points are measured.
    icount = the number of tuples accessed.
    tcount = the number of tuples output as answer substitutions.
    ctime  = time for generating an access program T[msec].
    atime  = execution time of T[msec].
    etime  = ctime + etime.
We evaluate the LIP in order to make clear (1) how many meaningless backtrackings are reduced and (2) how good access path is selected by our computation rule GP. In (1), we measure both the LIP and the Prolog program for the same goal clauses whose atoms are sequenced as selected by the GP.

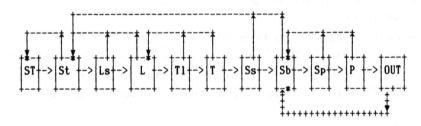

**Fig.16   Access Program**

For a goal G = ?-St(S,_),Ls(S,L),L(L,_),T1(T,L),T(T,_),Ss(SB,S),Sb(SB,?SNAME),

Sp(P,SB),P(P,_), a general access program T as shown in Fig.16 is generated. Results of execution of Prolog program and T are shown in Table 1. From this table, icount and tcount in our method are less than Prolog. This means that our method can decrease the number of backtrackings and redundant refutations. Our method needs an additional compilation time. In our system, a large amount of data are accessed. Problem is how to reduce the number of tuples accessed. Access time to the database dominates the total time. The compilation time, i.e. ctime, can be neglected compared with the access time, atime. Hence, even if the network data structure and goals are more complicated, our method can be applied.

Table 1  Result

|        | Our system | Prolog |
|--------|------------|--------|
| icount | 609        | 48333  |
| tcount | 88         | 880    |
| ctime  | 1321       |        |
| atime  | 34436      |        |
| etime  | 35757      | 171649 |

Table 2.

|   |        | GP1    | GP2    | Prolog |
|---|--------|--------|--------|--------|
|   | icount | 51     | 1623   | 5621   |
|   | tcount | 10     | 880    | 1060   |
| 1 | ctime  | 890    | 3894   |        |
|   | atime  | 9322   | 253169 |        |
|   | etime  | 10212  | 257063 | 178145 |
|   | icount | 2821   | 521    | 655    |
|   | tcount | 880    | 88     | 88     |
| 2 | ctime  | 892    | 1041   |        |
|   | atime  | 242366 | 83341  |        |
|   | etime  | 243258 | 84362  | 69665  |
|   | icount | 4581   | 4833   | 1710   |
|   | tcount | 880    | 880    | 880    |
| 3 | ctime  | 813    | 1117   | 3976   |
|   | atime  | 248689 | 499977 | 253776 |
|   | etime  | 249499 | 501094 | 257752 |

Next problem is which access path our system generates. In Table 2, $cost_1$ is used in GP1 and $cost_2$ in GP2. Prolog indicates that a goal clause written by an database expert is processed by the Prolog program. Table 2 shows that GP does not select always good access paths. An access program is composed of two parts, one for finding a refutation and the other for finding answer substitutions. The former aims at decreasing icount and the latter aims at decreasing tcount. Decreasing icount does not necessarily mean decreasing tcount. So, we think a method that if a large number of answer substitutions are retrieved, an access program is generated so as to minimize the number of answer substitutions, i.e. tcount, otherwise so as to minimize the number of tuples accessed, i.e. icount.

## 6. CONCLUDING REMARKS

In this paper, we present a Prolog interface on the conventional network database system. This system is now operational on M-380Q. Users can retrieve data from the network database system as if it were a Prolog system.

In our system, redundant refutations which give the same answer substitutions are prevented by accessing navigationally the network database without making intermediate files. Our method can not only be applied to the network database system but also the relational database system. The relational database system provides tuple-at-a-time interface like cursor [9] in addition to the non-procedural SQL interface. Our method can apply to the tuple-at-a-time interface. In another method, intermediate results are created. we think that it is difficult to efficiently access the intermediate files because they do not provide efficient access path other than a sequential access method.

Our system cannot necessarily generate an optimal access program. We are considering the method by taking usage of knowledge of database application experts on access paths. At present, we try to provide a transaction functions[23] which manipulate the network database system atomically.

**REFERENCES**

[1]  "FACOM OS IV/F4 MSP AIM/DB," Fujitsu.
[2]  Apt,R. and van Emden,M.H., "Contributions to the Theory of Logic Programming," JACM,Vol.29,No.3, 1982, pp.841-862.
[3]  Cambell,J.A., "Implementations of Prolog," Ellis horwood limited, 1982.
[4]  Chang,C.L., "On Evaluation of Queries Containing Derived Relations in a Relational Data Base," Logics & Database, Plenum Press, 1981.
[5]  Chikayama, "FACOM UTILISP Manual," Univ.of Tokyo.
[6]  Clocksin,W.F. and Mellish,C.S., "Programming in Prolog," Springer-Verlag, 1984.
[7]  CODASYL DDL Committee, "CODASYL Data Description Language," Journal of Development, 1973, 1978.
[8]  Codd,E.F., "A Relational Model of Data for Large Shared Data Bank," CACM, Vol.13,No.6, 1970, pp.337-387.
[9]  Date,C.J., "An Introduction to Database Systems," Addison-wesley, 1981.
[10] Dayal,U., et al., "Query Optimization for CODASYL Database Systems," Proc. of the ACM SIGMOD, 1982, pp.138-150.
[11] Enderton,H., "Mathematical Introduction to Logic," Academic Press, 1972.
[12] Gallaire,H., Minker,J., and Nicolas,J.M., "Logic and Database: A deductive Approach," ACM Computing Survey, vol.16, No.2, 1984, pp.153-185.
[13] Henschen,L.J. and Naqvi,S.A., "On Compiling Queries in Recursive First-order Databases," JACM, Vol.31, 1984, pp.47-107.

[14] Hevner,A. and Yao,S.B., "Query Processing on a Distributed Databases," Proc. of the 3rd Berkeley Workshop, 1978, pp.91-107.

[15] Kobayashi,I., "Classification and Transformations of Binary Relationship Schemata," Sunno Institute of Business Administration, 1985.

[16] Kowalski,R., "Logic for Problem Solving," Research Studies Press, 1979.

[17] Lloyd,D., "Foundation of Logic Programming," Springer-verlag, 1985.

[18] Ohsuga,S., "Developing a Deductive Relational Database for Uniform Handling of Complex Queries," JIP(IPSJ), 1983, pp.123-137.

[19] Olle,T., "The CODASYL Approach to Data Base Management," John Wiley & Sons, 1978.

[20] Takizawa,M., "Distributed Database System-JDDBS," JARECT, Ohm-sha and North-holland,Vol.7, 1983, pp.262-283.

[21] Takizawa,M., "Deductive Network Database System," Journal of JSAI, Vol.2, No.2, 1987, pp.182-191.

[22] Takizawa, M., et al., "Logic Interface System on Navigational Database System," Lecture Notes in Computer Science, Springer-Verlag, No.264, 1987, pp.70-80.

[23] Takizawa, M., "Transaction Management by Prolog," Proc. of the Logic Programming Conf., ICOT, 1987.

[24]Warren, D. H. D., "Efficient Processing of Interactive Relational Database Queries Expressed in Logic," Proc. of the VLDB, 1981, pp.272-281.

[25] Ullman,J.D., "Implementation of Logical Query Languages for Databases," TODS,Vol.10,No.3, 1985, pp.289-321.

# EUODHILOS: A General-Purpose Reasoning Assistant System

## — Concept and Implementation —

Toshiro MINAMI, Hajime SAWAMURA

International Institute for Advanced Study of Social Information Science (IIAS-SIS),
*FUJITSU LIMITED*, 140 Miyamoto, Numazu, Shizuoka 410-03, Japan
E-mail: {tos,hajime}%iias.fujitsu.junet@uunet.uu.net

and

Kaoru SATOH, Kyoko TSUCHIYA

Software Development Laboratory, *FUJITSU LABORATORIES LTD.*,
1015 Kamikodanaka, Nakahara-ku, Kawasaki, Kanagawa 211, Japan

## Abstract

The concept of the general-purpose reasoning assistant system is presented. We have developed the first version of a system named EUODHILOS as a prototype of that kind of system. It assists the user in describing the syntax of the logical expressions, defining a variety of logics which consists of axioms, inference rules, and rewriting rules, and also in constructing proofs for theorems under the logic so defined. Proofs are constructed under the support of the facility named "sheet of thought", which is an interactive and visual proof editing environment. Proofs are expressed and edited in the tree structured forms of the natural deduction-like style.

## 1. Introduction

In these days, logics play important and even essential roles in many fields like mathematics, computer science, artificial intelligence, and so on. In fact, various logics such as first-order, higher-order, equational, temporal, modal, intuitionistic, and type theoretic logics are used in these fields, and human reasoning activities based on these logics appear in daily work.

Here the phrase "human reasoning" is used to denote the process consisting of the following three phases.

(1) Making mental images about the objects and concepts.

(2) Making logical models which describe the mental images.

(3) Examining the models to make sure that they are sufficient.

The process begins with the first phase when one becomes aware of some mental images of objects and concepts having some structures and also wants to clarify what they are. To clarify the mental images, one has to describe them formally. A formal framework for describing objects and concepts is called a "logic" in this paper. A "logical model" is a logical description which specifies some mental image.

The second phase is for making logical models. Since the language is important for describing objects, one defines the syntax of the language at the beginning. In this phase, one has to determine what objects, concepts, and relations appear in the universe of discourse. The logical structure of the world of objects can be described by giving the axioms and derivation rules. The derivation rules are given in forms of such as inference and rewriting rules.

In the third phase, one derives results from the logical model. One comes to know many formal properties of the model. At the same time, one examines the correctness of the model. The model is insufficient if some properties which are expected to hold by the image of the objects fail to prove in the model. In this case, one has to modify some or all of the logical expressions about the objects. Sometimes one has to modify not only the logical expressions, but also the definition of the language used for the modeling.

Since human beings reason in various fields, it is valuable to help them by a computer-based system. The purpose of the reasoning assistant system is to make the human reasoning process accurate and being more efficient with the aid of the computer.

Two major subjects are pursued for realizing a reasoning assistant system. The first one is the "generality" of the system. Here the phrase "general-purpose system" indicates that it is free from any specific logic. As S. K. Langer told [Langer 25], we recognize that "Every universe of discourse has its logical structure." That is a thought that for each object which we mention, there must be a logic best suited for expressing about it. In order to assist human reasoning for the object, the reasoning assistant system must have the ability to allow the user to describe all the existing logical structures and manipulate the expressions under those logics. Our system EUODHILOS (pronounced "you-oh'-dee-los") is named as an acronym of the phrase by Langer. This reflects our intention to emphasize the generality of the system.

The other subject is the "user-friendliness" of the system. We investigate the reasoning-oriented human-computer interface that can be established as an aspect of reasoning supporting facilities. A system having good interface so that it can be used easily, is helpful for one to conceive ideas in reasoning. Furthermore, a reasoning methodology, which often reminds us of programming methodology, needs to be investigated.

We aim at building an ideal reasoning assistant system; which can be used for general-purpose and is used easily. EUODHILOS is a prototype of such a system. We intend to clarify the concept of the ideal general-purpose reasoning assistant system through developing and using EUODHILOS.

In Section 2, the reasoning assistant system is characterized through the comparisons to several other types of system which can be used for assisting human reasoning, specifically to theorem provers, proof checkers, and proof constructors. In Section 3, an overview of EUODHILOS is illustrated. In the succeeding two sections, its two significant features are described. In Section 4, the feature of defining logics is explained. In Section 5, the feature of assistance for constructing proofs, called "sheet of thought", is explained. In Section 6, some of the other features of EUODHILOS are illustrated. In Section 7, some concluding remarks and the directions for future research are stated.

## 2. Characterization of the Reasoning Assistant System

We consider the following four as the system-types which can be used for assisting human reasoning:

(i) reasoning assistant system
(ii) automated theorem prover
(iii) proof checker
(iv) proof constructor

In the rest of this section the reasoning assistant system is comparatively characterized with other types of system. In Subsection 2.1 the reasoning assistant system is introduced, and its characteristic features are exhibited. In Subsections 2.2 to 2.4, it is compared with each of the other types of system.

## 2.1 Reasoning Assistant System

The purpose of the reasoning assistant system is to support the whole phases of human reasoning process. The concept of the system comes from the philosophy of Langer [Langer 25] introduced in Section 1, and the recognition that the (mathematical) reasoning proceeds through "Proofs and Refutations" [Lakatos 76].

The following two major characteristic features of the system reflect these underlying concepts respectively:

(i) General-purpose
(ii) Possession of user-friendly proof editing environment

Figure 2.1 is an illustration of how the reasoning assistant system is used. In the upper half of the figure which corresponds to the feature (i), the user specifies each of the

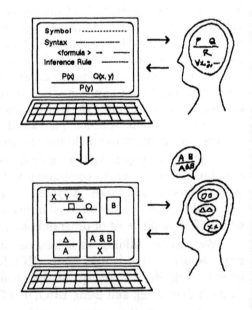

**Figure 2.1** Reasoning Assistant System

components of a logic, i.e., symbols, syntax of expressions including (logical) formulas, inference rules, etc. In the lower half of the figure, corresponding to (ii), the user tries to construct proofs of theorems under the logic defined in the previous step. Proofs are searched by trial and error.

EUODHILOS is the only one reasoning assistant system. In the system, partially constructed proofs, which are called proof fragments, appear scatteringly on a sheet of thought. The user edits these proof fragments by the editing commands such as create, delete, extend (derive), connect, separate, and so forth. The sheet of thought is the environment for creating theorems and their proofs. The theorems on the sheet can be saved so that they may be reused in the later proofs for other theorems. They can be used just in the same way as axioms.

## 2.2 Automated Theorem Prover

An (automated) theorem prover is a system which searches a proof of a given formula. Figure 2.2 illustrates how the theorem prover is used. In the upper half of the figure, a user tries to prove a formula. The user starts by putting an assumption of the formula. But he has no idea how to proceed for completing the proof. In the lower half of Figure 2.2, the user gives the formula to the theorem prover. The system finds out a proof, and displays it on the screen.

The theorem prover is different from the other types in that the proofs of theorems are given by the system. In other types of systems, including the reasoning assistant system, proofs are given by the user.

The situation in Figure 2.2 is, in fact, an ideal one. Considering the current state of the art of the proof-finding power of theorem provers, there is little hope of finding practically useful proofs automatically by computers. From this observation, theorem provers are to be used for finding only those proofs which fill small gaps which appear in a large proof. If the gap in a proof is small, the prover can find the proofs effectively. On one hand human beings are good at making a plan how to find a proof; on the other, they are not good at doing things accurately. Machines are on the contrary to human beings.

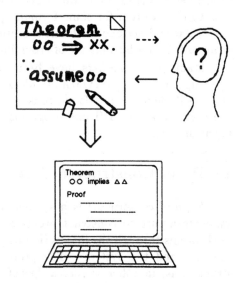

Figure 2.2 Theorem Prover

This is the reason why we pay attention to support the process of human reasoning by the computer. The capacity of computers for finding proofs can be used as a part of a reasoning assistant system.

## 2.3 Proof Checker

In this paper, a system is called a proof checker if it checks the correctness of a proof described by the user. Figure 2.3 is an illustration of how the proof checker is used. In the upper half of the figure, the user makes a proof of a theorem. A human proof may contain some careless mistakes including small gaps in a proof. The checker provides a language for describing human proofs. By using this language, the user describes the proof. In the lower half of the figure, the user gives the description of the proof to the checker. If the checker finds errors in the proof, it shows them on the screen. We can see an error indication in the figure.

When a user has a proof and wants to verify its correctness, a proof checker is one of the best tools for him. But when one begins to find a proof for some formula, proof constructors described in the next section is more suitable for his purpose of proof finding.

Many proof checkers have been developed up to now. AUTOMATH [de Bruijn 70] is a proof checker in which the user can specify how the proofs are constructed. PL/CV2 [Constable 82] is used for proving the correctness of PL/I like programs. CAP-LA [ICOT 86] deals with the proofs on linear algebra.

**Figure 2.3** Proof Checker

## 2.4 Proof Constructor/Editor

A proof constructor is a system which supports a user to construct proofs as well as theorems through the interaction between the user and the system. The proof construction is, in other words, a "proof editing." Users edit proofs, precisely proof fragments, by inputting, deleting, and combining the proofs. From this point of view, a proof constructor is a proof editor. The function of the proof constructor is included in a reasoning assistant system as an aid to proof constructions.

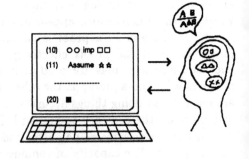

**Figure 2.4** Proof Constructor

Figure 2.4 is an illustration of how the proof constructors are used. The user interactively uses a proof constructor by entering some commands and tries to find a proof of some theorem.

Many proof constructors have been developed up to now. For example, LCF [Gordon 79], FOL [Weyhrauch 80], EKL [Ketonen 84] and Nuprl [Constable 86] are well known.

The purpose of Nuprl is very similar to ours. It aims at providing the proof construction environment for various logics. But the approach to the realization of it is different from those of the reasoning assistant systems. Nuprl has a fixed underlying logic and other logics are defined by using the expressions in this logic. In the approach of reasoning assistant system, even the syntax of the logic is specified by the user. It aims at the complete realization of logic free systems which can assist human reasoning in the various fields. Proof construction methodologies are also different. In Nuprl, proofs are constructed only by refinement, while in the reasoning assistant system, proofs are constructed by three types of deductions; i.e. by forward, backward (same as refinement), and interpolating deductions. The interpolation is a deduction which fills a proof gap between two formulas. Another difference is on user-interfaces; that is, Nuprl has been based on character displays, while EUODHILOS uses bit-map displays so that symbols can be expressed as its natural shape on a paper.

The significant difference between the proof constructors and the reasoning assistant systems is that in the former, underlying logics are fixed, while in the latter, underlying logics can be defined by the user. There are merits and demerits for fixing the underlying logics. As a merit, it is easy to introduce some specific procedures suited to the logic. As a demerit, if the system is applied for general cases of human reasoning, the fixation of logic may restrict the reasoning about some objects under consideration. In such a case, a general framework treating a variety of logics is required.

# 3. Overview of EUODHILOS

EUODHILOS is a prototype of the general-purpose reasoning assistant system. Its first version is now working on the sequential inference machine PSI on an operating system named SIMPOS.

It is designed by considering the following issues:

(1) Realization of a logic-free reasoning system, based on the philosophy in [Langer 25].

(2) Provision of an environment to be used easily to those who are not necessarily familiar with computers.

(3) Support of logical thought, symbolic or logical manipulations done by human reasoners.

(4) Environment for experimenting logical model construction based on the philosophy in [Lakatos 76].

The issue (1) is reflected to EUODHILOS in its logic definition feature which is shown in Section 4. For (2), it is implemented under the overlapping window system with bit-map display. It can be used easily because most of the operations are achieved by selecting the menu item with the mouse. For (3) and (4), the major tools used in EUODHILOS are "editors." The user can modify the language definitions, logic definitions, proof constructions, and so forth directly through the visual editor windows. Considering the importance of the proof construction, the system provides a special proof editing environment called "sheet of thought", which is an interactive, easy to use, and visual proof constructor.

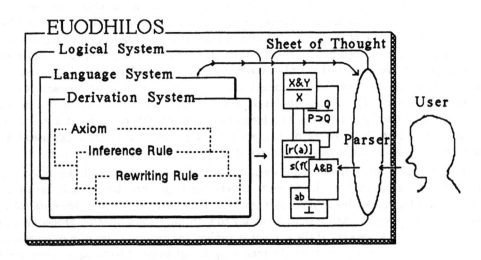

**Figure 3.1** An Overview of EUODHILOS

Figure 3.1 shows an overview of EUODHILOS. The system consists of two major parts, one for defining a user's logical system and the other for constructing proofs in a sheet of thought. The former is concerned with the second phase of human reasoning discussed in Section 1. It provides the feature for defining the syntax of logical expressions called (well-formed) formulas and the logical structure of the mentioned objects, as well. The latter is concerned with a proof construction which corresponds to the third phase of human reasoning. It is a proof editing environment, where the user constructs the proofs by trial and error. On the sheet of thought, proofs are expressed in the form reflecting their derivation structures. In EUODHILOS proofs are represented in natural deduction style, i.e. a tree structure, they are shown in their familiar representation.

Among the various features of EUODHILOS, we put stresses on the following topics:

(i) Defining Logics
(ii) Constructing Proofs (Sheet of Thought)

In the following Sections 4 and 5, the features of defining logical expressions and supporting to construct proofs on the sheet of thought are explained respectively mainly based on the specification for the current (the first) version of EUODHILOS.

# 4. Defining Logics

## 4.1 Language Description Feature of EUODHILOS

In EUODHILOS, a language system to be used is designed and defined by the user at the first stage. The language system consists of the specifications of the syntax of the logical expressions (i.e. formulas). The syntax of the expression is given by using definite clause grammar (DCG)[Pereira 80] in the first version. We intend to modify DCG by adding the operator-declarations in the second version in order to decrease the amount of descriptions. From the description in DCG, a bottom-up parser called BUP[Matsumoto 83] can be automatically generated. We modify the BUP algorithm by adding the function so that the augmented operators can be treated.

The system generates not only a parser, but also an unparser for the defined language. The unparser translates from the internal expressions into external ones which can be understood by the user. The parser and unparser are used in all the following phases of symbol manipulations. When an expression is entered, the parser is invoked for checking the validation of it. At the same time the internal structures of the expression of the language are constructed as well. When derivation commands are given by the user, the internal expressions of the formulas are manipulated and new internal expressions are generated. These expressions are presented to the user after translated into the external ones by the unparser.

Figure 4.1 in the next page is an example description of the first-order logic in DCG with operator and symbol declarations.

## 4.2 Derivation Description Feature of EUODHILOS

A derivation system in EUODHILOS consists of axioms and derivation rules which are given as inference and rewriting rules. A finite set of formulas is given as the axiom system. Inference rules are given in a natural deduction-like style presentation by the user. An inference rule consists of three parts; the first one is the premises of a rule, each of which may have an assumption, the second is the conclusion of a rule, and finally the third is for the restriction that is imposed on the derivations of the premises, such as variable occurrence conditions (eigenvariable). Well-known typical styles of logic presentations such as Hilbert's style, Gentzen's style, equational style can be treated within this framework.

Schematically, inference rules are given in the natural deduction style format as follows:

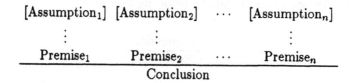

Syntax description:

```
formula('⇒'(F1,F2))→formula(F1), "⇒", formula(F2)
formula('∧'(F1,F2))→formula(F1), "∧", formula(F2)
formula('∨'(F1,F2))→formula(F1), "∨", formula(F2)
formula('¬'(F))→"¬",formula(F)
formula(F)→atomic_formula(F)
atomic_formula(F)→"(",formula(F),")"
atomic_formula(F)→predicate_symbol(P),"(",term_list(TL),")",
                  {F=..[P|TL]}
term_list([T])→term(T)
term_list([T|TL])→term(T),",",term_list(TL)
term(T)→function_symbol(F),"(",term_list(TL),")",{T=..[F|TL]}
term(T)→variable_symbol(T)
term(T)→constant_symbol(T)
```

Operator declaration:

```
"⇒":  xfx, 100
"∧":  yfx, 50
"∨":  yfx, 50
"¬":  fy, 30
```

Symbol declaration:

```
predicate_symbol:  "p"-"r"
function_symbol:   "f"-"h"
variable_symbol:   "x"-"z"
constant_symbol:   "a"-"e"
```

Meta symbol declaration:

```
formula:  "P"-"T"
term:     "A"-"D"
```

**Figure 4.1** A description of the first-order logic

In this format, each of the assumption parts is optional. If a premise has the assumption, it indicates that the premise is obtained under the assumption, and otherwise it is obtained unconditionally. An inference rule may have a condition on the eigenvariable. An inference rule is applied if all the premises are obtained in this manner, and the restrictive condition is satisfied. Then, the conclusion is obtained by the application of the rule.

Rewriting rules are presented in the following format:

$$\frac{\text{Pre\_Expression}}{\text{Post\_Expression}}$$

A rewriting rule indicates that it is applied to an expression when the formula has a subexpression which matches to the pre-expression part of the rule. The resultant expression is obtained by replacing the subexpression with the expression corresponding to the post-expression part of the rule. Rewriting rules have no condition of application in the first version.

Iterating the applications of the derivation rules described above, one can get a derivation (tree). The following Figure 4.2 is an example of the derivation using both inference and rewriting rules.

$$\frac{\dfrac{\dfrac{\dfrac{\dfrac{\dfrac{\forall xyz.(x+y)z = xz + yz}{(a+0)b = ab + 0b}\ (\forall\text{E})}{ab = ab + 0b}\ (x+0 \to x)}{0 = 0b}\ (x = y \to x + z = y + z)}{0b = 0}\ (x = y \to y = x)}{\forall x.0x = 0}\ (\forall\text{I})}$$

**Figure 4.2**   A derivation in EUODHILOS

# 5. Constructing Proofs

In EUODHILOS an environment called the "sheet of thought" provides the assistance to find proofs of theorems by trial and error. This originates from a metaphor of work or calculation sheet and is apparently analogous to the concept of sheet of assertion due to C. S. Peirce [Peirce 74]. It allows one to draft a proof, to compose proof fragments, detach a proof, to reason by using lemmas, and so on.

On the sheets of thought, proof fragments (in other words, partially constructed proofs) are the elementary units for manipulation. Proof fragments are newly created as assumptions, axioms, or theorems of the theory, which are composed, and deleted according to the operations given by the user.

In a sheet of thought, applications of inference and rewriting rules are possible in the same style as those users use on the paper. This naturally induces that the appearance of a proof structure on the sheet is also the same as that on the paper. This way of treating is considered as an example of the proof visualization.

It is desirable that reasoning during proof construction can be done along the natural way of thinking of human reasoners. Therefore EUODHILOS supports the typical method for reasoning, that is, forward (or bottom-up) reasoning, backward (ortop-down) reasoning, interpolation (i.e. filling the gap between proof fragments) and reasoning in a mixture of them. They are accomplished interactively by manipulating the fragments on a sheet of thought. It is planned to incorporate not only such a proving methodology but also methodology of science (e.g., Lakatos' mathematical philosophy of science [Lakatos 76], Kitagawa's relativistic logic of mutual specification [Kitagawa 63], etc.).

As an example of deduction process on a sheet, we will illustrate how one can proceed the forward deduction. In order to deduce forward by applying an inference rule, one has to start by selecting the formulas used as premises of the rule. The selection is achieved with the mouse by clicking the desired formula. Then the user may select the inference rule by calling the operation menu of the sheet, or he may enter a formula as the resultant formula. If the user selects a rule, then by the "do it" command (action) the system applies the rule to the premises and deduces the resultant. If the user indicates the resultant formula, then the system searches the list of deduction rules and tries to find one which is applicable to this deduction.

Among the editing functions on a sheet of thought such as delete, copy, move, undo, separate, etc., we will illustrate two of them; connection and separation.

# (1) Connection

The user can connect two proof fragments if they have equal formulas, where one of them must be a resultant of a fragment and the other a hypothesis of another fragment.

In order to connect the two proof fragments, one selects the two formulas by clicking them with the mouse at first. One of the two is a resultant, and the other is a hypothesis which must be equal to the resultant. And then, he invokes the operation menu and selects the "connect" item. As the result, the proof fragments are connected into the one fragment. Figure 5.1 is an illustration of this operation. The two fragments in the left part of the figure are connected at the formula "B", and the fragment in the right part is obtained.

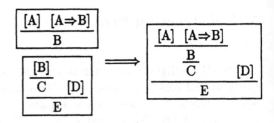

**Figure 5.1** Connection at B

# (2) Separation

This operation is just the inverse of the connection. When the user indicates a formula in a proof fragment and selects the command "separate" in the operation menu, then the fragment is separated into two parts at the position of the selected formula.

Suppose, for example, we have a proof fragment like the right one in the Figure 5.1. If we point the formula "B" in the proof fragment and select the separate command in the command menu, then we can get the two proof fragments which appear at the left part of Figure 5.1.

An example of the screen image of sheet of thought in EUODHILOS is indicated in Figure 5.2.

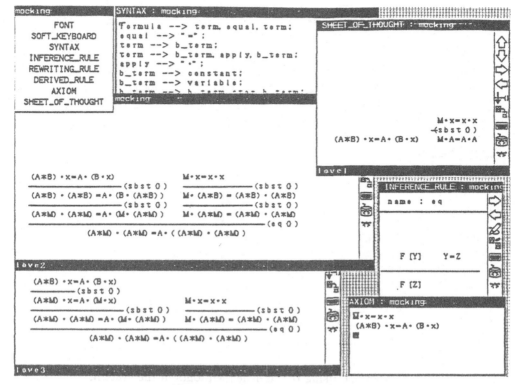

**Figure 5.2** Sheet of Thought

# 6. Other Facilities for Reasoning

In order to make the system user-friendly and easy to use, we have to pay much attention to the visualization of things. For this purpose, the bit-mapped display with multi-window environment, mouse, icon, pop-up menu, etc. are exploited in the implementation of EUODHILOS. The followings are available as the user-interface facilities for inputting formulas, visualizing formulas, and assisting reasoning.

## 6.1 Software Keyboard and Font Editor

The software keyboard and the font editor are used to design and input special symbols often appearing in various formal systems. It is a matter of course that provision of special symbols which reasoners are accustomed to use makes it possible to reason in a natural way of thinking on a computer. The user designs the fonts of the symbols in the dot matrix pattern of them by using the built-in font editor. These fonts are assigned on the software keyboard and are used with the corresponding keys. In Figure 6.1, one can see a software keyboard on which user-defined symbols such as ∨, ∧, ⇒, ∃, etc. are attached.

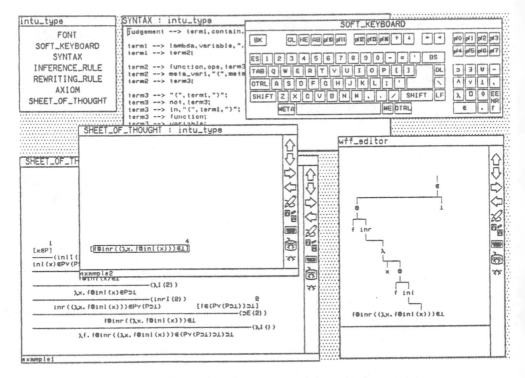

Figure 6.1 Using the user-defined fonts in the system.

## 6.2 Formula Editor

The formula editor is a structure editor for logical formulas. It aims to simplify inputting formulas by displaying complicated formulas. In addition to ordinary editing functions, it provides some formula rewriting functions. It can be used not only for entering formulas, but also for just displaying the structure of formulas clearly. This is a visualization of formulas. You can see the formula editor in the bottom-right corner of Figure 6.1.

## 6.3 Stationery for Reasoning

Independently of a logic under consideration, various reasoning tools such as decision procedures become helpful and useful in reasoning processes. In a sense it may also play a role of a model which makes up for a semantical aspect of reasoning. You can display and erase the stationery at any time within the system. Currently, a logic calculator for Boolean logic is realized as a desk accessary. Figure 6.2 indicates what it looks like on the screen.

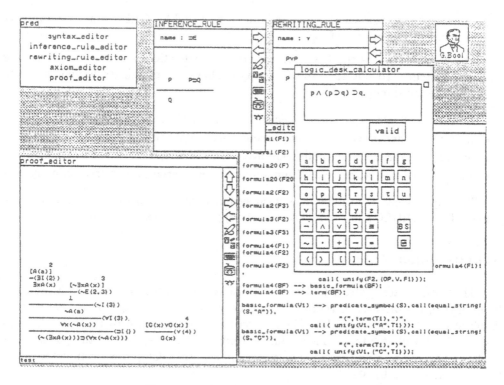

Figure 6.2 Boolean logic calculator

# 7. Concluding Remarks and Directions for Future Research

The first version of EUODHILOS is now available and the second version is under development. The system is being improved by reflecting the experience of using it.

So far, we have dealt with logics, such as first-order logic (NK), propositional modal logic (T), intensional logic (IL), combinatory logic, and Martin-Löf's type theory. Many logics can be treated in the current version. Though, some logics such as tableau method can not be treated in the current framework for logic description. We intend to extend the framework so that these "irregular" logics can be treated in the system.

From the experiments so far in EUODHILOS, the followings become aware.

(i) Describing the syntax of logical expressions is difficult at first. But, by making good use of the experience, it becomes easier. If the system keeps descriptions for typical logics as a library, the description of a new logic is an easy task even for beginners.

(ii) On a sheet of thought, users are free from deduction errors. On the paper, they may make mistakes in deriving a new formula when deduction rules are applied. The difference is important, because the users have to pay attentions only to the decision how to proceed the proof on the sheet of thought.

(iii) The reasoning assistant system can be used as a tool for CAI. In the system, users can deal with a variety of logics.

The current state is the first step toward the realization of a practical reasoning assistant system. To put the step forward, we have to investigate various subjects including the followings:

- Treatment of relationships between meta and object theories
- Maintaining dependency relations among various theories
- Opening up various new application fields of reasoning
- Improvement and refinement of human-computer interface for the reasoning system

The experiments with different logical systems have shown the potential and usefulness of EUODHILOS in the realm of logics appearing in various fields.

## Acknowledgements

The authors are grateful to Dr. T. Kitagawa, the president of IIAS-SIS, and Dr. H. Enomoto, the director of IIAS-SIS, for their ceaseless encouragements. We wish to thank also to Mr. T. Hai for his contribution to our project and to Dr. K. Kobayashi and Mr. Y. Takada for their many valuable comments on the draft of the paper. This work is a part of the major research and development of FGCS project conducted under the program set up by MITI.

## References

[Constable 82] R. L. Constable, S. D. Johnson and C. D. Eichenlaub : An Introduction to the PL/CV2 Programming Logics, *LNCS* **135**, Springer–Verlag, 1982.

[Constable 86] R. L. Constable et al. : Implementing Mathematics with the Nuprl Proof Development System, *Prentice–Hall*, 1986.

[de Bruijn 70] N. G. de Bruijn : The Mathematical Language AUTOMATH, its Usage, and some of its Extensions, In M. Laudet, D. Lacombe, L. Nolin and M. Schutzenberger (eds.), *Symposium on Automated Demonstration*, Springer–Verlag, pp.29-61, December 1970.

[Gordon 79] M. J. Gordon, A. J. Milner and C. P. Wadsworth : Edinburgh LCF, *LNCS* **78**, Springer–Verlag, 1979.

[Goguen 83] J. A. Goguen and R. M. Burstall : Introducing Institutions, *LNCS* **164**, Springer–Verlag,pp.221-270, 1983.

[Griffin 87] T. G. Griffin : An Environment for Formal Systems, *ECS-LFCS-87-34*, University of Edinburgh, 1987.

[Harper 87] R. Harper, F. Honsell and G. Plotkin : A Framework for Defining Logics, *ECS-LFCS-87-23*, University of Edinburgh, 1987.

[Ketonen 84] J. Ketonen and J. S. Weening : EKL — An Interactive Proof Checker, User's Reference Manual, *Dept. of Computer Science*, Stanford University, 1984.

[Kitagawa 63] T. Kitagawa : The Relativistic Logic of Mutual Specification in Statistics, *Mem. Fac. Sci. Kyushu University*, Ser. **A**, 17,1, 1963.

[Lakatos 76] I. Lakatos : Proofs and Refutations — The Logic of Mathematical Discovery —, J. Worrall and E. Zabar (eds.), Cambridge University Press 1976.

[Langer 25] S. K. Langer : A Set of Postulates for the Logical Structure of Music, *Monist* **39**, pp.561-570, 1925.

[Matsumoto 83] Y. Matsumoto, H. Tanaka, H. Hirakawa, H. Miyoshi and H. Yasukawa : BUP : A Bottom-Up Parser Embedded in Prolog, *New Generation Computing* **1**, pp.145-158, 1983.

[Peirce 74] C. S. Peirce : Collected Papers of C. S. Peirce, Ch. Hartshorne and P. Weiss (eds.), *Harvard Univ. Press*, 1974.

[Pereira 80] F. C. N. Pereira and D. H. D. Warren : Definite Clause Grammars for Language Analysis — A Survey of the Formalism and a Comparison with Augmented Transition Networks, *Artificial Intelligence* **13**, pp. 231-278, 1980.

[Smullyan 85] R. Smullyan : To Mock a Mockingbird, and Other Logical Puzzles Including an Amazing Adventure in Combinatory Logic, *Alfred A. Knopf Inc.*, 1985.

[Weyhrauch 80] R. W. Weyhrauch : Prolegomena to a Theory of Mechanized Formal Reasoning, *AI Journal* **13**, pp. 133-179, 1980.

[Mizoguchi 85] F. Mizoguchi et al. : Prolog and Its Applications 2, *Souken Syuppan*, 1985. (in Japanese)

[ICOT 86] ICOT CAP-WG : The CAP Project (1)-(6), *Proc. 32nd Annual Convention IPS Japan*, 1986. (in Japanese)

[Satoh 86] K. Satoh et al. : Well-Formed Formulas Editor for the Reasoning Assistant System, *Proc. 33rd Annual Convention IPS Japan*, 1986. (in Japanese)

[Minami 86a] T. Minami and H. Sawamura : Proof Constructors for the Reasoning Assistance, *Proc. 33rd Annual Convention IPS Japan*, 1986. (in Japanese)

[Minami 86b] T. Minami and H. Sawamura : A Construction of Computer-Assisted-Reasoning System, *Proc. 3rd Conf. JSSST*, 1986. (in Japanese)

[Tsuchiya 87] K. Tsuchiya et al. : Well-Formed Formulas Editor for the Reasoning Assistant System, *Proc. 35th Annual Convention IPS Japan*, 1987. (in Japanese)

[Minami 87] T. Minami and H. Sawamura : Proof Construction with Working Sheets — A Consideration on the Methodology for Computer Assisted Reasoning —, *Proc. 35th Annual Convention IPS Japan*, 1987. (in Japanese)

[Sawamura 87] H. Sawamura and T. Minami : Conception of General-Purpose Reasoning Assistant System and Its Realization Method, *Proc. WG of Software Foundation IPS Japan (87-SF-22)*, 1987. (in Japanese)

# Logic Based Lexical Analyser LAX

Ryôichi Sugimura
Matsushita Electric Industrial Co.,LTD.
Kôji Akasaka

Yukihiro Kubo
Institute for New Generation Computer Technology (ICOT)
Yûji Matsumoto
Kyoto University

## Abstract

This paper describes a method of Japanese morphological analysis which runs in a sequential or parallel logic programming language. In the method presented here, a morphological dictionary is compiled into a logic program which executes lexical analysis deterministically.

Morphemes and their categories are written in a morphological dictionary. The categories are used as inputs to a non-deterministic finite state automaton (NFSA).

The dictionary is compiled into a TRIE structure in which morphemes can be quickly looked up using an index search mechanism such as those provided in logic programming languages like ESP or Prolog.

The layered stream technique, which records search space in recursively structured data, is applied in analysis. All solutions are given at the end of analysis. The analysis output can be used as input to the syntactic analyser, SAX, which can also be executed in parallel logic languages.

This method can process unknown morphemes which are not in the dictionary in linear order. This paper also reports the evaluation of this method in sequential languages.

# 1 Introduction

This paper presents a morphological analysis method which can be executed both in parallel and sequential languages. In this method, a morphological dictionary is transformed into sequential logic programming languages, such as ESP or Prolog, or parallel logic programming languages, such as GHC [8]. These programs analyse a sequence of Japanese characters deterministically [7].

Each word entry in the dictionary contains the appropriate morphological information. The analysis procedure in LAX can be regarded as the breakdown of the input Japanese string into a concatenation of sub-strings that correspond to words with some constraints. This mechanism can be represented as a non-deterministic finite state automaton (NFSA) [5]. The layered stream technique [6] is applied to obtain multiple solutions. This method gives high performance both in sequential and parallel logic languages. The method uses local ambiguity packing [Tomita 85].

Section 2 describes the form of the lexical dictionary. Each lexical entry has the sequence of surface characters, a category, and two kinds of special features: special constraints on concatenation and state transition. This section presents the model of concatenation in terms of a NFSA.

The compiled dictionary has a TRIE structure [3], in which lexical entries are searched for at high speed with the indexed search mechanism provided by logic programming languages.

Section 3 presents an elementary parallel algorithm. This algorithm can be regarded as a parallel version of Cocke-Kasami-Younger algorithm or the bottom up chart parsing algorithm method [4] used for regular grammars.

Section 4 presents a practical algorithm which is obtained by optimising one of the elementary parallel algorithms. In this algorithm, the number of processes required is reduced drastically, and data structures of morphological constructions are packed. All results are given at the end of analysis without backtracking, and unknown morphemes can be found in the algorithm. The results can be used as input to the parser SAX [10].

Section 5 describes optimisation for sequential implementations and section 6 evaluates the sequential implementation.

# 2   Dictionary

## 2.1   Overview of the Lexical Dictionary

Four kinds of information should be declared for each morpheme. The first two are easy to describe: they are the surface of the morpheme and its category. The third and fourth entries are described later.

For readers unfamiliar with the problem posed by Japanese orthography, a few words of introduction are in order. A normal Japanese sentence is written using both *Kanji* (Chinese characters) and *Kana* (Japanese phonetic characters, each representing a syllable). The input is generally a mixed sequence of both kinds of characters.

It should be noted that when the input is *Kana* only , heuristics must be utilised to obtain a morphological analysis. However, we are not concerned with this special case.

A recent study of Japanese morphology [5] reports that finite state automata have just enough power to analyse strings of this kind. We define two more features for each morpheme. The first is the input category of a morpheme for finite state automata and the second is the transition state. These are the third and fourth kinds of information.

## 2.2   Rules for Concatenation

This section explains the rules for *concatenation*. In our approach, morphological analysis is performed by applying rules restricting the legal *concatenation* of adjacent morphemes. Before going further, we define the notation.

We define a Japanese string ($string_u$:$[n]$ ) as a finite sequence, $u : [n] \rightarrow A$, where $n$ is a natural number denoting the length of $u$, and $A$ is a set of Japanese characters. Thus, if $u : [n] \rightarrow A$ is a string and $n > 0$, for every $i \in [n]$, $u(i)$ is some element of $A$.

A Japanese string as an entry of a lexical dictionary usually has lexical ambiguities; thus we define a function, *get_entries*, which obtains lexical entries corresponding to a string. As shown in (1) and (2), each morpheme is a triple, ($string_u$:$[n]$, $A, B$), where $A$ and $B$ are the left- and right-hand restriction for string. We will use $S_{LF}$ to refer to the set of left-hand-side features of morphemes. The symbol $\stackrel{u}{\Longleftarrow}$ denotes the left-hand-side feature of $morpheme_u$. Similarly, $S_{RF}$ is the set of right–hand–side features of morphemes, and $\overset{u}{\Longrightarrow}$ denotes the right–hand–side feature of $morpheme_u$.

$get\_entries(string_u:[n])$

$\overset{\text{def}}{=} \quad string_u:[n] \rightarrow \{morpheme_{u1}:[n] \ldots morpheme_{uk}:[n]\} \subset S_{entries}$ (1)

where $\quad S_{entries} \overset{\text{def}}{=} \{(string_u:[n], A, B) | A \in S_{LF} \bigwedge B \in S_{RF}\}$ (2)

We will use expressions of the form $morpheme_u:[n]$ to denote elements of the set $S_{entries}$. It is sometimes convenient to refer to $\overset{u}{\Longleftarrow}$ and $\overset{u}{\Longrightarrow}$ by the functional expressions $leftf(morpheme_u:[n])$ and $rightf(morpheme_u:[n])$.

Restrictions on legal concatenations are expressed by the predicate $C_{rule}$. The intention is that two morphemes, $morpheme_u:[m]$ and $morpheme_v:[n]$, can be *concatenated* if the right context of $morpheme_u:[m]$ is related to the left context of $morpheme_v:[n]$ as shown in figure 1.

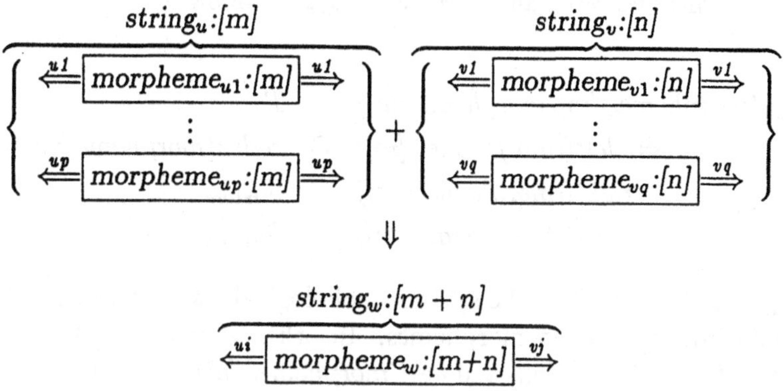

$$string_w(i) = \begin{cases} string_u(i) & \text{if } 1 \leq i \leq m \\ string_v(i-m) & \text{if } m+1 \leq i \leq m+n \end{cases}$$

$$\text{where } C_{rule}(\overset{ui}{\Longrightarrow}, \overset{vj}{\Longleftarrow}) = T$$

Figure 1: Concatenation of morphemes

In the traditional method [11], $C_{rule}$ is defined as in line (3) and the functions $leftf$ and $rightf$ are realized as in lines (5) and (6). Here, $leftf$

and *rightf* will return a natural number. $Set_{connect}$ in line (3) consists of a finite number of pairs $(Pre, Post)$ where $Pre \in S_{LF}(S_{LF} \subset N)$ and $Post \in S_{RF}(S_{RF} \subset N)$ ($N$ is a finite set of natural numbers). In [11], the cardinality of $N$ is less than 300.

$$C_{rule}(morpheme_u\!:\![m], morpheme_v\!:\![n])$$
$$\stackrel{\text{def}}{=} \quad (rightf(morpheme_u\!:\![n]), leftf(morpheme_v\!:\![n])) \in Set_{connect} \quad (3)$$
$$\in \quad \{T, F\} \quad (4)$$
$$\text{where} \quad rightf(morpheme_u\!:\![m]) \in N \quad (5)$$
$$leftf(morpheme_v\!:\![n]) \in N \quad (6)$$

In this traditional method, the definition of $Set_{connect}$ is difficult for grammar writers to handle, since the same number occurring in sets $S_{LF}$ and $S_{RF}$ will have different meanings. An element in $Set_{connect}$ does not have anything that makes it easy to handle. However, in the LAX system, we define the functions *rightf* and *leftf*, and predicate $C_{rule}$ as follows.

$$C_{rule}(morpheme_u\!:\![m], morpheme_v\!:\![n]) = T \quad (7)$$
$$\Leftrightarrow leftf(morpheme_u\!:\![m]) \cap rightf(morpheme_v\!:\![n]) \neq \phi$$
$$rightf(morpheme_u\!:\![m]) \subset S_{feature} \quad (8)$$
$$leftf(morpheme_v\!:\![n]) \subset S_{feature} \quad (9)$$

$S_{feature}$ in (8) and (9) is the set of morphological features which represents the relationships between morphemes. In other words, $C_{rule}$ holds exactly when $rightf(morpheme_u\!:\![m])$ and $leftf(morpheme_v\!:\![n])$ have only one common element, as shown in line (7).

If the rules are of this form, the process of finding legal concatenation in LAX can be formalized as a non-deterministic finite state automaton as follows.

$$M = (K, \Sigma, \delta, Q_o, F) \quad (10)$$
$$K \stackrel{\text{def}}{=} \{X | X = (\{rightf\}, string_m\!:\![n])\} \quad (11)$$
$$\text{where } \{rightf\} \subset S_{feature}$$

$$\Sigma \stackrel{\text{def}}{=} \{X | X = string_i : [n]\} \tag{12}$$

$$\delta((q, string_j : [m]), string_i : [n]) = \bigcup_M (rightf(M), string_k : [m+n]) \tag{13}$$

$$\text{where } M \in get\_entries(string_i : [n]) \wedge C_{rule}(q, leftf(M))$$

$$\delta(q, \varepsilon) = (q, string_0 : [0]) \tag{14}$$

$$\delta(q, ax) = \bigcup_{p \in \delta(q,a)} \delta(p, x) \tag{15}$$

$$\text{where } q \in K, a \in \sigma, x \in \sigma^*$$

$$\delta(S, x) = \bigcup_{(q, input\_string) \in S} \delta(q, x) \tag{16}$$

$$\text{where } S \subset K, x \in \sigma^*, q \in F$$

The NFSA $M$ is defined in (10). $K$ is the set of states of $M$, and $\sigma$ is the set of alphabets for $M$. $\delta$ is the transition function. $Q_o$ is the initial state, and $E$ is the final state.

$K$ is the set of right restrictions $\Longrightarrow$ as defined in (11).

$\sigma$ is the set of Japanese strings that are in entries of the LAX lexical dictionary. The string look–up process in the lexical dictionary is realized as a TRIE structure, and takes a finite interval of less than 0.5 msec in the worst case. Therefore, we start our discussion assuming that Japanese strings in the dictionary have already been found.

The definition of the transition function, $\delta$, is slightly complicated. If the Japanese string $string_a : [n]$ has more than one $\stackrel{a}{\Longleftarrow}$, then $\delta(q, a)$ is defined as shown in (13).

The definition of $\delta$ in (14), (15) and (16) is the same as the usual definition for an NFSA.

In LAX, plural transition tables (**TrTbl**) can be used as shown in figure 2. Therefore, the elements of $S_{feature}$ are defined as follows.

$$S_{feature} \stackrel{\text{def}}{=} \{X | X = \textbf{Name\_of\_TrTbl(State)}\} \tag{17}$$

$$\text{where } \textbf{State} \text{ is the name of a state in Trtbl}$$

The multiple transition table is very convenient for representing rules of derivation and rules of inflection in separate forms. See [12] and [13] for details.

Figure 2 shows the analysis of the Japanese word " 痛めるな " [*itameruna*] (do not hurt: 痛める = to hurt, な= do not). In this figure, the input category $I_{dm}$ of the word stem, 痛 (word stem of the verb "hurt"), is accepted in the initial state, $S_{dj}$. Then, the next state is $S_{di}$ or $S_{dj}$. The next input character is め. *leftf(め)* is accepted in the state $S_{di}$ and the next state becomes $S_{dk}$ or $F$, that is, the final state. The next character is accepted in the state $S_{dk}$ and the next state becomes $S_{fl}$ or $F$. $S_{fl}$ is the state in the inflection table. The last input, な, is accepted in the inflection table and the word 痛めるな is accepted.

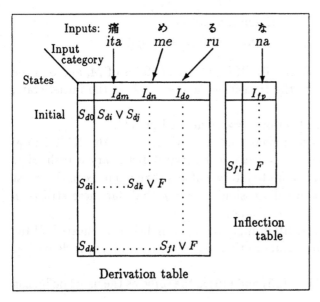

Figure 2: Multiple transition table

## 2.3 Expansion of NFSA

The LAX system also provides a "handle" which allows the lexicon-writer to build arbitrary data structures in parallel with the analysis.

The arbitrary data structures can be attached by assigning the function shown in (19) to each element of $S_{feature}$. This function enables us to attach some data structures to $\Longleftarrow$ and $\Longrightarrow$; using them, we can write programs to construct morphological semantic information, which will be described further in section 2.4.

$$info(X) \quad \rightarrow \quad \{\text{Some data structures}\} \qquad (18)$$
$$where \quad X = leftf(morpheme_x:[n]) \vee X = rightf(morpheme_x:[n])$$
$$morpheme_x:[n] \in S_{entries} \qquad (19)$$

## 2.4 Format of the Dictionary

The syntax of the dictionary in the LAX system is outlined below. Each entry has the following structures.

$$begin(\textbf{Category of morpheme}). \qquad (20)$$
$$\textbf{SURF} \quad :: \quad \textbf{TrTbl}_\textbf{a}([\textbf{St}_\textbf{a1}, ...]) \qquad (21)$$
$$\&\& \quad [\textbf{TrTbl}_\textbf{b}([\textbf{St}_\textbf{b1}, ..]), ...] \qquad (22)$$
$$\$\$ \quad [[in(Input), \textbf{Common\_Procedures}], \qquad (23)$$
$$\textbf{TrTbl}_\textbf{b}(\textbf{St}_\textbf{b1}, \qquad (24)$$
$$[\textbf{procedure}_\textbf{b11}, send(O)], \qquad (25)$$
$$[\textbf{procedure}_\textbf{b12}, call\_sax(O_2)]])... \qquad (26)$$
$$end(\textbf{Category of morpheme}). \qquad (27)$$
$$\vdots \qquad (28)$$

Morphemes with the same category are defined between lines (20) and (27). The category name of morphemes is written in lines (20) and (27),

In line (21), the surface character of a morpheme is written first. :: is a delimiter. Then, $leftf(Morpheme)$ is written. $leftf(Morpheme)$ can be regarded as input to the NFSA. If the current state is $rightf(Morpheme_u)$ = {動詞派生接辞め (word stem for the verb "me"), ウ系強変化マ (word stem for the verb "ma") } and the input is $leftf(Morpheme_v)$ = {動詞派生接辞め}, then $string_v:[n]$ will be accepted according to the definition of $C_{rule}$ defined between (7) and (8).

In (22), $rightf(Morpheme)$ is defined.

In (23) to (26), we can write programs which correspond to the next state transitions.

In (23), common programs can be written. Programs written in this part are activated when the morpheme is accepted. $in(I)$ is a function to obtain information from the preceding morpheme. $in(I)$ is the realization of the complex function $info(leftf(morpheme))$ as shown in (19) and (9).

$$in(I) \stackrel{\text{def}}{=} I = info(leftf(Morpheme))$$

From (24) to (26), programs which correspond to the next state transitions can be written. The predicate $call\_sax$ is used to call the syntactic analyser SAX. The predicate $send$ is used to attach some information to the left–hand–side feature of the morpheme. $send$ is $info(rightf(morpheme))$.

$$out(O) \stackrel{\text{def}}{=} O = info(rightf(Morpheme))$$

When $C_{rule}(\stackrel{u}{\Longrightarrow}, \stackrel{v}{\Longleftarrow})$ is true, information on the right–hand–side and left–hand–side features is unified.

# 3  Elementary Algorithm

The elementary algorithm is executed by multi-processes which are layered in a well formed substring table, as shown in figure 3.

In figure 3, the input string is いためるな [i-ta-me-ru-na] (do not fry). In this figure, a string of *Kana* is used as input to the LAX for expository reasons. The characters are numbered from 1 (い) to 6 (the punctuation mark '。 ').

$p_{ij}$ represents a search process. F1 to F6 represent the raw numbers of table 3.

In the LAX dictionary, a process, $p_{RC}$, looks up morphemes corresponding to the string which starts from the character at R and ends at C-1. For example, process $p_{23}$ looks up morphemes which have た as the surface. Search processes $p_{12}$ to $p_{67}$ can be executed simultaneously.

Each process is connected through streams (data paths) which the searched morphemes are passed through. Outputs from the processes at column C are merged to be the input to processes at raw C. For example, outputs from $p_{14}$, $p_{24}$ and $p_{34}$ are merged to be the inputs to $p_{45}$ and $p_{46}$; $p_{14}$, $p_{24}$ and $p_{34}$

look up morphemes corresponding to the string which ends at ゟ; and $p_{45}$ and $p_{46}$ look up morphemes corresponding to the string which starts from ゟ. Therefore, connecting these processes by a stream, we can concatenate morphemes.

An outline of the elementary algorithm is as follows.

1. Activation of processes

   (a) Activate $(N(N + 1)/2) + 1$ processes corresponding to an input string which has $N$ Japanese characters and a Japanese punctuation mark.

   $(N(N + 1)/2)$ processes correspond to $N$ Japanese characters. Activated processes are linked with streams which are indicated by the arrows in figure 3.

   (b) $\xrightarrow{top}$ indicating the initial state of the NFSA is put in the stream to the processes at raw 1.

   (c) Data from $p_{(N+1)(N+2)}$ is the result of analysis.

2. An activated process PNK then executes the following algorithm

   (a) Wait for input $M_{in}$.

   (b) If the input data is *nil*, indicating the tail of the stream, output *nil* and stop. Otherwise, go to the next step.

   (c) Look up morphemes $M_{ref}$ which correspond to the string starting from N and ending at $K - 1$. If $M_{ref}$ exists, go to the next step. Otherwise, stop.

   (d) Call $C_{rule}$ to check whether $M_{in}$ and $M_{ref}$ can be concatenated or not. If they can be concatenated, concatenate $M_{ref}$ and $M_{in}$, then output the concatenated morpheme. Go to 2a.

This method makes it possible to perform parallel lexical analysis, although there are still some problems in practical use, as follows.

1. Although $((N + 1) \times N/2) + 1$ processes will be activated in 1a, few of these processes will be able to look up morphemes $M_{ref}$ at 2c. Therefore, the efficiency of analysis will drop because of this useless activation.

2. The elementary algorithm cannot handle unknown lexical entries.

3. The elementary algorithm produces each result separately so that the worst complexity will be as follows.

$$O = \sum_{i=0}^{n-1} a^{i+1} \times \frac{(n-1)!}{(n-1-i)!i!}$$
$$= a(1+a)^{n-1}$$

where a is the worst ambiguity of the morpheme and

n is the character length of the input sentence

Therefore, there should be a packing algorithm. As described in section 5, this reduces the complexity to $O(n^3)$ as follows.

$$O = \sum_{i=1}^{n-1} i \times (n-i) \times a^2$$
$$= \frac{a^2 \times (n^3 - n)}{6}$$

where a is the worst ambiguity of the morpheme and

n is the character length of the input sentence

$$\overbrace{\underbrace{C_1, C_2, \ldots, C_i}_{i}, \underbrace{C_{i+1}, \ldots, C_n}_{n-i}}^{n}$$

# 4 Practical Algorithm

In this section, a practical algorithm which activates minimal processes, can handle the unknown lexical entries, and has complexity $O(n^3)$ is represented. First, efficient activation of the processes is represented. Second, the data flow with packing is described.

## 4.1 Making Process Activation Demand-Driven

This sub-section describes an efficient way to minimize unnecessary activation of processes. At the beginning of the analysis, a 'dict' process is activated for each input character as shown in figure 4.

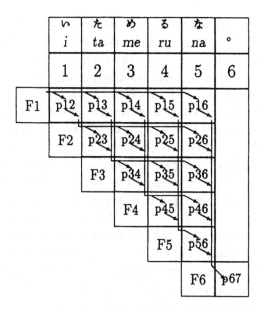

| | い<br>i | た<br>ta | め<br>me | る<br>ru | な<br>na | 。 |
|---|---|---|---|---|---|---|
| | 1 | 2 | 3 | 4 | 5 | 6 |
| F1 | p12 | p13 | p14 | p15 | p16 | |
| | F2 | p23 | p24 | p25 | p26 | |
| | | F3 | p34 | p35 | p36 | |
| | | | F4 | p45 | p46 | |
| | | | | F5 | p56 | |
| | | | | | F6 | p67 |

Figure 3: Data flow in the basic algorithm

| | い<br>i | た<br>ta | め<br>me | る<br>ru | な<br>na | 。 |
|---|---|---|---|---|---|---|
| | 1 | 2 | 3 | 4 | 5 | 6 |
| F1 | dict | p13 | p14 | | | |
| | F2 | dict | | | | |
| | | F3 | dict | p35 | | |
| | | | F4 | dict | | |
| | | | | F5 | dict | |
| | | | | | F6 | dict |

Figure 4: Process activation in the practical algorithm

$N + 1$ 'dict' will be activated when an input string has $N$ characters and a punctuation mark. (In figure 4, six 'dict' processes were activated.) 'dict' looks up morphemes which correspond to the string from the point at which 'dict' was placed. (For notation, we use function $position(dict_{process})$ to indicate this point.) For example, the 'dict' process at F1 in figure 4 looks up morphemes corresponding to strings which start from い in the first column. If there are morphemes corresponding to いた in the dictionary, the 'dict' at F1 will activate sub-process P13. Similarly, if いため is in the dictionary, the 'dict' at F1 will activate sub-process P14. If there is no morpheme corresponding to いためる, no process is activated. For convenience, the notation $refmorph(dict)$ or $refmorph(PXY)$ will be used in this paper to represent a set of morphemes corresponding to the substring to which 'dict' or PXY is attached. A 'dict' process and its sub-process can be obtained as programs by compiling the lexical dictionary of the LAX. For example, let us consider the tiny lexical dictionary shown in figure 5. It can be represented as a TRIE structure, as shown in figure 6, and then compiled into a 'dict' program, as shown in figure 7. To simplify the representation, figure 7 shows only the look-up processes.

| Surface | Category |
|---------|----------|
| い | Word stem of the noun 胃 (*stomach*) |
| [i] | |
| いた | Word stem of the adjective 痛 (*sore*) |
| [ita] | |
| いた | Word stem of the verb 傷 (*to hurt*) |
| [ita] | |
| いため | Word stem of the verb 炒め (*to fry*) |
| [itame] | |
| いため | Word stem of the noun 板目 (*wood grain*) |
| [itame] | |
| いたく | Word stem of the nominal verb 委託 (*trust, to entrust*) |
| [itaku] | |

Figure 5: Example of a LAX lexical dictionary

In figure 7, the first argument of 'dict' is the character to which 'dict' corresponds. The second argument is the next sequence of input characters.

```
[い,    word-stem-of-noun(胃)
[i]
        [た,    word-stem-of-adjective(痛),
        [ta]
                word-stem-of-verb(傷),

                [め,   word-stem-of-verb(炒め),
                [me]
                        word-stem-of-noun(板目)],

                [く,   word-stem-of-nominal-verb(委託)]
                [ku]
        ]
]
```

Figure 6: The LAX dictionary as a TRIE structure

The last argument returns the result of the search.

Let us see what happens when we input the sequence [い, は, め, る]. The 'dict' corresponding to the first character, い, will accept this sequence. Therefore, 'dict' will obtain the word-stem-of-noun(胃). Next, 'dict' calls い([は, め, る],RR,Ir), and this call does not bring any more results, so that no redundant processes which search for sub-strings such as [い, は], [い, は, め] or [い, は, め, る] will be activated.

With regard to the efficiency of the search, the program in figure 7 is fast because logic programming languages like Prolog search for clauses using the first argument hashing. The TRIE structure enables us to utilise this hashing mechanism easily, making the 'dict' process perform its search rapidly.

As stated above, compilation of the lexical dictionary enables us to minimise the number of activated processes, and to look up morphemes quickly.

## 4.2   Data and Its Flow in the Practical Algorithm

This section describes the data flow between 'dict' and its sub-processes, then presents a data packing mechanism which makes the complexity of the

```
dict(ん,R,I) :- R = [H|RR],
                I = [[word-stem-of-noun(胃)]|Ir],
                ん(H,RR,Ir).
ん(た,R,I)    :- R = [H|RR],
                I = [[word-stem-of-adjective(痛)],
                     [word-stem-of-verb(傷)]|Ir],
                んた(H,R,Ir).
ん(_,_,[]).
んた(め,R,I) :- I = [[word-stem-of-verb(炒め)],
                    [word-stem-of-a-noun(板目)]].
んた(く,R,I) :- I = [[word-stem-of-nominal-verb(委託)]].
んた(_,_,[]).
```

Figure 7: Prolog program for the 'dict' process

practical algorithm $O(n^3)$.

### 4.2.1  Data flow

The 'dict' processes described in section 4.1 are connected with each other through data streams, as shown in figure 8.

The data stream structure is shown in figure 9. This structure represents the trace of morphological analysis, and can be regarded as an application of the layered stream technique.

Unlike the SAX, which analyses inputs according to CFG with the layered stream technique, LAX does not place any identifier between the rules.

In figure 9, ⟨r-features⟩ corresponds to *rightf(morpheme)*. ⟨array of results⟩ enables the packing of resultant data, described in the next section. In the practical algorithm, a different type of data will flow into a 'dict', which should distinguish the data to be processed in it. For example, in figure 8, the results from P14 will be passed through the 'dict' in lines F1, F2 and F3 before flowing into the 'dict' in F4, in which the results should be processed. Therefore, in the practical algorithm, each item of data has a tail position number representing the process by which it should be processed. (We use the function *position(data$_{data}$)* to mark this position.) Cor-

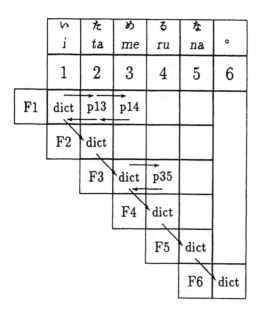

Figure 8: Data flow in the Practical Algorithm

⟨data stream⟩ ::= [⟨array of data⟩]

⟨array of data⟩ ::= ⟨data⟩, ⟨array of data⟩

⟨array of data⟩ ::= ⟨data⟩

⟨data⟩ ::= [⟨position⟩,
⟨r-features⟩,
⟨results⟩]

⟨position⟩ ::= $N(1 \leq N \leq$ length of input)

⟨r-features⟩ ::= [⟨re⟩, ..., ⟨re⟩]

⟨re⟩ ∈ $S_{feature}$

⟨results⟩ ::= [⟨surface of a morpheme⟩,
⟨morphological category⟩,
⟨array of results⟩]

⟨array of results⟩ ::= []

⟨array of results⟩ ::= ⟨results⟩,
⟨array of results⟩

Figure 9: Structure of Data stream

[
  [2,[*rightf*(胃)], [胃,word-stem-of-noun,[]]],
  [3,[*rightf*(痛)],[痛,word-stem-of-adjective,[]]],
  [3,[*rightf*(傷)],[傷,word-stem-of-verb,[]]],
  [4,[*rightf*(炒め)],[炒め,word-stem-of-verb,[]]],
  [4,[*rightf*(板目)],[板目,word-stem-of-noun,[]]]
]

Figure 10: Example of data in the stream

responding to *position(data$_{data}$)*, each 'dict' is tagged with the position number *position(dict$_{process}$)* when it is activated. For example, in figure 8, the 'dict' in line F1 is tagged with 1 and the 'dict' at line F3 is tagged with 3 at the beginning of the analysis.

Let us trace the example computation in detail. First, the token [1, [end(*top*)],[]] is given to the 'dict' in line F1. This can be regarded as initializing the NFSA.

The 'dict' at F1 will output the token [2, *rightf*(胃), [胃, word-stem-of-noun,[]]] after calling $C_{rule}$ to check whether *top* and word–stem–of–noun(胃) can be concatenated.

The 'dict' in F1 activates P13, and P13 activates P14 in succession. Then, the data stream coming out from the 'dict' in F1 into the 'dict' in F2 is now as shown in figure 10.

### 4.2.2 Concatenation with data packing

On receiving the inputs, as shown in figure 10, the 'dict' in F2 picks up data whose *position(data$_{data}$)* is 2, and outputs data whose *position(data$_{data}$)* is greater than 2 to the 'dict' in line F3. The 'dict' in F2 will check whether the data picked up can be concatenated with a morpheme corresponding to character strings starting from point 2. If there is no such morpheme, the 'dict' in F2 will output [] and stop. Otherwise, the 'dict' in F2 will work like the 'dict' in F3.

The 'dict' in F3 inputs data as follows.

[
    [3,[*rightf*(痛)],[痛,word-stem-of-adjective,[]]],
    [3,[*rightf*(傷)],[傷,word-stem-of-verb,[]]],
    [4,[*rightf*(炒め)],[炒め,word-stem-of-verb,[]]],
    [4,[*rightf*(板目)],[板目,word-stem-of-a-noun,[]]]
]

Let us suppose that, using the 'dict' in F3, a morpheme め is found as follows.

$$leftf(inflect(め)) \cap rightf(word\text{-}stem\text{-}of\text{-}adjective(痛)) \neq \phi$$
$$leftf(め) \cap rightf(word\text{-}stem\text{-}of\text{-}verb(傷)) \neq \phi$$

Then, the output from the 'dict' in F3 will be as follows.

[
    [4,[*rightf*((め))],[め,inflect,
                  [  [痛,word-stem-of-adjective,[]],
                     [傷,word-stem-of-verb,[]]]]]],
    [4,*rightf*(炒め),[炒め,word-stem-of-verb,[]]],
    [4,*rightf*(板目)),[板目,word-stem-of-noun,[]]]
]

Figure 11: Packed data

The result shown in figure 11 is very important. In LAX, combinatorial ambiguities which occur in concatenation are not propagated to any other concatenation. If there are ambiguities, they are packed as shown in figure 11. Therefore, the complexity becomes $O(n_3)$. Details of complexity will be discussed in section 5.

## 4.3   Summary of the Practical Algorithm

This section summarizes the practical algorithm.

1. Activation of 'dict' processes

   (a) Activate $N+1$ 'dict' processes corresponding to each input string which has $N$ Japanese characters and a Japanese punctuation mark.
   Each 'dict' should have a *position(dict$_{process}$)*.
   $N$ 'dict' processes correspond to $N$ Japanese characters.
   Activated processes are linked with streams as indicated by the arrows in figure 8.

   (b) *rightf(top)*, indicating the initial state of the NFSA, is put in the stream to the processes at raw 1.

   (c) Data from the 'dict' at $N+1$ is the result of analysis.

2. Algorithm for the 'dict' processes
   The 'dict' processes activated in line 1 continue as follows. A 'dict' has many sub-processes, which are connected with each other through communication streams, as shown in figure 12. Each sub-process can be characterised by its *input* and process and its *output* to its connected processes. From this line, the function *input(Data)* represents the data input of each process, and the function *output(Data,Process$_N$)* represents the data output to the *Process* whose number is $N$. Numbers in figure 12 correspond to the following item numbers.

   (a) Do *input(Data)*.
   If *Data* is the *tail* of a data stream, do *output(tail,Process$_{2b}$)* and stop.
   Otherwise, do *output(Data,Process$_{2b}$)*.
   Go to 2a.

   (b) The *filstr* process
   Do *input(Data)*.
   If *Data* is the *tail* of a data stream, do *output(tail,Process$_{2c}$)*, *output(tail,Process$_{2d}$)*, *output(tail,Process$_{2e}$)*, and stop.
   If *position(Data$_{data}$)* is equal to *position(dict$_{data}$)*,
   do *output(Data,Process$_{2c}$)* and *output(Data,Process$_{2d}$)*.
   If *position(Data$_{data}$)* is greater than *position(dict$_{data}$)*,
   do *output(Data,Process$_{2e}$)*.
   Go to 2b.

(c) The *filcon* process

input(Data).

Check whether $C_{rule}$(Data, refmorph(dict)) is true or not. If it is true, concatenate Data and refmorph(dict) to make new morphemes and output(new morphemes,$Process_{dict:pro:5}$). Go to 2c.

(d) The PXY sub-process

    i. Do input(Data).

    If Data is the *tail* of a data stream, output(tail,$Process_{2(d)ii}$) and stop.

    Otherwise, do output(Data,$Process_{2(d)ii}$), recursively call PXY, and do output(Data,$Process_{dict:pro:4}$).

    Go to 2(d)i.

    ii. Do input(Data).

    If Data is the *tail* of a data stream, do output(tail,$Process_{2(d)ii}$) and stop.

    Check whether $C_{rule}$(Data,refmorph(sub_pro)) is true or not. If it is true, concatenate Data and refmorph(sub_pro) to make new morphemes and do output(new morphemes,$Process_{dict:pro:5}$).

    Go to 2(d)ii.

(e) Do input(Data).

If Data is the *tail* of a data stream, and it is the first input data, then process the unknown word, else do output(Data,$Process_{thenextdict}$) and stop.

Otherwise, do output(Data,$Process_{thentextdict}$).

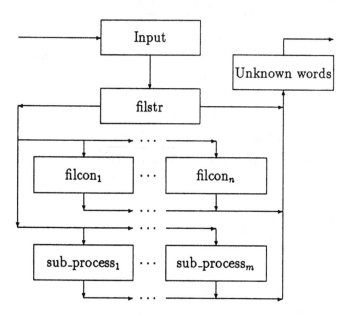

Figure 12: 'dict' procedure

# 5  Complexity

This section discusses the complexity of the elementary and practical algorithms in sequential and parallel execution.

## 5.1  Complexity in Sequential Execution

First, the elementary algorithm has the following complexity. In the following expressions, $n$ is the number of input characters and $T$ is the total amount of time required to obtain all solutions, so that complexity is that of $T$ related to $n$. We assume that any input substring corresponds to $a$ morphemes. All adjacent morphemes can be concatenated. $d$ is the time required for dictionary search. $c$ is the time required to check and concatenate a pair of morphemes. $i$ is the number of delimiting positions, as shown in the chart under the expressions. $a^{i+1} \times {}_{n-1}C_i$ is the time required to check and concatenate all the pairs of morphemes when there are $i$ delimiters in character strings.

Morpheme look-up is realised with the TRIE structure, and the search time for a morpheme of $m$ characters takes $d \times m$ where $d$ is the time required to trace the TRIE structure. Thus, the total look-up time for a sub-string contains $j$ input characters, $d \sum_{i=1}^{n} i(n-i+1)$. Thus, we have:

$$T = c \sum_{i=0}^{n-1} (a^{i+1} \times {}_{n-1}C_i) + \sum_{j=1}^{n} dj(n-j+1) \tag{29}$$

$$= c \times a(1+a)^{n-1} + d\frac{n(n+1)(n+2)}{6}$$

$$\text{where } a, n \geq 1, \quad c, d > 0$$

$$O(T) = O(a^n) \tag{30}$$

and thus,

$$\overbrace{C_1, C_2, \ldots, C_a}^{morpheme_1}, \overbrace{C_{a+1}, \ldots, C_b}^{morpheme_2}, \cdots, \overbrace{C_{m+1}, \ldots, C_n}^{morpheme_{i+1}}$$
$$\qquad 1 \qquad\qquad\quad 2 \qquad\; i$$

There should be a limitation on the morpheme length so that the maximum character length of a morpheme can be set to $l$. If $l$ is greater than $n$, the complexity becomes $O(a^n)$. Otherwise, it becomes as follows. It is impossible to obtain one expression for 31 because we cannot obtain any expressions for polynomials whose maximum degree is 'n'.

$$T \quad = \quad cA_n \tag{31}$$

where

$$A_k \quad = \quad \sum_{i=1}^{l} A_{k-1} \ (k > l) \tag{32}$$

$$A_k \quad = \quad ca^k (k \leq l) \tag{33}$$

where $c > 0, k > l$

Then the complexity of the practical algorithm is as follows:

$$T \quad = \quad c\sum_{i=1}^{n-1}(i \times (n-i) \times a^2) + \sum_{j=1}^{n} dj(n-j+1)$$

$$= \quad \frac{a^2 \times (n^3 - n)}{6} + d\frac{n(n+1)(n+2)}{6}$$

$O = O(n^3)$      where a is the worst ambiguity of the morpheme and n is the character length of the input sentence

$$\overbrace{C_1, C_2, \ldots, \underbrace{C_i}_{i}, \underbrace{C_{i+1}, \ldots, C_n}_{n-i}}^{n}$$

If the maximum length of the morpheme is $l$, the complexity is given by:

$$T \quad = \quad c\sum_{i=1}^{n} a^2 + d\sum_{j=1}^{l} j(n-j+1) \tag{34}$$

$$= \quad c \times a_2 \times n + d(1+l)l/2 \times n + K \tag{35}$$

$$\text{where } K = -d\sum_{j=1}^{l} j^2 + \sum_{i=1}^{l} \tag{36}$$

$$O \quad = \quad O(n) \tag{37}$$

The conclusion to be drawn is clearly that packing is critical to the algorithm.

## 5.2 Complexity in Parallel Execution

We define the time complexity of a parallel execution in terms of the time from the beginning to the end of parallel execution. In parallel execution, the dictionary search process can run simultaneously, so that the search time is proportional to the maximum length of morphemes. However, the concatenation processes cannot run simultaneously, because a process suspends itself until the preceding process outputs data to it. Therefore, in parallel execution, the time complexity will be proportional to the input length.

# 6 Algorithm for Sequential Logic Languages

This section describes an implementation of the LAX algorithm in terms of the sequential logic programming language, ESP. ESP, which can be executed on the PSI or PSI-II machine, is an object oriented Prolog and has an array structure called the *stack vector*. Using the stack vector, we can access each logical variable with an index.

Due to the execution time and the memory efficiency consideration, it is not a good idea to simulate the layered stream mechanism sequentially for the implementation of the LAX algorithm. We have therefore adopted another mechanism, the *tableau method*, in place of the layered stream mechanism. In this method, a tableau stores the analysis, and analyses breadth-first. This method is also a sort of parallel algorithm, which our implementation simulates sequentially.

First, the sequential version of the LAX algorithm is explained. Next, the result of efficiency evaluation of this algorithm is reported.

## 6.1 Sequential Algorithm

This algorithm consists of two phases. In the first phase, it looks up all the morphemes that occur in the input sentence and stores them in a stack vector (*tableau*). These morphemes are the only candidates for the morphemes that belong to the correct interpretation of the input sentence. This phase is implemented as a *clause indexing* search on the programs compiled from the TRIE structure. Fundamentally, this part of the algorithm is the same as in the parallel version.

In the second phase, the algorithm attempts to connect two adjoining morphemes. If analysis fails in some position, namely, if there are no two morphemes connected with each other at that point, it calls the error recovery process that connects the last two morphemes. We can therefore obtain an almost correct analysis even when there are some *unknown words*, or words that are not entered in the morphological dictionary, in the input sentence. This enables us to process sentences flexibly that contain unknown words.

○ The sequential LAX algorithm:

· *Input*: a string of $n$ characters

· *Output*: the result of morphological analysis (a packed structure)

• First phase:

Make a stack vector of size $n + 1$, and set the right-hand feature of the start of the sentence and left-hand feature of the end of the sentence to the first and last positions of the stack vector, respectively. For each number $i$ ($1 \leq i \leq n$), do the following.

o Look up all the morphemes that start from the $i$th character and register them in the stack vector at the $i$th position. Each morpheme has two kinds of features, the left-hand feature and right-hand feature, and is represented as a list structure with its tail unbound.

• Second phase:

For each number $i$ ($1 \leq i \leq n$), do the following.

o For each morpheme of size $l$ stored at the $i$th element of the stack vector, pick up the morphemes at the $(i + 1 - l)$th element of the stack vector. If two adjoining morphemes can be concatenated, unify the left-hand morpheme with the tail of the right-hand morpheme.

If no morpheme can be connected to any adjoining morpheme, and if no morpheme stored at less than the $i$th position is connected to the morpheme stored at greater than the $i$th position, then select one morpheme which is connected to the morpheme stored at less than the $i$th position and connect it to one of the adjoining morphemes.

If there is no sequence of morphemes from the start of the sentence to the end of the sentence, that is, analysis fails, search the missing morphemes backwards and connect them so that there is at least one sequence of morphemes.

## 6.2  Evaluation of Sequential Algorithms

This section reports the evaluation of the sequential LAX algorithm. We adopt two texts as the test sentences. One is a biography 「キュリー夫人」 ("Madame Curie"), and the other is an article about nature conservation entitled 「自然を守る」 ("Nature Conservation"). These are in the textbooks for the fifth and sixth grades of elementary school, respectively. Appendix A shows an extract of the text 「自然を守る」 ("Nature Conservation") for evaluation. Table 1 shows the size of the texts and of morphological dictionary entries. We use the same affix dictionary to analyse each text, and provide a word stem dictionary for each text.

The analysis of these texts was performed on a PSI-II machine with the SIMPOS 4.1 operating system.

Appendix B is part of the result of the analysis for the second text 「自然を守る」 ("Nature Conservation"), and shows the length (number of characters), number of ambiguities and analysis time for each sentence. LAX can analyse each sentence in less than 100 msec even when there are many ambiguities.

| Text | 「キュリー夫人」<br>"Madame Curie" | 「自然を守る」<br>"Nature Conservation" | Total |
|------|------------------|--------------------------|-------|
| Number of sentences | 126 | 82 | 208 |
| Word stems | 780 | 450 | 1230 |
| Derivational and<br>inflectional affixes | 520 | 520 | 520 |

Table 1: Contents of the test texts and their dictionaries

This result shows that the LAX sequential algorithm can analyse Japanese sentences in linear order.

# 7 Conclusion

This paper described the LAX algorithm, its time complexity and its implementation on a sequential logic based machine. It also reported the evaluation of the result of analysis for two types of Japanese sentences. We believe that there are two areas for further research. One is to refine the algorithm to allow a more precise retrieval of unknown words. The second is to implement the parallel LAX algorithm in terms of GHC.

# A Sample Sentences

Extracts of the text 「自然を守る」 ("Nature Conservation")

1. 人間が、この地球の上で生き続けていくためには、どうしても、自然の恵みに頼らなければならない。

2. 私たちが毎日食べる物も、住んでいる家も、着る服も、もとはといえば、みな自然界から手に入れた物である。

3. 人間は、その優れた技術を使って、自然から得た物を巧みに加工し、自分たちの生活を豊かにしている。

4. 人間にとって、自然は、限り無い資源の宝庫なのだ。

5. また、人間は、宅地を造るために、山を切り崩して平地にしたり、交通を便利にするために、森を切り開いて道路を造ったりしている。

6. あるいは、電気を起こすために、川の流れをせき止めてダムを建設したり、工業地帯にするために、海を埋め立てて陸地に変えたりしている。

7. つまり、人間は、いろいろな方法で自然に手を加えているのである。

8. このように、人間は、自然が生み出す物を資源として利用する一方、自分たちに都合の良いように自然の姿を変えて生活している。

9. この地球上で、人間だけが、自然の資源を思う存分利用したり、自然を改造したりする知恵と力とを備えた生物なのである。

10. しかし、それだからといって、人間が思いのままに自然の姿を変え、その資源を手当たり次第に自分たちの物にしてしまってもいいのだろうか。

# B  Result of Analysis

Sample text: 「自然を守る」 ("Nature Conservation")

| Sentence number | Number of characters | Ambiguities | Analysis time (msec) |
|---|---|---|---|
| 1 | 46 | 2 | 57 |
| 2 | 50 | 4 | 56 |
| 3 | 47 | 2 | 43 |
| 4 | 24 | 1 | 23 |
| 5 | 61 | 4 | 58 |
| 6 | 64 | 4 | 62 |
| 7 | 31 | 2 | 34 |
| 8 | 59 | 2 | 67 |
| 9 | 56 | 8 | 58 |
| 10 | 65 | 12 | 85 |
| 11 | 64 | 8 | 89 |
| 12 | 57 | 4 | 70 |
| 13 | 16 | 2 | 24 |
| 14 | 18 | 2 | 19 |
| 15 | 20 | 1 | 15 |
| 16 | 26 | 4 | 49 |
| 17 | 21 | 1 | 17 |
| 18 | 45 | 1 | 46 |
| 19 | 26 | 1 | 23 |
| 20 | 21 | 1 | 14 |
| 21 | 45 | 3 | 42 |
| 22 | 27 | 1 | 32 |
| 23 | 24 | 2 | 32 |
| 24 | 43 | 3 | 34 |
| 25 | 39 | 1 | 46 |
| 26 | 33 | 4 | 44 |
| 27 | 38 | 4 | 37 |
| 28 | 63 | 6 | 81 |
| 29 | 66 | 1 | 88 |
| 30 | 60 | 6 | 74 |

# References

[1] Akasaka, K., Sugimura, R. and Matsumoto, Y., "Chikuji : Shorikei-jô deno LAX no Mondai-ten to sono Kaiketsu-hô" ("Problems in LAX in sequential implimentation, and their Solutions" (in Japanese)), *Proceedings of the 35th Conference of Information Processing Society of Japan*, pp.1355–1356, 1987

[2] Aizawa, T. and Ebara. T., "Mechanical Translation System of Kana Representations to Kanji-kana Mixed Representations" (in Japanese), *NHK Gijutsu-Kenkyû*, Vol.25 No.5, pp.23-60, 1973

[3] Kamiwaki, T. and Tanaka, H., "Jisho no TRIE Kôzô-ka to Jukugo Shori" ("Idiom Handling Using the TRIE Structure Dictionary" (in Japanese)), *Proceedings of the Logic Programming Conference '85*, pp.329–340, 1988

[4] Kay, M., "Algorithm Schemata and Data Structures in Syntactic Processing", *Technical Report*, CSL-80-12, XEROX PARC., Oct. 1980

[5] Mizutani, S., "Kokubunpô Shibyô" ("Sketch of Japanese Grammars" (in Japanese)), *Bunpô to Imi I*, Asakura Nihongo Kôza No.3, Asakura Shoten, 1983

[6] Okumura, K. and Matsumoto, Y. , "Layered Stream wo Mochiita Heiretsu Pogramming" ("Parallel Programming using Layered Stream" (in Japanese)), *Proceedings of the Logic Programming Conference '87*, pp223–232, 1987

[7] Sugimura, R., Akasaka, K. and Matsumoto, Y., "Heiretsu Keitaiso Kaiseki System LAX no Jitsugen" ("Imprementation of Parallel Morphological Analyser LAX" (in Japanese)), *Proceedings of the 35th Conference of Information Processing Society of Japan*, pp.1323-1324, 1987

[8] Ueda K., Guarded Horn Clauses, *ICOT Technical Report* No.103, 1985

[9] Earley, J., "An Efficient Context-free Parsing Algorithm", *CACM*, Vol13, No.2, pp.94-102, 1970

[10] Matsumoto,Y and Sugimura, R., "Ronri-gata Gengo ni Motozuku Kôbun Kaiseki System SAX" ("Logic Programming Based Parser SAX" (in Japanese)), *Computer Software*,Vol3, No.4, 1986

[11] Yoshimura,K., Hidaka, I. and Yoshida, S., "Nihon-go Bun no Keitaisokaiseki ni okeru Saichô-itchi-hô to Bunsetsu-sû Saishô-hô nitsuite" ("Saichô-itchi and Bunsetsu-sû Saishô-hô in Morphological analysis " (in Japanese)), IPSJ-NLU 30-7, 1982

[12] Morioka, K., "Goi no Keisei" ("Formation of a Vocabulary" (in Japanese)) *Gendai-go Kenkyû Series 1*, Meiji-Shoin, 1987

[13] Sano, H., Akasaka, K., Kubo, Y., and Sugimura, R., "Go-Kôsei ni Motozuku Keitaiso Kaiseki" ("Morphological Analysis with Derivation and Inflection" (in Japanese)), *Proceedings of the 36th Conference of Information Processing Society of Japan*, 1988

[14] Mukai K., A System of Logic Programming for Linguistic Analysis Based on Situation Semantics, Proceedings of the Workshop on Semantic Issues in Human and Computer Languages. Half Moon Bay. CSLI 1987

# Extraction of Characteristic Facts and Abstract Generation

Naoyoshi TAMURA, Tomomi KAMIO, Masato KUROSAKI

Yokohama National University

156 Tokiwadai Hodogayaku Yokohama 240, Japan

## Abstract

This paper presents a formalization of the summary generation process, which takes a set of observed facts as input and generates its summary in the form of natural language text. Our assumption is that human summarization process consists of the following four phrases : (1) reconstructing the original semantic structure in his/her mind from observed facts, (2) extracting the characteristic facts from the reconstructed structure, (3) constructing the surface structure of text in the macroscopic view and finally (4) generating a natural language text from the surface structure. Our system generates newspaper-like texts in the domain of baseball games. The implementation is also briefly presented.

## 1 Introduction

In this paper we present a formalization of the summary generation process, which takes a sequence of observed facts as input and generates a summary in natural language text from the facts. We also present a part of its implementation which is written in C-Prolog.

Among the wide current studies of text or story understanding, text summarization is one of the difficult themes which require highly advanced processes of semantic analysis. In summary generation, the mechanism to decide whether a fact is important or not is primarily significant. The following approaches seem to be typical: (1) an approach based on the frequency of key words, (2) an approach based on scripts [7], (3) an approach based on the connective relation between sentences [2,8], (4) an approach based on the story grammars and rules for summarization [6]. We assume that the human process of extracting characteristic facts can be described only with semantic information manipulation. Therefore we focus on semantic information processing and consider the input information, which is a series of facts (we will call this facts observation), to have no surface structure. And we restrict the domain of summarization to be so small that sufficient understanding and deep inferences can be performed for as many cases as possible.

Our system basically uses summarization rules in the extraction process. However, there are some text generation systems which decide the degree of refinement of generated texts with the importance decision mechanism based on semantic analysis [1,3]. In our system the semantic information is represented in networks. We aim at construction of the human model of interest, the importance decision mechanism and the summarization model by arranging all of the networks.

The world to which we apply our summarization system is that of games with wins and defeats, especially the world of baseball game. The reasons why we chose this are the overall goals of a group (to win the game, to hit a ball at a chance, to defend at a disadvantage) is obvious, it is possible to appropriately formalize the game by simplifying rules of baseball and sufficient inferences are possible in the small domain.

Our aim is to generate sentences in newspaper-like style which we think it is easy to deal with outwardly, not only because we want to lighten a burden on the generation process but also because our final object is to build a sports journalist robot who can write news from the scorebook of a game.

In chapter 2, we present a formalization of the extraction process in the most abstract model, and we extensively study the model of human interests, the existence of a reader and the hierarchy of semantic representation. In chapter 3, we concretely reconsider the extraction process again for an implementation. Especially, we study the similarities of our importance decision mechanism with the connectionist model. In the final chapter, chapter 4, we present an implementation of our system and some inner representations of knowledge or information. We also explain each sentence of generated texts.

## 2　A model of summarization process

In this chapter, we present a model of the human summarization process which comprehends a sequence of facts and generates a text as a summary.

### 2.1　A model of extraction

First, we study the process of summary generation and present a model of extraction.

Given information about a series of facts, we divide the summary generation process into three phases.

1. Deletion of uninteresting information and extraction of interesting information: a deletion phase of uninteresting information and information from which any other interesting information cannot be derived.

2. Transformation to "the macroscopic structure" (the surface structure) and the text planning: We will call a structure stating assertions of a mass (members participate in events) in the macroscopic view "the macroscopic structure". The macroscopic structure is reconstructed from facts of each element in order to generate more natural sentences. In our objective world, the world of baseball games, structures collectively describing a movement of a team or describing win or loss of a team are macroscopic ones, whereas descriptions of each member's movement are microscopic ones. Topic of paragraphs or documents correspond to such structure.

3. Generation of surface sentences: We consider the text generation phase as an isomorphism except for a rhetorical transformation.

We define the process of the extraction of characteristic facts as in Definition 1. In the definition, each domain of discourse is a set of information, more concretely speaking, which corresponds to a set of assertions and rules about facts. And we think the deletion and the extraction of information are influenced "personal interests", so we deal with human interests as a parameter in the process of the summary generation.

**Definition 1 (Extraction process)**

The *extraction process* is defined as followings.

1. Let $F$ be a set of information about series of original events to be considered, the act of observation is an application of the function $o$ to $F$. We define the result $O$ to be an *observation*.

$$O = o(F)$$

2. The *reconstruction* $R$ of original events is constructed by an application of the function $r$ to the observation $O$ and the knowledge $K$ of an objective world. By this application some obvious facts which were deleted at the observation are supplied.

$$R = r(O, K)$$

3. The set $S$ of *characteristic facts* is constructed by an application of the function $s$ to the reconstruction $R$ and parameter $P$ of human interests.

$$S = s(R, P)$$

In our application of this definition, the knowledge $K$ of an objective world consists of rules of baseball, some information about each player and so on. The outline of the summarization process is shown in Fig.1. Though we will mention in more details in section 3.1, the input of the system is currently the observation $O$.

Let us consider "the quantity of knowledge" as the number of assertions in a domain, where each element is an assertion for a knowledge. Fig.2 shows the domain and the region of each function (i.e. set of original events $F$, reconstruction $R$, observation $O$ and characteristic facts $S$). Next, we study the relation of each domain.

1. The observation $O$ is included in the set $F$ of original events, because $O$ has less information than $F$.

$$O \subset F$$

2. The reconstruction $R$ has more information than the observation $O$ because $R$ is made from $O$ by a supplementation of some obvious facts.

$$O \subset R$$

3. The set $S$ of characteristic facts is a subset of the reconstruction $R$.

From Fig.2 we find the followings. ($\bar{O}, \bar{R}$ stand for the complement set of $O, R$, respectively.)

$S \cap O$ is the important information from the observation.

$R \cap \bar{O}$ is the important information supplemented by the inference and is obvious to the observer.

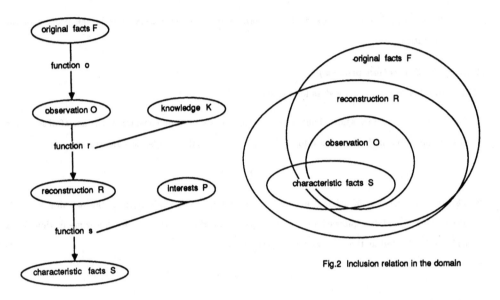

Fig.1 Model of extraction process

Fig.2 Inclusion relation in the domain

$S \cap \bar{R}$ is the information of human interests supplied at the extraction process.

Definition 2 represents a transformation from a description of each event to a description of re-structured in macroscopic view.

### Definition 2 (Transformation to the macroscopic structure)

A *macroscopic structure (surface structure)* $M$ is generated by function $m$ from a set of characteristic facts $S$ and a parameter $P$ describing human interests.

$$M = m(S, P)$$

The parameter $P$ of human interests indicates what standpoints the macroscopic structure is viewed from, for example in a baseball game, $P$ is used to indicate whether one scene is favorable to one team or not favorable to the other team.

### 2.2 Model of human interests

The parameter of human interests, which appeared in Definition 1, is referred at the characteristic facts' extraction and the transformation to the surface structure. This parameter was introduced to model the human interests (or view points) which a man referes at writing text from a series of events. Hereafter, this we will call this model *the model of (human) interests*, or simply *interests*. The model of human interests is represented by a set of items about what the man is interested in. The model of human interests depends on the objective world of summarization. Also, there are some common interests among people and some kinds of personal interests of a man who generate summaries or surface structures, although both view points are not strictly distinguishable. We show an example model of human interests, which is represented in natural language. The items are selected for the summarization of baseball games, and are partially implemented as rules of a production system.

[The model of human interests]

1. Common view points among almost people

    (a) the issue of the game

    (b) score (tie, reverse, home run, etc.)

    (c) activity of favorite players

    (d) evolution of severely changing game

    (e) unexpected scene

    (f) points-expected scene

2. Specific view points of summary writer

    (a) the issue of the favorite/notfavorite team

    (b) score or chance of the favorite/notfavorite team

    (c) activity of favorite/notfavorite players

    (d) standpoint (either offense of one team or defense of the other)

In this model, (1) seems to be common interests among almost people. (1-d) and (1-e) relate to a method in which events not matching a script remain in the summary. We thought items in (2) represent a personalities of the writer who likes/dislikes a specific team. On the other hand we can say that items in (2) also represent common interests in a sense the he has favorite/notfavorite particular one team. In this sense we can think of models of specific interests focused on runnings or, extremely speaking, the second base. In actual newspaper articles of professional baseball league, victory in a season and the record of players usually become a major subjects of discussion. To generate newspaper-like texts, more precise models of interests are necessary, in which time transitions and the relation to other games have to be taken into account. However we left these problems to be future works.

## 2.3 Existence of a reader

The process told in Definition 1 proceeds from the inference of original events to the extraction of characteristic facts. We think such a process of summarization corresponds to one in which the summary writer has his own standards of extraction and he doesn't recognize the existence of a reader. On the other hand there may be another style of summary generation, i.e. the summary writer has a reader model and through the model the writer proceeds with the summarization while he is considering reader's ability of reconstructing the points of original events from the summarization. In this section we present the summarization process with a reader model.

At first, we abstractly redefine Definition 1. Let $i$ be a function which has the domain and the region both on the world of knowledge $K(R, O, S \in K)$ and infers a set of information as much as it can infer. Conversely let $s$ be a function to get summaries from a set of information.

$$i, s : K \to K$$

Then the process of Definition 1 can also be represented by the following way:

$$R = i(O) \qquad \{reconstruction\ from\ the\ observation\ O\}$$

$$S = s(R) \qquad \{summarization\ from\ the\ reconstruction\ R\}$$

where the writer generates summaries on the base of his interests only.

Now

$$R' = i(S)$$

represents one more reconstruction from the summary by inference $i$, and

$$S' = s(R')$$

represents one more summarization from the re-reconstruction.

We next define a function $s_n$ which repeats reconstructions and summarization $n$ times.

$$s_0(x) \equiv s(i(x))$$

$$s_{n+1}(x) \equiv s(i(s_n(x)))$$

And moreover let $S_n$ be equal to $s_n(O)$ i.e.,

$$S_n \equiv s_n(O)$$

then the sequence $S_1, S_2, S_3, \ldots$ corresponds to the polishing of summaries.

Fig.3 represents the model of summarization process considering the existence of readers. In this summarization model the summary writer knows the existence of readers. However, the writer thinks readers are interested in the same points that the writer has and readers can infer in the same way that the writer does.

We can study more precise models of summarization. For example, distinguishing interests of a reader (or the knowledge of a reader's world) from that of the writer will make a model with more respect for readers. In these summarization models deletion is the only operation, however, summaries are to be polished not only by deletion of information but also by restoration of deleted information. To formalize the restoration, extension of inference mechanism, such as reference to the reconstruction $R$ which is the information with no deletion performed, is necessary.

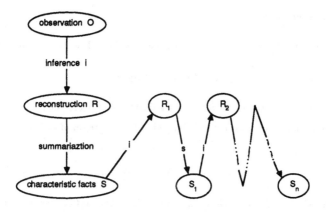

Fig.3 Model of summarization process considering
the existence of a reader.

## 2.4 Transformation to macroscopic structure

Each event in the reconstruction of original events were described separately. However, the information represented by several sentences usually can be processed together. Moreover, when the summarization process has finished, the whole text is often gathered into one sentence. Thus there is an hierarchy in representation level. We call this hierarchy *the hierarchy of representation*. We divide this hierarchy into three levels.

1. fine description level: each sentence in the text summarization and each player's movement in our application.

2. middle description level: a summary for one paragraph in text summarization and topics in a game in our application.

3. inclusively description level: a theme in the text summarization and win or loss in our application.

## 3 Extraction of characteristic facts

In this chapter, we formalize more concretely the observation which is the input of the system, the inference process of original events and the extraction process of characteristic facts.

### 3.1 Definition of the observation

At first, let us define what is the input to be summarized. A series of events to be summarized is a sequence of facts in which a group cooperates to accomplish a goal, for instance to win a baseball game. The input is defined as follows. This is called set of events observation.

**Definition 3 (Observation)**

1. An *event* is a triple of a *time point*, an *agent* and an *action*. Therefore the domain of event is

$$Evt = Tp \times Agt \times Act$$

where $Tp$ stands for an ordered set representing time points (this relation is denoted by e.g. $t1 < t2$), $Agt$ stands for a finite set of agents and $Act$ stands for a finite set of actions.

2. An *observation* is a set of events.

$$O = \{evt1, evt2, \ldots\}$$

In our system, which deals with the world of baseball games, $Agt$ corresponds to a set of players of both teams, and $Act$ to a set of simplified action.

$$Act = \{hit(1), hit(2), hit(3), homerun, out, gethome, \ldots\}$$

Note that all facts that occurred in the objective world are not entered into the system. The sequence of events is entered into the system through some kind of means such as an observer. In this style of input we must recognize the existence of a filter on the objective world. But viewing the observation as abstractly represented original events, we take the existence of a filter as a future work.

## 3.2 Semantic network and inference

In this section we define the form of semantic network and the inference process for original events as a function on the network.

**Definition 4 (Semantic network)**

1. A set of *nodes* $N$ consists of a set of *names* $W$ and a set of *values* $D$.

$$N = W \cup D$$

2. A set of *link names* $Lbl$ is given as follows.

$$Lbl = \{case\ labels\} \cup \{attribute\ names\} \cup \{next, isa, stateA, stateB, effect, \ldots\}$$

3. A set of *link* $L$ is given as follows.

$$L = \{(n_1, l, n_2) \mid n_1, n_2 \in N, l \in Lbl\}$$

4. A *knowledge* $K$ is represented in the network as follows.

$$K = (N', L')$$

where $N' \subset N, L' \subset L$.

Given an observation $O$, the initial semantic network is built as following definition.

**Definition 5 (Initial semantic network)**

For each event in the observation $O$, i.e.

$$(tp, agt, act) \in O,$$

there exists an *event node* named $e$, and *the initial semantic network* $K_0 = (N_0, L_0)$ has the following links.

1. $(e, isa, act) \in L_0$,

   which represent that event $e$ belongs to a class $act$.

2. $(e, agent, agt) \in L_0$,

   which represent that an agent of event $e$ is $agt$.

3. $(e, stateB, s_i) \in L_0$,

   which represent that *the state node* before event $e$ occurs is $s_i$.

4. $(e, stateA, s_{i+1}) \in L_0$,

   which represent that the state node after event $e$ occurs is $s_{i+1}$.

5. $(s_i, next, s_{i+1}) \in L_0$,

   which represent that there is a relation *next* (relation of temporal ordering) between state node $s_i$ and $s_{i+1}$, provided that

$$tp_i < tp < tp_{i+1}$$

   for the event $(tp, agt, act)$ where time points of state nodes $s_i$ and $s_{i+1}$ correspond to $tp_i$ and $tp_{i+1}$, respectively.

6. $(e, next, e') \in L_0$,

   which represent that there exists an event $e'$ after the event $e$ (relation of temporal ordering).

When some events occur in the same time point, we treat them as a group on the network and consider these events as one event. Trivial facts and inferable facts from other facts are usually omitted from the observation when given as an input. But, we assume that facts represented as a group include all exceptional related facts. This is because exceptional related facts are difficult to reconstruct. Therefore, there is no inference for group facts (Definition 6, 3-a).

The inference on the initial semantic network is performed as follows.

**Definition 6 (Inference process)**

For a initial semantic network $K_0 = (N_0, L_0)$, we define *the process of inference* as a construction of semantic network

$$K = (N', L')$$

according to 2 and 3 given as follows.

1. For a state node $s$, we call a set of link

$$s^* \equiv \{(s, l, v) \mid l \in \{attribute\ names\}, v \in N\}$$

   the *state of* $s$.

2. Attach a set of link

$$S_i^* = fs(e, s_{i-1})$$

to each state node in the initial semantic network $K_0$, where function $S_i^* = fs(e, s_{i-1})$ maps occurring event $e$ and state $s_{i-1}^*$, which is the state before event $e$ occurs, to next state. And

$$(e, stateB, s_{i-1}) \in L_0,$$

$$(e, stateA, s_i) \in L_0,$$

$$(s_{i-1}, next, s_i) \in L_0.$$

3. Replace event node $e$ in the initial semantic network $K_0$ by a set of node $fe(e, s_i)$, where $s_i$ stands for a state before event $e$ occurs (which is indicated by a link named $stateB$), and function $fe$ is defined as follows:

   (a) When $e$ is a group event node,

   $$fe(e, s_i) = e,$$

   i.e., inference is not performed.

   (b) Otherwise

   $$fe(e, s_i) = \{events\ derived\ from\ event\ e\ at\ state\ s_i\}$$

Fig.4 show an example semantic network in our application. Some of the node names and link names which are specially used in the net are explained as follows.

1. nodes

   | | |
   |---|---|
   | event#N | represents an event node. |
   | state#N | represents a state node related to an event. |
   | team#N | represents an object at middle description level. |
   | game#N | represents an object at inclusively description level. |
   | other atoms | |

2. links

   | | |
   |---|---|
   | effect | links an effected node. |
   | cause | links a cause node. |
   | other case labels | |

The situation presented by Fig.4 is as follows: at second half of the first inning, when Shinozuka and Matsumoto are on the second and the third base, respectively, batter Hara makes a timely two base hit, then Shinozuka and Matsumoto come back to home base and turn the table to score 1-2.

Note that this scene is extracted as a characteristic facts because turning the table is in the model of interests told at section 2.2.

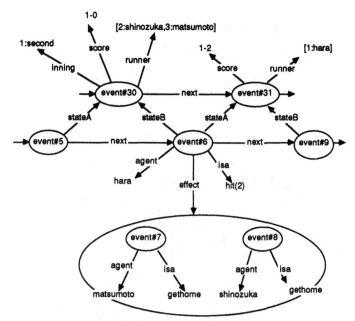

Fig.4 An example of semantic network.

## 3.3 Extraction process of characteristic facts

In this section, we formalize the extraction process of characteristic facts. The principle of extraction is based on weighting on the network: 1) Select significant items according to the model of human interests mentioned in section 2.2 and give them initial values of importance, 2) Compute new value of importance for each node by summing up the multiplication between values of importance of those nodes which connect to the node and the predifined weights of links between them.

### Definition 7 (Importance decision function on semantic network)

The importance decision function $p$ on a semantic network

$$K = (N', L')$$

is defined as follows.

1. Define the first importance decision function

$$p_0 : N \to R$$

   where $R$ is the domain of real number.

2. Define weight for each link name

$$w : Lbl \to R.$$

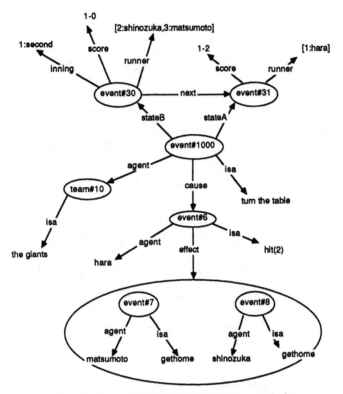

Fig.5 An example of semantic network in more macroscopic view.

For each link $(n_i, l, n_j)$, let *the weight of the link* be

$$w_{i,j} = w(l).$$

3. the $m + 1st$ *importance decision function* $p_{m+1} : N \to R$ is defined by

$$p_{m+1}(n_i) = \sum_j w_{j,i} p_m(n_j).$$

4. when

$$\sum_i \mid p_{m+1}(n_i) - p_m(n_i) \mid^2 < \delta$$

for some threshold number $\delta$, we define $p_m(n)$ to be *the importance decision function* $p(n)$ for semantic network $K = (N', L')$.

We can think our extraction mechanism of characteristic facts on the connectionist model. Making importance factors correspond with activity levels on neural net, the computation of importance decision function $p$ is very similar to that of activity level of connectionist model. On the other hand, we use the model of human interests to initialize the importance factors, however, assignment to the weight of links is also thought to be a kind of the model of human interests. These problems are left to be further works.

## 3.4 Transformation to macroscopic structure (planning)

In order to generate natural and readable texts, transformation from microscopic description to macroscopic structure and how to make that structure into text (planning) is very important. So far, we considered the extraction process and the transformation process separately. However, in the implementation, it is more effective to use the information obtained at the extraction of characteristic facts for the transformation to the macroscopic structure or planning. Moreover, theoretically, we think that such transformation to macroscopic structure has its meaning in the process of extraction. Because of these reasons, formalization is not sufficient. In chapter 4 we will show several examples of the transformation using experimental results.

Fig.5 shows a transformed macroscopic structure obtained from that of Fig.4. In Fig.4 events are found on the focus of each player, but in Fig.5 the view point is moved to higher level, i.e., the team level, where the agent of the representative event (event#1000) is a team (team#10). Fig.5 corresponds to the sentence "The Giants turned the table by Hara's two-base hit ..."

## 4 Implementation and experiment

In this chapter we present our summary generation system based on the formalism shown in chapter 2, 3, and we also present texts generated by the system from observations of (imaginary) baseball games.

### 4.1 Implementation

Our system is built on a Prolog system and the semantic network is represented in DCKR [5]. An example of network in DCKR is as follows, which corresponds to event#6 in Fig.4. '#' and ':' found in the followings are infix operators (xfx) with precedence 200 and 250, respectively.

```
sem(event#6,stateB:state#30).
sem(event#6,stateA:state#31).
sem(event#6,next:event#9).
sem(event#6,agent:hara).
sem(event#6,isa:hit(2)).
sem(event#6,effect:event#7).
```

Searching is quite simple by DCKR representation, such as omission of inverse links. Note that our DCKR representation is simple because searching doesn't need any complex operations on the isa hierarchy.

Rules of inference for the reconstruction (Definition 4,5,6) are written in production rule format and we implemented a very simple production system for them. The format of the rule is

*pattern on the semantic network* ==> *transformation on the network*

*pattern on the semantic network* is written in a conjunction (or disjunction) of prolog clauses in DCKR format, and *transformation on the network* is mainly to assert a new relation of objects. Even though for simplified baseball rules mentioned in section 3.1, production rules are so complicated that we will not mention them any more.

We defined the importance decision function in Definition 7 and mentioned the relation to the connectionist model, however, the function has not yet implemented.

Grammar for the generation of surface sentences consists of about 40 DCG rules, whose nonterminal symbols have difference lists and a pointer to a macroscopic structure on the semantic network as parameters.

## 4.2 Parameters of the system

We have parameterized several concepts in the summary generation process as follows.

1. Common view points of human interests (eg. score or the issue of the game).

2. Personality of summary writer (eg. favorite player/team).

3. Existence of a summary reader (i.e. whether to make another inferences or not).

4. Importance decision function (i.e. weights of links and initial values of nodes).

Here we have implemented two models of interests as common view points, that is 1 in the above list. Other parameters are not implemented so the system generate summaries at the neutral standpoint and pays no attention to the summary readers.

[Interests 1]

1. turning the table

2. same points

3. getting ahead

4. "if hit ..."

5. three consecutive strikeouts in a pitcher's game

6. home run

[Interests 2]

1. turning the table

2. winning hit

3. three consecutive strike-outs in a pitcher's game

4. home run

Each item represents following situations:

"same points" is a situation where both teams get to the same points.

"getting ahead" is a situation where a team gets point(s) after "same points" situation.

"turning the table" is a situation where losing team defeats another.

"if hit ..." is a situation where one team would get some points if a hit were made.

"three consecutive strikeouts in a pitcher's game" is a situation where a pitcher gets three consecutive strikeouts in a pitcher's game. Here, we define a pitcher's game is the game in which the total score of both team is less than two. This is based on the assumption that strike-out is a characteristic fact in a pitching game though it is not in hitting games.

"winning hit" is a situation where that hit causes the victory.

### 4.3   Input and generated texts

Next we show a part of input (the observation). In the input

        event(28,[(out,cromatie),(out(2),yoshimura)])

represents that "cromatie" was put out and "yoshimura" was also put out on the second base (out(2)) at time point 28.

Prolog clauses given below are two parts of the observation, the former represents a defense of "Hanshin" team at first half of the first inning, the latter represents that of "Giants" team at second half of the third, respectively.

The input to our system is the observation of the following form only, and information such as "first half of the first inning" is inferred automatically by the system. We made experiments for three more imaginary games. (cf. Appendix A)

        event(1,[(hit(2),mayumi)]).
        event(2,[(hit(1),tao)]).
        event(3,[(gethome,mayumi),(out,kakefu),(out(2),tao)]).
        event(4,[(strikeout,bass)]).

            ...

        event(24,[(hit(1),matsumoto)]).
        event(25,[(hit(1),shinozuka)]).
        event(26,[(walk,yoshimura)]).
        event(27,[(strikeout,hara)]).
        event(28,[(out,cromatie),(out(2),yoshimura)]).

            ...

### 4.4   Results and discussion

In this chapter we present two results by two models of interests (shown in section 4.2) from one (input) observation and explain some expression generations. Because texts generated are in Japanese, we give word-to-word translations of the outputs. The originals in Japanese texts are given at Appendix B. The time taken to generate texts for one model is about four minutes (in elapsed time, Sun-3/140, C-Prolog Interpreter). Results from other three inputs are also given in the Appendix A.

### [Game 1, Interests 1: word-to-word translation]

(1)Giants won the severely hitting game. (2)At first half of the first inning, Hanshin gained the first one point by Mayumi's two-base hit, Tao's hit and Mayumi's get-home during Kakefu's out. (3)At second half of the first inning with no out, losing one point, Giants tied by Matsumoto's hit, Matsumoto's advance to the second base during Shinozuka's out and Yoshimura's timely hit. (4)Also at second half of the second, Giants added one point by Nakahata's home run. (5)At first half of the third inning with no out, losing one point, Hanshin turned the table by Kido's walk, Kido's advance to the second base during Ikeda's out, Mayumi's timely hit, Kakefu's two runners home run and Bass's home run. (6)At second half of the third inning with score 5-2, Giants got a full base by Matsumoto's hit, Shinozuka's hit and Yoshimura's walk, but lost the chance by Cromatie's out, (7)however at the last inning, ended the game by Shinozuka's hit, Yoshimura's two-base hit and Hara's clinching home run.

Sentence (1) is a macroscopic expression for the whole game.

Sentence (2) has subject "Hanshin" instead of some player by the transformation to macroscopic structure. This sentence is extracted from "getting ahead" view point, however, because the score at this time is 0-0 the system generate "gained the first one point" as a surface phrase. Such a mechanism is built into the grammar as constraints.

Sentence (3) represents a situation from "same points" view points.

Sentence (4) represents a situation from "home run" view points.

In sentence (5),"advance to the second base during Ikeda's out, Mayumi's timely hit ..."(「...2 塁に進塁, 真弓のタイムリー」) represents a situation from "same points" view point and "turned the table by Kakefu's two runners home run and Bass's home run" (「掛布の2ラン, バースのホームランで逆転」) represents a situation from "turning the table" and "home run" view points.

Sentence (6) represents a situation from "if hit ..." view point.

Sentence (7) represents a situation from "turning the table" view point but the inning is last one so the system generates "end the game" (「さよなら勝ち」).

### [Game 1, Interests 2: word-to-word translation]

(1)Giants won the severelly hitting game. (2)At second half of the second inning with score 1-1, Giants added one point by Nakahata's home run. (3)At first half of the third inning with one out, score 1-2, Hanshin turns the table by Mayumi's timely hit, Kakefu's two runners home run and Bass's home run. (4)At second half of the last inning with no out, score 5-3, Giants settled the game by Shinozuka's hit, Yoshimura's two-base hit and Hara's three runners home run.

Note that the generated text by Interest 2 is shorter than by Interest 1, because there is less items in Interests 2.

Sentence (1) is a macroscopic expression for the whole game.

Sentence (2) represents a situation from "home run" view point. Because the system has no interests in "same points" and "getting ahead" view points the situation occurred before this situation is not extracted.

Sentence (3) represents a situation from "turning the table" view point.

In sentence (4) "settled the game by ... Hara's home run" (「原の3ランで試合を決めた」) represents a situation from "winning hit" view point. Note that in Interests 1 this situation was extracted from "turning the table" view points so the surface sentences in both Interests are different.

## 5 Discussion and further research

In this paper we have formalized the summarization process, that is reconstruction of the original events from an observation and the extraction mechanism of characteristic facts. And we have also presented our summary generation system and explained the transformation to the surface structure through generated texts. In those texts, considerably advanced expressions are found. The reason seems to be that by limitation of the objective world to baseball game, goals of each event in the world are clear, that decision of connectives between sentences are simple because, for instance, advantage of one team is disadvantage of the other, and that the system can cover almost all of transformation to surface structures.

Some processes are not fully formalized and implementation has not completed. Finally we collect these problems which are still left to be further research.

1. Investigation and formalization of the transformation to macroscopic structures and the planning.

2. More realistic model of human interests. In actual newspaper scripts of base ball games, contents are selected not only by events in one game but also by events in the past games. How does the system use such an information ?

3. Investigation of the existence of readers. We must study the convergence of 'polishment' model when the system distinguishes the world of summary writer and readers.

4. Relation to the connectionist model in the extraction process. How does the system assign initial values to nodes and weights to links in the importance decision function ? Convergence and so called local minimum must be investigated.

5. More natural sentence generation. Because of poor grammar, only stereotyped sentences are generated in our system. Not only newspaper-like style but also any styles of sentences would be generated. Pronominalization, omission of subjects and varying sentence styles are also important.

6. Investigation of the relation between the parameter of human interests and texts generated.

## Acknowledgement

We are grateful to Prof. Hozumi Tanaka of the department of computer science, Tokyo Institute of Technology and members of artificial intelligence research group AIUEO for their valuable suggestive opinions.

## Bibliography

[1] K. Hasida, S. Ishizaki, and H. Isahara. A connectionist approach to the generation of abstracts. In G. Kempen, editor, *Natural Language Generation*, pages 149–156, Martinus Nijhoff Publishers, 1987.

[2] J.R. Hobbs. Coherence and coreference. *Cognitive Science*, (3):69–90, 1979.

[3] Kakiuchi, Makimoto, Uehara, and Toyoda. Explanation generation on manualless system. ICOT NLS WG, 1986.

[4] K. Kita, E. Komatsu, and H. Yasuhara. Summarization support system, cogito. Preprints Work.Gr.for Natural Language Processing, 1986. IPSJ, 86-NL-58-7.

[5] H. Koyama and H. Tanaka. Definite clause knowledge representation. In *Logic Programming Conference.'85*, pages 95–106, ICOT, 1985. (in Japanese).

[6] D.E. Rumelhart. Notes on a schema for stories. Academic Press, 1975.

[7] R. Schank and R. Abelson. *Script Plans Goals and Understanding*. Lawrence Erlbaum Associates, 1977.

[8] K. Uchiumi and M. Shigenaga. Abstract generation of english text. Preprints Work.Gr.for Natural Language Processing, 1986. IPSJ, 86-NL-54-8.

## Appendix A. Results of the generation (English translation)

**[Game 2, Interests 1]**

Hanshin won by one side game. At first half of the first inning with no out, Hanshin gained the first one point by Mayumi's hit, Mayumi's advance to the second base during Tao's out and Kakefu's timely two-base hit. Also at first half of the third inning, Hanshin added three points by Tao's walk, Kakefu's two runners home run and Bass's home run. At second half of the third inning with no out, score 5-1, the Giants loaded bases by Egawa's hit, Shinozuka's hit and Yoshimura's walk, but lost the chance by Cromatie's strikeout. At the last inning with no out, score 5-1, Hanshin added one point by Bass's home run.

**[Game 2, Interests 2]**

Hanshin won by one side game. At first half of the first inning with one out, Hanshin settled the game by Kakefu's timely two-base hit and Bass's timely hit. Also at first half of the third inning, Hanshin added three points by Tao's walk, Kakefu's two runners home run and Bass's home run. At the last inning, Hanshin added one point by Bass's home run.

## [Game 3, Interests 1]

Hanshin shut out the Giants by pitcher's game, such as Ikeda's three strikeouts at the third inning and Egawa's three strikeouts at the fifth inning. At first half of the first inning with no out, Hanshin got the first point by Mayumi's hit, Mayumi's advance to the second base during Tao's out and Kakefu's timely two-base hit. At ssecond half of the first inning with no out, score 1-0, the Giants lost the chance by Hara's strikeout in spite of Matsumoto's hit, Shinozuka's hit and advance to the third base during Yoshimura's out.

## [Game 3, Interests 2]

Hanshin shut out the Giants by pitcher's game, such as Ikeda's three strikeouts at the third inning and Egawa's three strikeouts at the fifth inning. At first half of the first inning with no out, Hanshin settled the game by Mayumi's hit, Mayumi's advance to the second base during Tao's out and Kakefu's timely two-base hit.

## [Game 4, Interests 1]

The Giants won by one side game. At second half of the first inning with no out, the Giants added four points by Matsumoto's hit, Shinozuka's hit, Matsumoto's advance to the third base and Shinozuka's advance to the second base during Yoshimura's out, Hara's two points timely hit and Cromatie's two runners home run. At first half of the second inning with no out, score 0-4, Hanshin added one point by Bass's home run.

## [Game 4, Interests 2]

The Giants won by one side game. At second half of the first inning with no out, the Giants settled the game by Matsumoto's hit, Shinozuka's hit, Matsumoto's advance to the third base and Shinozuka's advance to the second base during Yoshimura's out, Hara's two points timely hit and Cromatie's two runners home run. At first half of the second inning with no out, score 0-4, Hanshin added one point by Bass's home run.

## Appendix B. Results of the generation

### [Game 1, Interests 1]

(1)試合は打撃戦で巨人がさよなら勝ち. (2)一回表無死, 阪神は真弓の二塁打, 田尾のヒット, 掛布のアウトの間に真弓がホームインして1点を先制. (3)1点差で迎えた一回裏無死, 巨人は松本のヒット, 篠塚のアウトの間に松本が2塁に進塁, 吉村のタイムリーで同点. (4)二回裏にも, 中畑のホームランで1点を加えた. (5)

1点差で迎えた三回表無死，阪神は木戸の四球，池田のアウトの間に木戸が2塁に進塁，真弓のタイムリー，掛布の2ラン，バースのホームランで逆転．(6)5－2で迎えた三回裏無死，巨人は松本のヒット，篠塚のヒット，吉村の四球で満塁，しかしクロマティのアウトでチャンスを逃した(7)が，最終回裏には，篠塚のヒット，吉村の二塁打，原の3ランでさよなら勝ち．

### [Game 1, Interests 2]

(1)試合は打撃戦で巨人がさよなら勝ち．(2)1－1で迎えた二回裏無死，巨人は中畑のホームランで1点を加えた．(3)1－2で迎えた三回表一死，阪神は真弓のタイムリー，掛布の2ラン，バースのホームランで逆転．(4)5－3で迎えた最終回裏無死，巨人は篠塚のヒット，吉村の二塁打，原の3ランで試合を決めた．

### [Game 2, Interests 1]

試合はワンサイドゲームで阪神が勝った．一回表無死，阪神は真弓のヒット，田尾のアウトの間に真弓が2塁に進塁，掛布のタイムリー二塁打で1点を先制．三回表にも，田尾の四球，掛布の2ラン，バースのホームランで3点を加えた．5－1で迎えた三回裏無死，巨人は江川のヒット，篠塚のヒット，吉村の四球で満塁，しかしクロマティの三振でチャンスを逃した．5－1で迎えた最終回表無死，阪神はバースのホームランで1点を加えた．

### [Game 2, Interests 2]

試合はワンサイドゲームで阪神が勝った．一回表一死，阪神は掛布のタイムリー二塁打，バースのタイムリーで試合を決めた．三回表にも，田尾の四球，掛布の2ラン，バースのホームランで3点を加えた．最終回表にも，バースのホームランで1点を加えた．

### [Game 3, Interests 1]

試合は池田の三回の三者三振，江川の五回の三者三振などの投手戦で阪神が完封勝ち．一回表無死，阪神は真弓のヒット，田尾のアウトの間に真弓が2塁に進塁，掛布のタイムリー二塁打で1点を先制．1－0で迎えた一回裏無死，巨人は松本のヒット，篠塚のヒット，吉村のアウトで三塁，しかし原の三振でチャンスを逃した．

### [Game 3, Interests 2]

試合は池田の三回の三者三振，江川の五回の三者三振などの投手戦で阪神が完封勝ち．一回表無死，阪神は真弓のヒット，田尾のアウトの間に真弓が2塁に進塁，掛布のタイムリー二塁打で試合を決めた．

### [Game 4, Interests 1]

試合はワンサイドゲームで巨人が勝った．一回裏無死，巨人は松本のヒット，篠塚のヒット，吉村のアウトの間に松本が3塁に進塁，篠塚が2塁に進塁，原の2点タイムリー，クロマティの2ランで4点を加えた．0－4で迎えた二回表無死，阪神はバースのホームランで1点を返した．

[Game 4, Interests 2]

試合はワンサイドゲームで巨人が勝った. 一回裏無死, 巨人は松本のヒット, 篠塚のヒット, 吉村のアウトの間に松本が3塁に進塁, 篠塚が2塁に進塁, 原の2点タイムリー, クロマティの2ランで試合を決めた. 0－4で迎えた二回表無死, 阪神はバースのホームランで1点を返した.

# Knowledge Representation and Reasoning for Discourse Understanding*

**Satoshi KINOSHITA, Hiroshi SANO, Teruhiko UKITA,**
**Kazuo SUMITA, and Shin'ya AMANO**
**Toshiba Corp. R&D center**
**1, Komukai Toshiba-cho, Saiwai-ku,**
**Kawasaki 210, Japan**

**ABSTRACT**

Extra-linguistic knowledge is necessary for discourse understanding. In this paper, we classify the knowledge, and present a framework to describe it using frames and rules. With this framework, it is easy to represent an IS-A hierarchy, which is based on a classification by different viewpoints, and to describe functions of objects as declarative knowledge. Furthermore, to treat ambiguities in discourse understanding and to process utterances based on assumptions, the system has a world mechanism for inference. Lastly, we report the evaluation of this framework through the knowledge representation of a VCR and the conversation experiment by the dialogue system.

## 1. Introduction

Context processing technology is most important in building a question-answering system which reads sentences and answers the user's questions, or a machine translation system which translates sentences correctly, based on their contexts. Determining anaphoric reference and complementing ellipses are two of the most fundamental problems in context processing, and they are especially difficult in understanding conversations.

For context understanding, it is obvious that the extra-linguistic knowledge and reasoning based on it are necessary as well as the linguistic one. However, how the extra-linguistic knowledge should be represented and used has not been fully discussed. In this paper, we propose a framework for representing the extra-linguistic knowledge, which is a multi-paradigm knowledge representation system based on frames and rules.

Knowledge representation based only on frames is insufficient in the following points.

(a) In classifying the concepts in a task domain, we can classify them in a different way by changing the view point, but frames cannot express the taxonomy based on such classification simply.

(b) Negative expression and inference concerning negation are insufficient.

(c) We cannot describe the behavior of objects and logical relations between attributes as declarative knowledge.

*This work is supported by ICOT (Institute for New Generation Computer Technology).

The framework we propose here solves these problems. Moreover, the inference system is based on a world mechanism, which offers multiple hypothetical worlds for discourse analysis and problem solving.

We have been developing a consulting system which helps the user to use electrical equipment such as a VCR (video cassette recorder) through conversation. We then report the appraisal of the framework, which is obtained through the description of knowledge for this task and experiment of the consulting system.

## 2. Knowledge and inference for context understanding
### 2.1 Knowledge for context understanding

Let's discuss "context understanding" before thinking about "knowledge" for it. We use the term "context understanding" in two meanings. One is understanding context itself, that is, understanding the contents of whole sentences or understanding the topic or the structure of the conversation. The other is understanding each sentence correctly in the flow of the context, that is, determining the meaning of a sentence by resolving anaphoric reference and ellipsis, using the information of the context. But these two meanings are complementary. If we can't understand the meaning of each constituent sentence, we can't understand the meaning of the whole piece of text, and in some cases, understanding one sentence helps understanding the whole. Furthermore, if an ambiguity exists in a sentence that can't be resolved in semantic analysis, the context may be able to give the answer. Since an utterance in conversations depends on its context very much, the second meaning -understnding a sentence in the context flow- is more important. In this paper, we will use the term mainly in this meaning.

Needless to say, there are two kinds of knowledge for understanding a sentence. One is linguistic knowledge such as a grammar, and the other is extra-linguistic knowledge, knowledge of the world around us. In this paper, we focus on the latter and just call it "knowledge".

As knowledge necessary for context understanding, we classify the knowledge into 4 categories as listed below.
(a) Knowledge of objects
(b) Knowledge of events
(c) Relationships between events
(d) Concept hierarchy (thesaurus)

(a) Knowledge of objects

We use the term "objects" to distinguish entities or things, with, or without, physical existence. Intuitively they correspond to what is denoted by nominals. Knowledge of objects in a task domain is essential for understanding a sentence.

When we read a sentence, we sometimes can't understand, nor even imagine, the meaning of the whole sentence even though we can understand the meaning of each word. This sort of situation may be caused by lack of knowledge of what properties the object in the sentence has by nature. We think this is the same reason that Minsky proposed frames to recognize objects[Minsky 75]. The most systematic knowledge of an object is a model. Having a model of an object helps the understanding of sentences about it.

(b) Knowledge of events

"Events" distinguish some kind of action, state or movement of an object. If we talk about something, we can't describe it without a predicate and other objects, i.e. in a form of an event. So we must have knowledge of events. Although this seems to be rather linguistic, knowledge that what kind of object may be an event agent, source or goal is strongly connected to the world.

(c) Relationships between events

Determining anaphoric referents and complementing elliptic information are the most fundamental problems of context understanding. For this, we have to recognize the relationships between the sentences being processed and the context. For example, Schank proposed a method of using knowledge about typical sequences of events, called scripts [Schank 77], but the method cannot analyze sentences which cannot be matched to the scripts, this means it lacks flexibility. In order to solve this problem, Wilensky tried to recognize the relationship between events as a goal and a plan for it [Wilensky 83]. We have this sort of knowledge and utilize it to understand sentences. In our current task, we recognize knowledge of procedures to use a VCR.

(d) Concept hierarchy

Concept hierarchy is necessary in context understanding because we use various expressions to refer the same object in a dialogue. Let's consider the following sentences.

(1) Did you push the play-back switch?

(2) Yes, I pushed the switch.

Except when using pronouns, we use different expressions that mean different concepts when we refer to the same entry, as in the example above: a 'switch' is a super class of a 'play-back switch'.

## 2.2 Inference for context understanding

We can see various kinds of inference in the process of context understanding (for example [Rieger 75 and Ishizaki 86]). Here we will discuss an inference framework for treating ambiguities of interpretation.

The most important requirement for an inference system, for context understanding, is a framework to describe the situations according to the various interpretations of an ambiguous sentence simultaneously. As an example, let's consider the utterances below.

(3) I put a cassette tape into the VCR, and pushed the play-back switch.

(4) But it didn't work.

Assume that the candidates for 'it' are 'cassette tape 001', 'VCR 001', and 'playback switch 001' ('001' denotes instances). Then the hearer (system) can assume three situations as interpretations shown in Figure 1. We call each situation described in a box a 'hypothetical context world' or simply a 'context world'.

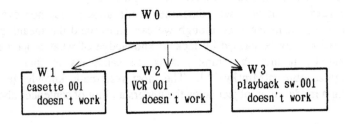

Figure 1  Example of context worlds

The process of context understanding is to select the most appropriate context world. To do so, we must evaluate every possible interpretation. But in some cases, we can't evaluate them unless we make some inferences from the interpretation first, which may change the contents of the working memory, and for that, we must be able to create context worlds simultaneously.

The interpretation which is decided by the context analysis is not always correct. If the system finds an inconsistency, it must resolve it. In the field of expert systems, Doyle proposed an inference system called TMS [Doyle 79]. A context understanding system should have this sort of inference system, and the world mechanism is a key to its realization.

Considering human language activity, we can find that we talk not only about objects and events in a real world but also about those in an imaginary world. So the system should process utterances based on conditionals. We think this is possible by utilizing context worlds. For processing such sentences, the system has only to create a new context world and process the following sentences in this world. The context world which corresponds to the imaginary world per se differs from the one which is created for context understanding, but can be processed in the same framework.

## 3. Design and realization of the knowledge representation system

As stated earlier, we are developing a consulting system which guides the usage of electrical equipment, such as a VCR, through a conversation with the user. In this chapter we show the concrete framework for knowledge representation of the task domain and the inference mechanism for understanding the user's utterance.

There are various knowledge representation paradigms, and the features of each have been discussed. We use 'frames' and 'rules' because of the ease in describing the concept hierarchy and the logical relation and in managing the described knowledge.

Figure 2 illustrates the composition of a knowledge base in the knowledge representation system. Knowledge of objects and events is described in a framework called a 'schema' that is composed of a frame part and a rule part. Knowledge of the relations between events, such as the causal relations, is described as a set of rules.

### 3.1 Knowledge representation
### 3.3.1 Knowledge representation using schema

Figure 3 shows a schema example (a part of the full description of a VCR). The schema is composed of a frame part and a rule part. Static knowledge is described in the frame part: such as super/sub class relations which compose an IS-A hierarchy, whole-part relations, and attributes of the object. In the rule part, actions or the behavior of the object is described.

There are two types of schemata in the knowledge base. One is an instance schema and the other is a class schema. Roughly speaking, an instance schema corresponds to a real object, and the information of the object is described in it. A class schema corresponds to a class of objects, and the restrictions of attributes or possible behavior of the objects are described.

### (A) Expression of knowledge by frames

As stated above, static knowledge such as an IS-A hierarchy is described in the frame part. As KRL [Bobrow 77], a frame is defined as a set of slots, and each slot is a set of facets. The features of the frame system in this paper are described below.

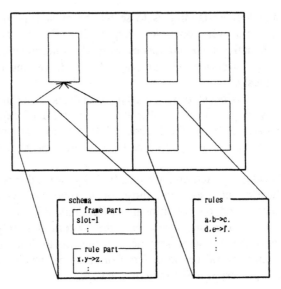

Figure 2   Composition of Knowledge Base

```
schema(cls, vcr_model_750,
        [(superC, type_of_sound_recording, [(value,[hi_fi_vcr])]),
         (superC, type_of_casette, [(value,[vhs_vcr])]),
         (has_part,        [(value,[power_switch, play_back_switch,...])]),
         (status,          [(car_num,1 ),
                            (enumeration,[stand_by,play_back, record, ...])]),
         (power,           [(car_num,1 ), (enumeration,[on,off ])]),
         (channel          [(car_num, 1),
                            (value_class, integer),
                            (value_condition, (_,V,(V>=1,V=<12))) ])
        ],
        [s_rule(power, power_on,VCR,
                        ( kr_schema(VCR,[(power,[off])],true),
                          event(push,1,[(object,[SW])]) ),
                        kr_schema(VCR,[(power,[on])],true),
                        [('$var_constraint',(
                            SW#power_switch :- part_of(SW,VCR) ))]),
         s_rule(power,power_lamp_on,VCR,
                        kr_schema(VCR,[(power,[on])],true),
                        kr_schema(LP,[(lamp_status,[on])],true),
                        [('$var_constraint',(
                            LP#power_lamp :- part_of(LP,VCR))])
        ]).
```

Figure 3    Schema example for a VCR (a part).
Kr_schema is a predicate that extracts or verifies slot values.
Words beginning with a capital letter denote variables.

## Representation of the concept hierarchy

We can classify one concept in different ways by changing the viewpoint, that is the feature we consider for discrimination. Figure 4 is a part of an IS-A hierarchy of our current task domain. If we classify a VCR, it can be classified in two different ways. Considering the type of cassette tape, we can classify it into 'VHS-type VCR' and 'Beta-type VCR', but by the type of sound recording, it is classified into 'hi-fi VCR' and 'monaural VCR'. So far, it has been difficult to describe such a hierarchy naturally, using conventional frame systems. In our system, it is described quite easily and naturally by attaching the viewpoint of the classification as additional information for a slot (See superC slot of Figure 3).

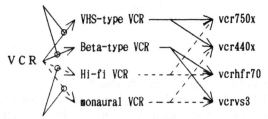

classification by recording of picture

classification by recording of sound

Figure 4  Example of classification from different viewpoints

This attachment of viewpoints is used in judging anaphoric referents. In a conversation, we use different expressions to refer to the same object, and sometimes they mean different concepts. In such a case, we can use the hierarchical relation between the concepts for the judgement.

Let's consider checking of identification of two objects; one is in the context and the other is in the sentence being processed. Assume that B is a concept of the former, and A is of the latter. If A and B are different, there are four possible relations between them.

(a) A is a sub-class of B.

Example: A:VHS VCR and B:VCR

(b) A and B are both sub-classes of a common concept C in the same viewpoint.

Example: A:television, B:VCR, and C:electrical equipment

(c) A and B are both sub-classes of a common concept C in a different viewpoint.

Example: A:VHS VCR, B:hi-fi VCR and C:VCR

(d) B is a sub-class of A (opposite case of a).

Example: A:VCR and B:VHS VCR

Figure 5 illustrates the above classification. An arrow between concepts is a subC (sub-class) link, and a dotted line around arrows is the viewpoint for the classification. Case (a) is the most general case. If two objects don't have any inconsistent property, we can judge that they are the same. In case (b), since these two objects essentially have inconsistent properties, we cannot recognize that they are the same object, but in the case of (c), it is possible to assume they are the same. Case (d) is the opposite case of (a). In this case, by judging that they are same, the information about the preceding object will increase.

The above example illustrates the case when a sub-class relation between two classes is direct. The same procedure should be applied for indirect relations among concepts.

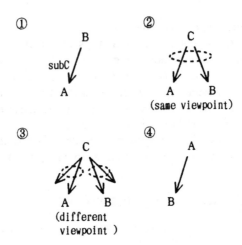

Figure 5 Relations between concepts

## Negative expression and the open/closed assumption

For a system which performs problem solving through a dialogue with a user, most data necessary for problem solving are unknown at the begining of inference. Furthermore an input sentence by the user may be a negative sentence. Although many systems based on Prolog treat negation on a closed world assumption, this is not always appropriate.

To solve this problem, we must have a framework to describe negation explicitly and also to describe whether the data used for reasoning are 'open' or 'closed'. 'Open' and 'closed' indicate the assumption for inference. If the system holds all the possible data about an item, we say the data are closed for the item, and if there is a possibility of another piece of data other than the current ones, we say the data are open.

In our knowledge representation, we can set a negative value as a slot value and add the information that the data for the slot are 'open' or 'closed'. With this framework, we can use the open/closed world assumption properly in the comparison of slot values and the reasoning based on them.

## Knowledge of events

We use case representation to describe an event. Using a schema, a case representation is described quite naturally by representing each case as a slot. Figure 6 shows an example description for a verb "rokuga-suru (to record something on a video tape)", where slots (agent, object and tool) have a special facet describing constraints on fillers of these cases. In this example, the constraint is that the agent, object and tool

```
schema(cls, record,
    [(superC,        [(value, [action])])]),
     (agent,         [(value_class, human_being)]),
     (object,        [(value_class, tv_program)]),
     (tool,          [(value_class, vtr)]),
     (obligatory_case,
                     [(value, [object, tool])]) )    ], []).
```

Figure 6 Event expression by schema.

must be a human, a TV program and a VCR respectively. The requirement for slot fulfillment, in implementing a task, is described in an 'obligatory-case' slot. These constraints are used to reduce search space in interpreting an input sentence.

## (B) Knowledge representation using schema rule

In addition to static knowledge, there is knowledge of functions of an object or logical relations between attributes. We use a rule in a schema called a 'schema rule' to describe this sort of knowledge.

In the case of a VCR, we have to represent how the internal state of a VCR changes by its operation. Figure 3 shows two schema rule examples. The first one describes that, if the power-switch of a VCR is pushed when the power is 'off', then the power will be 'on'.

To describe such knowledge using only a frame, we must describe it using attached procedures like if-added demons. Since there are many functions for usual devices, the clarity of the knowledge will be lost. By describing such knowledge using a schema rule, we can describe it as declarative knowledge, and the relation between the elements of knowledge will be kept clear.

Describing such knowledge of an object bit by bit, we get its model, and by forward reasoning with the knowledge, we can simulate its behavior. Lastly, these schema rules are inherited by lower classes like the slots of a frame and, therefore, economical description of functions is possible.

### 3.1.2 Knowledge representation using rule

In addition to knowledge described in a schema, we have to represent the relations between events such as the causal relation. In our framework, we use 'if-then' rules to describes knowledge of this sort.

For the current task, rules are used to represent procedures to operate a VCR and are prepared for every operational procedure, such as play-back and recording. Figure 7 is an example of a rule that describes how to play back a video cassette. The conclusion part holds the goal (to play back), and the conditional part holds the actions to accomplish it. Furthermore, every rule has some constraints on the variables. In the example, the variable 'SW' is constrained so that its content must be an instance of 'play-back switch' and be part of a VCR.

```
rule( operation, play_back,
    seq( event( put_on, 1, [( object,[PW])]),
          event( insert, 1, [( object, [K]), ( goal, [VTR])]) ,
          event( push, 1, [( object, [SW] )]) ),
    event( play_back, 1, [( object, [K]), ( tool,[VTR])] ),
    [('$var_constraint',(
       VTR # vtr;
       K # cassette;
       PW # power :- attribute_of ( PW, VTR) ;
       SW # play_back_switch :- part_of ( SW, VTR) ) )]).
```

Figure 7  Operation procedure example by rule.

### 3.1.3 Representation of time

In a task which only has to treat the present state of the apparatus, such as trouble diagnosis, there is little necessity to represent time. However, in guiding the usage of an apparatus, the order of the user's operations is quite important. Since we have a mechanism to describe context worlds, it is possible to represent the states of objects at various points in time by creating worlds for every point in time under consideration, but this representation makes it difficult to manage the context worlds. For this reason, we extend the data structure of a slot value of our frame system to be the pairing of its value and a time description. So every slot may have various values according to time.

### 3.2 Inference function

As a basic function, the system has an inference mechanism for frames to inherit slots or to check the restrictions of a slot, and a mechanism of forward/backward reasoning using rules. As we described, we have two kinds of rules; a schema rule in a schema and a rule in the rule base. In consultation about an apparatus, it is important that the system holds the state of the machine and predicts a possible state based on a simulation. In our system, this is performed by forward reasoning using schema rules.

Moreover, to realize the context world, we designed the system to create a working memory for reasoning according to each context world. Hereafter we call each working memory simply the 'world'. Using this mechanism, we can create context worlds for each possible interpretation in discourse analysis, and evaluate their properties simultaneously. Also in problem solving, we can process a sentence based on a conditional using this framework. This will be described in 4.2.

### 3.3 Implementation

We implemented the knowledge representation system on a PSI (Personal Sequential Inference machine) developed by ICOT. The programming language is ESP (Extended Self-contained Prolog). The size of the program is about 7000 lines including comment lines.

Since ESP is a kind of object oriented language, it is possible to translate all knowledge written in a schema to an object of ESP. However, in the current system, for ease of debugging and loading speed, we transform a set of schemata in one file to an object of ESP, and load it into the main memory.

Execution speed is not satisfactory because the system processes the frame data by interpretation. By compiling frame data to a Prolog program like DCKR (Definite Clause Knowledge Representation)[Tanaka 86], we can make the system faster.

### 4. Application and appraisal
### 4.1 Application in a dialogue system

We are developing an experimental question-answering system called ISAC (Information Service System by Analyzing Conversational Context) whose current task is consultation for operating a VCR, and we use the knowledge representation system as the knowledge module of the system.

Starting with SHRDLU[Winograd 72], many dialogue systems have been developed. The biggest difference between our system and SHRDLU is, that in SHRDLU, the world for conversation is closed and the system holds all information for inference, but in our system, the system can get information about the world only through the user's input.

This corresponds to a situation where an expert could consult via telephone conversation.

## Discourse analysis

Here we briefly introduce a procedure of discourse analysis for interpreting an input sentence[Ukita 88]. The procedure consists of four major steps; anaphora detection, referent candidate extraction, non-contradiction testing, and optimal candidate selection.

First the procedure detects anaphoric indicators in a sentence, which are pronouns or nouns, with or without definite articles. Furthermore, the omitted obligatory cases of the events (predicates) are detected as ellipses.

Next, for every anaphoric indicator, the procedure searches for referent candidates that have already emerged in the context. In the system, they are usually defined as instance schemata. If the procedure can't find an appropriate candidate for an indicator, it creates a new instance schema and treats it as the candidate. The inter-object relationships such as whole-part or attribute-value are also checked here.

When more than two possible interpretations remain after the non-contradiction test, the procedure tries to find causal links between the interpretations and the context, and decides on the most informative interpretation. This is the step of optimal candidate selection. In inspecting causal connections, the procedure searches for rules that describe the usage of a VCR. Let's consider an example sequence of sentences, whose preceding context contains a cassette tape and a practical image on a television set.

(5) I pushed the eject button. It didn't come out.

Assume that the referent candidates of "it" are the cassette tape and the image. To decide on the appropriate referent, the procedure finds a rule such as follows:

If (a cassette is inserted in a VCR),
and (the eject button is pushed),
then (the cassette comes out).

Using this rule, the procedure prefers the interpretation that the cassette didn't come out.

Currently we don't use schema rules which are described in a schema for this step. In referent candidate extraction, if an anaphoric indicator is a noun, the procedure searches for an object that is an instance of a concept meant by the noun. This is just the case in (a) and (c) described in Figure 5. We have to improve the discourse analyzing program to treat other cases.

## Problem solving

The current task of the consulting system is categorized into 3 sub-tasks as follows.

(a) Answering an inquiry about an operating procedure
 (example: Would you tell me how to play back this tape?)
(b) Solution of a fault which originates in an operation mistake
 (example: I pushed the play-back switch, but it didn't work.)
(c) Prediction of an action of the VCR
 (example: What happens if I push the play-back switch now?)

An input sentence is classified into one of these types, and the problem solving module for this type is activated. Finally the result of the task is output as a question or an answer to the user.

## Dialogue example

Figure 8 shows a conversation example using the experimental system. Before this user: ビデオテープを再生したい (I want to playback the video-tape)*

system: ビデオの電源を入れて、ビデオにカセットテープを入れて、
再生ボタンを押してください
(Please turn on the VTR power, insert the cassette into the VTR, and push
the play-back button.)

user: ビデオにカセットテープを入れて、再生ボタンを押した
(I inserted the cassette in the VTR and pushed the play-back button)*

system: はい、わかりました (OK)

user: 動かない ("It doesn't operate" or "It doesn't move")**

system: ビデオの電源はオンですか (Is the VTR power 'ON'?)

user: はい (Yes)

system: 再生ランプは点灯していますか (Is the play-back lamp lit?)

user: 点灯しています (It's lit)*

system: VHF出力端子はテレビに接続されていますか
(Is the VHF output terminal connected to the TV set?)

user: いいえ (No)

system: VHF出力端子をテレビに接続してください
(Please connect the VHF output terminal to the TV set.)

Figure 8    Dialogue example using the experimental system
    *  In Japanese, the subject is omitted.
    ** Japanese verb '動く (ugoku)' has several meanings.

conversation, the system was given the situation that there is a VCR and a television set, and that the initial state of the devices is such that the power is off. Unless such an initial state is given, the system asks the user about it and about his/her actions, and continues the consultation.

## 4.2 Evaluation of the framework of knowledge representation

We report the evaluation of our framework of the knowledge representation, which was gotten by representing knowledge about a kind of home hi-fi VCR. Using its operation manual, we represented the knowledge of the VCR, but didn't represent either knowledge concerning spatial relations, such as positions of switches, or knowledge which requires adjectival or adverbial expression for its representation.

### 4.2.1 Representation using schema

The number of concepts which are described in schemata is about 300. 120 schemata are concepts of events (verbs relevant to operations of the VCR), and 80 schemata are concepts of the VCR itself and its parts, such as switches and lamps. The rest are concepts of the attributes, such as channel, or of immaterial objects, such as a television program or a picture.

## Representation of the concept hierarchy

In describing an IS-A hierarchy, we can represent a classification based on different viewpoints easily and naturally. In the current hierarchy, there are only two sub-hierarchical structures: one is shown in Figure 4, and the other is a sub-hierarchy whose root concept is a 'terminal'. However we found the framework is quite valid.

## Negative expression and the open/closed world assumption

Since, in the current task, each slot can only have one value, we are unable to use the open/closed assumption to its full advantage. As for negation, when the knowledge representation system gets a command to fill a slot with a negative value, it will try, first, by reductio ad absurdum to infer a positive one. If this fails, the negative one will be used.

For example, since the slot 'power' in Figure 3 may only have the value 'on' or 'off' at one time, the slot will be set to 'off' if the negation of 'on' is provided. In a consultation, the user may answer the system's question with a negative sentence. So this reasoning is very useful to process such a sentence.

## Representation using schema rules

The functions of the VCR are described in about 170 schema rules: how it behaves according to an operation and how the state of the lamps is affected. Since these rules describe its model, we can simulate its behaivior, and this reasoning is quite useful for problem solving.

Currently we can't describe the events which happen continuously or iteratively under a certain state. For example, "If a VCR is in playback state, the cassette tape in it goes around" or "the display of the VCR's clock changes every minute". To describe this kind of knowledge, we have to extend our framework.

### 4.2.2 Representation using rules

The operation procedures of the VCR are described in about 30 rules. In describing the knowledge, we used the expressions in the operation manual as much as possible. However, we couldn't represent the following types of expressions as they are.

(a) The case of the purpose or the condition for an operation being described.

(example: "Please push the video button so as to put on the video lamp.")

In such a case, we neglected the purpose or the condition and wrote only the operation .

(b) The case of the goal of an operation being expressed as two events.

(example: "To watch a TV program while you record another program, ...")

In this example, we used a word that means 'a program on a different channel', but this is not always possible.

### 4.2.3 Inference in the world mechanism

In processing a conditional sentence (we will call it a 'hypothetical sentence'), we found inference within the world mechanism to be useful. To process a hypothetical sentence, the system first creates a new world, evaluates its potential, and continues the dialogue. Through the experiment, we found that our choice of world is important for processing the next sentence. As an example, let's consider a sequence of the user's input during a consultation.

(6) What happens if I push the recording switch now?

(7) What happens if I push the play-back switch instead?

(8) What happens if I push the fast forward switch after that?

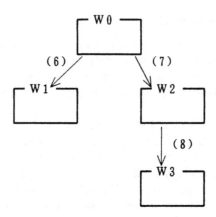

Figure 9 Example of world composition

Figure 9 illustrates an example of world composition in processing the sentences above. The world W0 is a world at which sentence (6) was input, and W1 is a world which is created in order to process (6). In processing (7), the supposition (pushing the play-back switch) must be evaluated instead of the supposition of (6), that is, we have to create a new world W2 whose parent is also world W0. Furthermore, in processing (8), we must evaluate it in the light of the supposition of (7), therefore we have to create W3 as a child of W2. For this, it is very important to manage relations between the context and the worlds.

## 5. Conclusions

In this paper, we discussed a classification of knowledge for context understanding, and a framework for its representation and reasoning based on this knowledge. We first classified the knowledge into four categories; knowledge of objects, knowledge of events, concept hierarchy, and relationships between events. The first three are described in a framework called a schema, and the last one is described by rules. Using schemata, we can naturally represent an IS-A hierarchy based on different viewpoints, and also describe a negative slot value, and use the open/closed assumption properly. Furthermore, by using schema rules, we can describe functions of an object and logical relations between attributes declaratively. As for inference, we pointed out the need for a context world for resolving an ambiguity in context understanding, and its validity in problem solving. Then we discussed our knowledge representation system which is implemented as a part of an experimental question-answering system for a VCR usage application. By representing the knowledge of the task domain, we found the above points to be advantages in our system. At present, there is some knowledge that can't be written in the current framework, but the framework reported here is thought basically applicable to context understanding in other task domains.

## References
[Bobrow 77] Bobrow,D.G. and Winograd,T., "An Overview of KRL, a Knowledge Representation Language", Cognitive Science, Vol.1, 1977, pp.3-46.
[Doyle 79] Doyle,J., "A Truth Maintenance System", Artificial Intelligence 12, 1979, pp.231-272.

[Ishizaki 86] Ishizaki,S. and Isahara, H., "Contextual Processing Technology", Vol.27, No.8, 1986, pp.897-905(in Japanese).

[Minsky 75] Minsky,M., "A framework for representing knowledge", in Winston,P. (ed.), The psychology of computer vision, McGraw- Hill, 1975, pp.211-277.

[Rieger 75] Reiger,C.J., "CONCEPTUAL MEMORY AND INFERENCE", in Schank,R. (ed.), Conceptual Infomation Processing, NORTH-HOLLAND, 1975, pp.157-288.

[Schank 77] Schank,R. and Abelson,R., "Scripts,Plans,Goals and Understanding", Lawrence Erlbaum Associates, 1977.

[Tanaka 86] Tanaka,H., "DCKR - Knowledge Represetation in Prolog and Its Application to Natural Language Understanding", in Nagao,M.(ed.), Language and Artificial Inteligence, Else Ver Science Publishers, B.V. (North Holland), 1987, pp.353-366.

[Ukita 88] Ukita,T., Sumita,K., Kinoshita,S., Sano,H., and Amano,S., "Preference Judgement in Comprehending Conversational Sentences Using Multi-Paradigm World Knowledge", Proc. of FGCS'88, 1988(to appear).

[Wilensky 83] Wilensky,R., "Planning and Understanding", Addison-Wesley, 1983.

[Winograd 72] Winograd,T., "Understanding Natural Language", Academic Press, 1972.

# Lecture Notes in Artificial Intelligence (LNAI)

Other volumes of the Lecture Notes in Computer Science relevant to Artificial Intelligence:

# Lecture Notes in Computer Science